The U.S. and Mexico:
Borderland Development and
the National Economies

About the Book and Editors

The U.S. and Mexico: Borderland Development and the National Economies
Lay James Gibson and Alfonso Corona Rentería

Addressing the economic aspects of ties between the United States and Mexico, this book looks at the structural characteristics of the border region and the flow of goods, services, capital, and people between the two countries. The contributors describe the cultural, economic, and demographic dimensions of the borderlands and focus on specific issues critical to the region, among them environmental pollution, migration, territorial issues, and the implications of border-zone industrial growth. Finally, the authors consider how these issues affect the national economies and relations between the two countries.

Lay James Gibson is professor and head of the Department of Geography and Regional Development at the University of Arizona, Tucson. **Alfonso Corona Rentería** is a professor of economics at the Universidad Nacional Autónoma de México.

The *U.S. and Mexico: Borderland Development and the National Economies

edited by Lay James Gibson
and Alfonso Corona Rentería

Westview Press / Boulder and London

A Westview Replica Edition

This is a Westview softcover edition, manufactured on our own premises using equipment and methods that allow us to keep even specialized books in stock. It is printed on acid-free paper and bound in softcovers that carry the highest rating of NASTA in consultation with the AAP and the BMI.

Published in 1985 in the United States of America by Westview Press, Inc., 5500 Central Avenue, Boulder, Colorado 80301; Frederick A. Praeger, Publisher

Library of Congress Cataloging in Publication Data
Main entry under title:
The U.S. and Mexico.
  (A Westview replica edition)
  1. Mexican-American Border Region—Economic conditions
—Addresses, essays, lectures. 2. Mexico—Economic
conditions—1971– —Addresses, essays, lectures.
3. United States—Economic conditions—1971–1981—Ad-
dresses, essays, lectures. 4. United States—Economic
conditions—1981– —Addresses, essays, lectures.
I. Gibson, Lay James. II. Corona Rentería, Alfonso.
III. Title: US and Mexico.
HC135.U16 1985   337.72'1'073   84-7510
ISBN 0-86531-870-0

Printed and bound in the United States of America

10   9   8   7   6   5   4   3   2   1

Contents

PART 1
BORDERLAND DEVELOPMENT

Tables, Figures, and Graphs

Figures and Graphs

Preface

For decades, scholars in the U.S. have studied Mexico and Mexican scholars have studied the United States. Only a relatively small part of these efforts has been focused on the economic aspects of ties between the two countries and even less attention has been given to the analysis of the structural characteristics of the U.S.–Mexico border region or to the flows of goods, services, capital, and people between these two neighbors. This book focuses squarely on these critical topics.

The sixteen chapters in the book are organized around two general themes: "Borderland Development" (Part 1) and "Institutional Structures, Flows, and the National Economies" (Part 2). The chapters in Part 1 deal with both the structure and character of the U.S.–Mexico Borderlands Region and specific development issues such as migration and the social and economic implications of border-zone industrial growth. Unlike the chapters in Part 1, those included in Part 2 take a macro-scale or nation-to-nation approach when discussing economic flows and linkages, migration streams, and territoriality issues involving the two nations.

The events of recent years have dramatically altered both the perceptions and realities of U.S.–Mexico relations. When organizing papers for a book such as this one, there is a strong temptation to be "trendy"—to grab hold of a "hot topic" and stretch it to the limit. But there is a risk in this approach—hot topics come and go. Inflation in both the U.S. and Mexico, the peso devaluations in Mexico, the energy crisis in the U.S., and the petroleum boom in Mexico are all topics that might be viewed in one light in 1980 or 1981 and in a very different light just a year or two later.

The chapters in this volume frequently deal with topics of perhaps exaggerated current interest, but the editors have made a genuine effort to be sure that they do more than describe issues that are in vogue. Papers selected for inclusion all share at least some of the following traits: they deal with major issues of lasting value, they have important policy implications, they offer a fresh perspective on an important topic, or they utilize methodologies that yield new insights into established issues. In more general terms, all chapters contribute to the special analytical perspectives gained by approaches that stress the importance of understanding the spatial structure of regions and the ways that regions are defined and bounded by flows of goods, services, capital, people, and ideas.

A total of ten chapters deal with the broadly defined theme of borderland development. All of these chapters are concerned with the U.S.–Mexico interface, but they are clearly not all cut from the same cloth. The chapters by Jorge A. Bustamante, Niles Hansen, and Kevin F. McCarthy deal with structural characteristics of the borderlands region. Hansen provides an overview of economic and demographic characteristics of both the U.S. and Mexican portions of the region; he stresses the asymmetric nature of U.S.–Mexico borderland relationships. Like Hansen, McCarthy presents an overview of regional structure, but his emphasis is more on social, cultural, and political factors than on the economic and demographic. McCarthy deals with that often confusing mix of factors which seem both to unite the Mexican and U.S. jurisdictions and at the same time make them separate entities. Bustamante's chapter develops more fully one of the themes discussed by McCarthy—national identity. He presents research findings for a number of Mexican cities that suggest that "cultural denationalization" is less likely to occur in border cities than in other parts of Mexico.

A second group of chapters in Part 1 focuses on the development of one side of the international border and on the actual and potential linkage effects between border regions and the respective national economies. Luis Suarez-Villa develops a model to describe the process of interregional movement of firms. He then goes on to discuss actual manufacturing shifts in the U.S. away from the northeast and to the borderlands; he investigates the particular role played by Mexico's Border Industrialization Program in promoting these shifts. James T. Peach, on the other hand, focuses exclusively on the U.S. side of the international border in his analysis of regional changes in income distribution. Jesús Tamayo and Alfonso Corona Rentería, like Suarez-Villa, are concerned with the ties between the relatively isolated border region and the national mainstream. Tamayo examines events that have, in recent years, had a substantial impact on the Mexican economy and then discusses their repercussions in the Mexican border region. Corona too is concerned with recent developments in the Mexican border zone's economic life. He concludes that national policy should focus on the development of new linkage structures that emphasize the strengthening of ties between the Mexican borderlands and Mexico's interior.

The final three chapters in Part 1 all focus on various aspects of Mexico's Border Industrialization Program (BIP). Joseph Grunwald's chapter, "Internationalization of Industry: U.S.–Mexican Linkages," offers a broad overview of the BIP and a detailed look at the workings of the U.S.-oriented "maquila" operations. He provides a comprehensive description of BIP products, location of plants, linkage patterns, employment, and the role of migration. He discusses policy implications of the BIP and gives special emphasis to the potential consequences of automation and its effects on labor utilization patterns. Haynes C. Goddard and Guillermina Valdes-Villalva both take a more issue-specific approach when dealing with borderlands industrialization. Goddard offers a technical analysis of the benefits and costs of the BIP. He quantitatively measures the BIP's contribution to foreign exchange reserves and the opportunity cost of utilizing labor in the BIP relative to wages paid. Valdes-Villalva, on the other hand, deals with both social and economic implications of the BIP. Her special emphasis is on the role of women in the labor force and the broader social and economic consequences associated with their participation in the BIP.

Part 2 includes six chapters that concern, in various ways, the "national economies." Olga Pellicer provides a broad overview of U.S.-Mexico economic relations as she traces the events of the 1976–1982 period that had a profound impact on financial flows. Her particular emphasis is on the role played by supply and demand for petroleum and its effect on national behavior and policy.

The chapters by John M. McDowell and Richard C. Jones both deal with migration. McDowell develops a general model that utilizes a theoretical/technical approach to understanding the welfare implications for both sending and receiving countries that experience labor migrations. Jones, on the other hand, offers a detailed analysis of data that describe the socioeconomic dimensions of migration of undocumented workers from Mexico to South Texas.

Mariano Bauer, Howard G. Applegate and C. Richard Bath, and Genaro Carnero Roque and Adolfo Aguilar Zinser deal with large questions of national policy, although their topics are all very different. Bauer is concerned with the one-sidedness of technology transfers and the effects of current patterns on Mexican economic independence. He points to the economic benefits that might be associated with increased efforts to internalize development of technology in Mexico. Whereas Bauer calls for the development of new policies, Applegate and Bath concentrate on the implications of existing policies—policies that establish the degree to which hazardous and toxic substances are regulated in the U.S. and in Mexico. They review current regulations and comment on the ways that these regulations affect commodity export and import policies and practices. Finally, the chapter by Roque and Zinser presents a Mexican perspective on questions of territoriality conflicts, especially conflicts involving the exploitation of resources from the sea.

Lay James Gibson
Alfonso Corona Renteria

Acknowledgments

Many individuals and institutions have helped to produce this book. Rebeca Quintana, managing director of Interdec, supervised the translation process—a substantial undertaking. Adolfo Aguilar Zinser, Jorge Bustamante, Haynes Goddard, Michael Greenwood, Michael Meyers, Leland Pederson, Ignacio Renero, Florencio Sanchez Camara, Arthur Silvers, and Edward Williams all contributed to the time-consuming task of commenting on drafts of the papers that are published here. Steven Turiano took on the job of bringing clarity to the graphics. Helen Horley typed—and retyped—the manuscript with patience and care. Finally, we wish to thank Barbara Schmidt, Christopher Wilna, and David Winder for their continuing interest, support, and encouragement.

The papers included here were drawn from those presented at the Second Conference on Regional Impacts of U.S.–Mexico Economic Relations: Challenges and Opportunities, which was held in Tucson, Arizona, in May 1983. Both the conference and the preparation of this book were funded by the Ford and Rockefeller Foundations. To both of these sponsors we are enormously grateful.

In addition, we want to acknowledge the ongoing efforts of El Colegio de México, the University of Arizona, Estudios Regionales Mexico–Estados Unidos, A.C., the Western Regional Science Association, and last but not least, Eliseo Mendoza Berrueto.

L.J.G.
A.C.R.

Part 1

Borderland Development

The Nature and Significance
of Border Development Patterns

Niles Hansen

Growth Trends in the 1970s

The seven Standard Metropolitan Statistical Areas (SMSAs) shown in Table 1 account for over 90 percent of the total population in U.S. border counties. All of these SMSAs grew more rapidly during the 1970s than during the 1960s. El Paso, which had the lowest 1970–1980 border SMSA population growth rate, still grew at over three times the corresponding national rate of 11 percent, and by well over the respective rates for the relatively rapidly growing South and West. McAllen's 56 percent rate of growth was five times that of the United States, and Tucson and Brownsville grew almost as rapidly. Of the 272 SMSAs that were officially defined as of 1980, McAllen ranked eleventh in terms of growth during the 1970s; Tucson ranked fifteenth, and Brownsville eighteenth. Moreover, in five of the seven border SMSAs, per capita personal income growth between 1975 and 1979 exceeded the corresponding rates for the South, the West, and the United States as a whole. The contiguous El Paso and Las Cruces SMSAs were the only exceptions.

Among the factors contributing to the phenomenal growth of border SMSAs have been manufacturing decentralization favoring the West and the South, climate and environmental amenities (as well as air conditioning to ameliorate the harsher aspects of the southwestern climate), migration of retired persons to the Southwest, and the diffusion of transportation, communications, education, and other social and economic infrastructures that have made it more feasible for people to live in once-remote areas. Moreover, the demographic and economic growth engendered by all of these phenomena has created expanding markets for new and existing firms in the services, trade, and construction sectors.

This chapter is based on research made possible by a grant from the National Science Foundation.

TABLE 1

Population Change, 1970–1980, and Per Capita Personal Income Change, 1975–1979 in U.S. Standard Metropolitan Statistical Areas Bordering Mexico, in the South and West, and in the United States

Area	Population (thousands)		Percentage Change, 1970–80	Per Capita Personal Income		Percentage Change, 1975–1979
	1970	1980		1975	1979	
San Diego	1,357	1,861	37	$5932	$8908	50.2
Tucson	352	531	51	5318	8319	56.4
Las Cruces	70	96	38	4152	6091	46.7
El Paso	359	480	34	4362	6207	42.3
Laredo	73	99	36	3392	5106	50.5
McAllen	182	283	56	3133	5024	60.4
Brownsville	140	210	49	3653	5731	56.9
South	63,000	75,000	19	5189	7753	49.4
West	35,000	43,000	23	6227	9279	49.0
U.S.	203,000	227,000	11	5845	8637	47.8

Sources: For population, U.S. Department of Commerce, Bureau of the Census (1981). For income, U.S. Department of Commerce, Bureau of the Census (1982).

TABLE 2

Population Change in Major Mexican Cities Bordering the United States, 1970–1980

| City | Population (thousands) | | Percentage Change, |
	1970	1980	1970–1980
Tijuana	277	542	96
Mexicali	267	495	85
Ciudad Juárez	407	680	67
Nuevo Laredo	149	272	83
Reynosa	137	240	75
Matamoros	138	258	87

Source: Consejo Nacional de Población (1982, 62–63).

As recently as 1940, Tijuana and Mexicali, both on the border with California, had modest populations of only 17,000 and 19,000 respectively. By 1970, these two cities, as well as Ciudad Juárez, on the border with Texas, ranked among the ten largest cities in Mexico. As the data in Table 2 indicate, the 1970–1980 population growth rate in each of Mexico's major border cities was greater than the corresponding national rate of 37 percent.

Urbanization on Mexico's northern border has been strongly influenced by the proximity of the United States, and it has been both a cause and an effect of migration from the interior. Minimum wage rates in Mexico vary by state and by economic subregions within states. The subregions on the border have relatively high rates; Baja California Norte has the highest in all Mexico (Schlagheck 1980, pp. 74–76), as well as the highest median monthly earnings (Greenwood 1978, p. 18). Even so, wage rates on the Mexican side of the border are considerably lower than those on the U.S. side, which in turn are low in relation to the United States as a whole. Thus, the growth of Mexico's border cities has been partly a result of opportunities to work across the border. These cities have served as a staging ground for persons who work in the United States on an undocumented basis, and they have attracted many persons who live in Mexico but cross the border regularly to work in the U.S. border cities. Prior to the peso devaluations of 1982, commuters and other Mexican border residents also did much of their shopping on the U.S. side. It has been estimated that, depending on the location, from 40 percent to 75 percent of the outlays of border area Mexicans have been spent on the U.S. side (Revel-Mouroz 1978, p. 15). Nevertheless, border transactions have traditionally been favorable to Mexico because of the large number of relatively wealthy U.S. tourists and shoppers who visit Mexican border cities.

In response to high unemployment rates, the Mexican government has been attempting to attract U.S. plants to the Mexican border area (Hansen 1981). The assembly plant, or *maquiladora,* program takes advantage of U.S. tariff code provisions that allow foreign-based subsidiaries of U.S. firms to assemble products whose parts were originally made in the United States and then to export the products to the United States with duties being imposed only on the value added (low-cost labor). In keeping with the new international division of labor, many U.S. firms have participated in this program, which currently provides some 130,000 jobs for Mexicans. In addition to the expenditures that Mexican workers have made on the U.S. side of the border, the *maquiladora* program has stimulated employment in "twin plants" located in U.S. border cities; and some firms that were originally attracted to the border area by the *maquiladora* program instead have decided to locate solely on the U.S. side. In the late 1970s Texas border cities proved particularly attractive in this regard because of large labor surpluses, relatively low wage rates by U.S. standards, and a relative absence of effective unions (Miller 1981).

All along the border there is mutual recognition of U.S.-Mexican interdependence. Despite national concerns about the presence of "illegal aliens" in the United States, the traditional use of undocumented Mexican workers in the U.S. border area has been "strongly supported by employers and borderlands families, church and relief agencies, politically responsive authorities (including immigration control agencies), and the Mexican government among others" (Stoddard 1976, p. 176). Moreover, the clash of Anglo and Mexican cultures has been diluted by the large and growing number of Mexican-Americans in the population and among local U.S. officials. Officials in sister cities have engaged in patterns of contact that are numerous, complex, and friendly. These contacts often have led to informal agreements and understandings with respect to transboundary cooperation in such matters as fire control, law enforcement, education, and health care. For the most part, local officials and elites have believed that what is good for one city is good for the other, and they have acted accordingly (Sloan and West 1976; Sloan and West 1977).

Effects of the Peso Devaluation on the U.S. Borderlands

Although many of the factors that contributed to the growth of the U.S. border economy during the 1970s are still operative, the devaluation of the peso—which during 1982 fell in value from about 25 to the dollar to 155 to the dollar—has had especially adverse effects on the Texas portion, where interdependencies with Mexican sister cities are particularly great. Because the peso devaluation was so recent, it is not possible at this writing to present a comprehensive and systematic evaluation of the consequences; nevertheless, the limited relevant data available are instructive.

Before 1982, the overvalued peso caused large numbers of Mexican consumers and investors to shift their spending to the U.S. market. For example, during 1980 and 1981 retail sales all along the Texas border grew at rates of over 30 percent per year; and bank deposits in the Lower Rio Grande Valley (the Brownsville and McAllen SMSAs) rose by 20 percent per year (Leatherwood 1983). During this period, Mexicans bought about 40 percent of the luxury condominiums on South Padre Island, in the Brownsville SMSA, but following the devaluation many could not maintain their payments. Realtors there "face an increasingly uncertain future," and "to the island's developers the devaluation has been especially disastrous" (Mieher 1982). South Padre Island is not the only place where Mexicans invested heavily in U.S. real estate, of course, though precise figures are difficult to obtain for specific areas.

Unpublished data provided by the Office of the Governor of Texas indicate that retail sales in Brownsville dropped by 68 percent between October 1981 and October 1982; during this same period retail sales in McAllen fell by over 85 percent. Home sales in the Lower Rio Grande Valley fell by 63 percent and building permits declined in value by 46 percent. Between the beginning of 1982 and the beginning of 1983, hotel and motel occupancy rates dropped from 75 percent to 41 percent in Brownsville, and from 92 percent to 62 percent in McAllen.

The data presented in Table 3 show that nonagricultural wage and salary employment in Texas declined by 1.6 percent between January 1982 and January 1983. Meanwhile, the state's unemployment rate rose dramatically from 5.9 percent to 8.5 percent (the national rate increased from 9.4 percent to 11.4 percent during this period). The economic boom that Texas experienced in the 1970s was clearly being tempered by the national business recession and the fading strength of the oil and gas sector. However, the economic situation in the border SMSAs was considerably worse than that in Texas as a whole, which no doubt reflected the adverse consequences of the peso devaluation. Total employment declines among the border SMSAs ranged from 4.4 percent in El Paso to 18.8 percent in Laredo between January 1982 and January 1983. At the beginning of 1983 the unemployment rate ranged from 13.3 percent in El Paso to 27.3 percent in Laredo, the highest in the nation. Employment declines in the trade sector were particularly pronounced, as might be expected in view of sharply curtailed purchases by Mexicans. During 1982,

TABLE 3

Nonagricultural Wage and Salary Employment and Percent Unemployed in Texas Border Standard
Metropolitan Statistical Areas, January 1982 and January 1983

	Brownsville	McAllen	Laredo	El Paso	Texas
Employment					
1982	65,700	83,150	37,500	170,400	6,271,700
1983	58,250	79,300	30,450	162,900	6,168,700
Percent Decline	11.3	4.6	18.8	4.4	1.6
Unemployment Rate					
1982	11.4	14.0	11.0	9.2	5.9
1983	17.7	20.5	27.3	13.3	8.5

Source: Texas Employment Commission (1983).

employment in trade in the McAllen SMSA fell from 28,800 to 26,150; in Brownsville, from 19,300 to 16,850; in Laredo, from 14,050 to 9,600; and in El Paso, from 42,550 to 40,350. For the four border SMSAs taken together, the drop in trade employment represented over 45 percent of the decrease in total employment.

Both the U.S. and Texas economic recessions have apparently bottomed out, and recovery should accelerate modestly through 1983 and into 1984. Nevertheless, the Texas border SMSAs are not likely to return soon to the rapid growth paths they were on during the 1970s. Dependence on Mexico, a positive factor when the peso was overvalued, has now become a liability. In 1982, Mexico's gross national product, adjusted for inflation, fell by 0.2 percent. This was the first decline in Mexico's GNP in 50 years. Investment in Mexico fell by 17 percent in 1982 in comparison with 1981, and the inflation rate was 99 percent; and, unless inflation can be brought under control, there may well be yet another devaluation of the peso. Moreover, in terms of per capita income, Brownsville, McAllen and Laredo are the three poorest SMSAs in the United States, which does not provide a promising basis for development that is not tied to conditions in Mexico.

In summary, the Texas border SMSAs are likely to experience little if any economic growth over the near term, though population may continue to increase as a result of high birth rates and the immigration of retired persons seeking a warm climate. In contrast, the Tucson and San Diego SMSAs, which as a whole are much less dependent on conditions in Mexico, should continue to grow on the basis of local advantages and the general national economic recovery. Tucson, however, should have the highest growth rate among border SMSAs because the attractiveness of San Diego will be dampened by its relatively high, and rising, cost of living.

Dependency and Interdependency in the Borderlands

While there is little question that the Mexican and U.S. borderlands are interdependent, the "asymmetric" nature of this relationship has frequently been deplored in Mexico. From the Mexican perspective, the principal problem with respect to the border has been how to gain some economic advantages from proximity while at the same time avoiding dependence upon the United States. For example, the *maquiladora* program has clearly expanded the industrial employment base in border cities of Mexico, but by their very nature the activities involved have no linkages with other Mexican firms; and, at least until the recent peso devaluation, a high proportion of the incomes of *maquiladora* workers has been spent on the U.S. side of the border. The net effect of the program has thus been to increase the dependence of the Mexican border area on the United States, rather than to integrate it more closely with the Mexican economy.

The dependency problem also arises in the cultural context. The inroads that U.S.-influenced values, expressions, and models of consumption have made among the people of the *frontera norte* (Monsiváis 1978) are typically deplored in Mexico City. However, what seems to be at issue here is less the economic well-being of the border residents than their attachment to the nation-state and the values it purports to represent. In this perspective, the *norteños* are in grave danger of becoming a people "without a clear consciousness of its historic experience, its identity, and its roots; and above all, unable to represent, express, and defend the national interests" (Castellanos Guerrero and López y Rivas 1981, p. 84). Thus, the Mexican central government should reduce the transboundary linkages that encourage dependency, as well as promote policies that would integrate the northern borderlands more closely with the rest of Mexico (Bustamante 1981).

Given the disparities in living standards between the United States and Mexico, as well as the past history of U.S. interference in Mexico's internal affairs, it can easily be understood why dependency is an important issue in Mexico. But two questions may be raised in this regard. First, would the people in the northern border regions of Mexico be better off if, say, an ocean were to exist where the United States is now? The rapid growth of Mexico's border cities has been largely a result of the voluntary migration of persons who have expected to gain something from being in proximity to the United States. Such migration may represent a gamble, but many people apparently have found the odds attractive. Moreover, one may wish that economic opportunities were better in the Mexican borderlands, but there is no rapid or easy way to give everyone a standard of living comparable to the U.S. average—not even in the United States.

And is the dependency of the *frontera norte* an issue that involves only the United States? Is there not also a great deal of dependency vis-à-vis the centralist government in Mexico City? It may be suggested that Mexico's border cities have difficulty controlling their own destinies in no small part because of the political control exercised by state, and more particularly federal, authorities. Important decisions affecting border communities are commonly made at the national level and implemented by national agencies. Historically, centralization of political power has hampered the resolution of border problems. For example, major local taxes have accrued to higher authorities; local officials have had to cope with deficient revenues and have not been able to control their own budgets (Martínez 1978, p. 110). To be sure, since the 1960s the traditional central government neglect of the *frontera norte* has been replaced by numerous programs specifically designed to promote border development. Survey results indicate that the great majority of border leaders feel that policymakers in Mexico City do understand their special problems (Sloan and West 1977).

But the significance of these phenomena is still controversial. Torres, for example, maintains that although per capita incomes are relatively high in Mexico's border cities, they still have poorly developed social and economic infrastructures (Torres Ramirez 1979, p. 86). Ugalde argues that the

> Mexican government has been willing to take advantage of the proximity and wealth of the United States in order to solve part of its own national unemployment problem and, at the same time, find the income necessary to maintain its political "stability." Since the Second World War, the privileges enjoyed by the border states have been given not so much to promote development and help solve local problems but rather to satisfy the political and economic interests of the country's power structure located in Mexico City (Ugalde 1978, pp. 108–109).

Ugalde stresses that central government investments along the border have not been intended to solve local unemployment problems, but rather to promote new job sources in order to attract the unemployed from other parts of Mexico. Such investments could increase interregional income disparities, but "the distribution of wealth is not a guiding principle of the government's domestic policy" (Ugalde 1978, p. 109).

In contrast, it has been pointed out that even if Mexican border development policies have been motivated by self-serving reasons on the part of federal officials, the positive effects in terms of expanded employment opportunities, greater availability of consumer goods, and access to new cultural centers should not be underestimated. Thus, Martínez concludes that it "can be argued that increased involvement by the central government in border affairs has diminished local autonomy, but there can be no doubt that the frontier has benefited greatly from the investment of public funds and from concessions to the business sector" (Martínez 1982, pp. 7–8).

There seems to be agreement that dependency, or lack of local autonomy, characterizes relations between the *frontera norte* and the U.S. side of the border, as well as relations between the *frontera norte* and Mexico City. Both relationships have nonetheless been associated with economic benefits for border communities. However, many nationalist arguments that deplore dependency on the U.S. side do not adopt the same position with respect to internal dependency. Indeed, the latter may even be regarded as a positive factor that works against national disintegration. Whatever the political merits of such arguments, they tend to shift attention away from the fact that the economies (and often the societies) of the Mexican and U.S. borderlands are closely interrelated and that dependency in this context is mutual, as the consequences of the recent peso devaluation have shown. Because there seems to be agreement that border problems often have unique dimensions—because of transborder interdependencies—it would seem reasonable to give more attention to ways by which local and regional solutions for local and regional problems along the border can be found. This further implies that such issues need to be dealt with in an international context, that is, increased consideration should be given to the creation of transboundary cooperation mechanisms that take account of local and regional realities but at the same time respect the essential sovereignty of each nation. Is there any experience to suggest that practical planning interests in border areas can be accommodated within an international setting that minimizes the difficulties created by central government bureaucracies, sensitivity concerning diplomatic protocol, and pride in national sovereignty? These issues have in fact been addressed in Western Europe, where national governments have recently agreed to facilitate relatively unfettered transboundary cooperation with respect to a wide range of local and regional problems that transcend borders.

Transboundary Cooperation: European Experience

Prior to the Second World War, international boundaries in Western Europe represented relatively rigid barriers between nations, but in the postwar period borders have become increasingly permeable to the mobility of persons, goods, services and information. Industrial and commercial expansion in border regions has clearly generated economic benefits. However, it also has induced or intensified numerous problems that cannot be resolved by one side of the border alone. These issues include environmental pollution, transportation, public health, workers who commute across borders, legal and educational differences and land use planning. Over the past dozen years a large number of experiments have been carried out between neighboring border regions in an attempt to find regional and local solutions to regional and local problems. While such efforts have taken place throughout Western Europe, they have been particularly marked in the vicinity of the Rhine. For example, the great majority of transboundary cooperation organizations that make up the Association of European Border Regions, which provides a mechanism for sharing experiences and promoting cooperation, are located in the Rhine Basin. It should be emphasized that transboundary cooperation efforts have nearly always been initiated directly by groups and individuals from border regions, and difficulties have been less the fault of the people directly concerned than of central government authorities. At least until recently, border region officials and planners have felt that the needs and aspirations of border populations have not been appreciated or understood in distant national capitals. Nevertheless, issues involving adjacent border regions have generally been dealt with in the respective national capitals because the only institutionalized means of communication across borders has been international law and diplomacy.

Moreover, it has been difficult to match the competence and powers of the relevant ministries in different countries, and there has seemed "to be no limit to the fantasy of State officials in devising difficulties to local cooperation across frontiers" (Strassoldo 1973, p. 9).

Throughout the 1970s it became increasingly evident that progress with respect to transboundary cooperation in Europe would require a legal basis for guaranteeing accords reached by neighboring regional and local authorities and for assuring central governments that national sovereignty would be respected in the process. Working through the Council of Europe, local and regional authorities from border regions, and national ministers responsible for regional planning, developed a European Outline Convention on Transfrontier Cooperation. In 1979 this European Convention was endorsed by the Council of Europe's Parliamentary Assembly and it has since been signed by Austria, Belgium, Denmark, France, Ireland, Italy, Luxembourg, The Netherlands, Norway, Sweden, Switzerland, and West Germany.

The nations that have signed the European Convention have agreed that they are resolved to promote transboundary cooperation "as far as possible, and to contribute in this way to the economic and social progress of frontier regions and to the spirit of fellowship which unites the peoples of Europe" (Council of Europe 1982, p. 2). Although not compelled to do so, each nation is indirectly encouraged to amend its domestic laws if this would encourage such efforts. The central governments' normal powers concerning the conduct of international relations are not affected by the European Convention, but they have agreed to consult with one another to resolve legal, administrative or technical difficulties that might hinder the development of transboundary cooperation.

The appendix to the European Convention is particularly important because it sets forth an array of agreements, statutes and contracts that could be used to formalize cooperative efforts in such areas as urban and regional development, transportation and communications, energy, environmental protection, education, health, tourism, disaster relief, culture, industrial development, and problems of workers who commute across borders. The model cooperative mechanisms represent a graduated system ranging from simple consultation to the establishment of permanent organizations. Thus, transboundary cooperation is implicitly treated as an evolving relationship that typically develops from a network of informal contacts to an increasing number and complexity of concrete arrangements that could eventually result in planning harmonization across borders.

Conclusions

The growth of interdependent sister cities along the U.S.-Mexico border has generated and will intensify a host of social, economic, and environmental problems that require transboundary cooperation if they are to be addressed effectively. Local authorities and civic leaders on both sides of the border have demonstrated their willingness to cooperate on a broad range of issues. These efforts have usually been highly informal—and therefore piecemeal and unsystematic—because these authorities and leaders have wished to avoid the complicated and often insensitive decision-making processes of the respective central government bureaucracies.

It might be supposed that Mexico's highly centralized administrative system would pose particularly great problems for the distant *frontera norte.* In the past this area was in fact neglected, but in recent years it has benefited economically from federal development policies. Moreover, border leaders have made substantial contributions to the formulation and implementation of these policies. It has even been argued that Mexican border leaders have an advantage over their U.S. counterparts in eliciting government decisions, because they can more easily take their case directly to the top (Martínez 1982, p. 7). It should be noted, however, that whatever the motives for Mexico's border development policies, it is generally agreed that border communities experience diminished local autonomy as a result; and this is hardly conducive to the development of locally-initiated formal transboundary cooperation mechanisms. U.S. border communities have more autonomy within their national framework, but the decentralized system often requires local officials "to clear several layers of power and a wider network of private-interest groups before they can achieve results" (Martínez 1982, p. 7). This is particularly evident with respect to a variety of critical water quality and apportionment issues (Mumme 1982). In this as in other areas involving border spillovers, U.S. local governments are asking for a greater measure of policy freedom in structuring their relations with their Mexican counterparts (Jamail and Mumme 1982, p. 59).

Many Western European border regions have problems similar in kind, if not always in degree, to those found in the U.S.-Mexican borderlands. Despite many traditional animosities, Western European nations recently have committed themselves to the promotion of transboundary cooperation among neighboring local and regional authorities, with a minimum of interference by central governments (whose essential sovereignty is nonetheless clearly recognized). It is noteworthy in the present context that such cooperation has not been precluded by the fact that one nation's administrative structure may be highly centralized (France, for example), while that of its neighbor may be characterized by decentralized federalism (West Germany, for example). The principal stimulus to European transboundary cooperation has been economic development, but the presence of similar ethnic and linguistic groups in neighboring border regions has also been a facilitating factor (Strassoldo 1973, pp. 43–44). Rapid economic development has also induced a great deal of informal transboundary cooperation in the U.S.-Mexico borderlands. The large numbers of Mexican-Americans who live in U.S. border communities provide an ethnic basis for cooperation with neighboring Mexican communities; this is especially the case in Texas, where such efforts have been most active. The proportion of the total SMSA population that is Mexican-American is 62 percent in El Paso; 77 percent in Brownsville; 81 percent in McAllen; and 92 percent in Laredo (U.S. Department of Commerce, Bureau of the Census 1982b, p. 1).

In the light of European experience, it would seem reasonable for the United States and Mexico at least to explore the possibilities for creating—even if only on an experimental basis—mechanisms to promote transboundary cooperation between respective border communities or regions. All along the border, but perhaps particularly on the Rio Grande (Rio Bravo) frontier, the interpenetration of Mexican and U.S. elements has brought about a novel culture that transcends the border. There are those in each country who view this phenomenon as a threat to national integrity. But it may also be regarded as an opportunity to further a genuine and lasting *rapprochement* between two great nations.

SUMMARY

Mexico and the United States are becoming increasingly interdependent in many respects, and it has been cogently argued that Mexamerica—a relatively distinct region comprising much of the southwestern United States and northern Mexico—may replace the Northeast–Great Lakes industrial area as the economically dominant and most populous region of North America by the end of this century (Garreau 1981). The symbiotic relations that bind Mexico and the United States are nowhere more evident than in the adjacent urban areas that lie along the international boundary from Brownsville-Matamoros on the Gulf of Mexico to San Diego–Tijuana on the Pacific Ocean.

This paper examines the nature of demographic and economic growth patterns in the Mexico-U.S. borderlands during the 1970s, with particular attention given to the U.S. side. Then the significance of the recently altered situation, brought about in large part by the devaluations of the peso in 1982, is considered, and the concept of mutual interdependency is evaluated in this context. It is argued that a greater degree of locally based transboundary cooperation is needed in order to deal more effectively with a host of problems that have international dimensions. Finally, some policy suggestions in this regard are made on the basis of recent European experience.

References

Bustamante, Jorge A. "La Conceptualizatión Programación del Desarrollo de la Zona Fronteriza Norte de Mexico." In *Estudios Fronterizos.* México, D.F.: Asociación Nacional de Universidades e Institutos de Enseñanza Superior. 1981.

Castellanos Guerrero, Alicia and Gilberto López y Rivas. "La Influencia Norteamericana en la Cultura de la Frontera Norte de México." In *La Frontera del Norte: Integración y Desarrollo,* edited by Roque González Salazar. México, D.F.: El Colegio de México. 1981.

Consejo Nacional de Población. *México Demográfico: Breviario 1980–81.* México, D.F.: Consejo Nacional de Población. 1982.

Council of Europe, *European Outline Convention on Transfrontier Cooperation between Territorial Communities or Authorities.* Strasbourg, France: Council of Europe. 1982.

Garreau, Joel. *The Nine Nations of North America.* New York: Avon Books. 1981.

Greenwood, Michael J. "An Econometric Model of Internal Migration and Regional Economic Growth in Mexico." *Journal of Regional Science* 18 (April 1978), pp. 17–31.

Hansen, Niles. *The Border Economy: Regional Development in the Southwest.* Austin: University of Texas Press. 1981.

Jamail, Milton H. and Stephen P. Mumme. "The International Boundary and Water Commission as a Conflict Management Agency in the U.S.-Mexico Borderlands." *The Social Science Journal* 19 (January 1982), pp. 45–62.

Leatherwood, Joseph, Jr. "Peso's Plummet Caught Us by Surprise." *San Antonio Sunday Express-News,* March 20, 1983, p. H-1.

Martinez, Oscar J. *Border Boom Town: Ciudad Juárez Since 1848.* Austin: University of Texas Press. 1978.

Martínez, Oscar. "Mexico's Northern Frontier and the National Political System: Accommodation to Changing Realities." *The Mexican Forum,* special number. Austin: Office for Mexican Studies, University of Texas, December 1982.

Mieher, Stuart. "Some Mexicans, Strapped by Peso Controls, Start Losing Condos in U.S. Resort Towns." *Wall Street Journal,* December 3, 1982, p. 25.

Miller, Michael V. *Economic Growth and Change Along the U.S.-Mexico Border: The Case of Brownsville, Texas.* San Antonio: Human Resources Management and Development Program, College of Business, University of Texas at San Antonio. 1981.

Monsiváis, Carlos. "The Culture of the Frontier: The Mexican Side." In *Views Across the Border: The United States and Mexico,* edited by Stanley R. Ross. Albuquerque: University of New Mexico Press. 1978.

Mumme, Stephen P. "The Politics of Water Apportionment and Pollution Problems in United States–Mexico Relations." U.S.-Mexico Project Working Paper Series, No. 5. Washington, D.C.: Overseas Development Council. 1982.

Revel-Mouroz, Jean. "Economie frontalière et organisation de l'espace: réflections à partir de l'exemple de la frontière Mexique–Etats Unis." *Cahiers des Amériques Latines* 18 (1978), pp. 9–16.

Schlagheck, James L. *The Political, Economic, and Labor Climate in Mexico.* Revised Edition. Philadelphia: Industrial Research Unit, The Wharton School, University of Pennsylvania. 1980.

Sloan, John W., and Jonathan P. West. "Community Integration and Policies Among Elites in Two Border Cities." *Journal of Interamerican Studies and World Affairs* 18 (November 1976), pp. 451–474.

———. "The Role of Informal Policy Making in U.S.-Mexico Border Cities." *Social Science Quarterly* 58 (September 1977), pp. 270–282.

Stoddard, Ellwyn R. "A Conceptual Analysis of the 'Alien Invasion': Institutional Support of Illegal Mexican Aliens in the U.S." *International Migration Review* 10 (Summer 1976), pp. 157–189.

Strassoldo, Raimondo. *Frontier Regions.* Strasbourg, France: Council of Europe. 1973.

Texas Employment Commission. *Texas Labor Market Reviews.* Austin: Texas Employment Commission. February 1983.

Torres Ramirez, Olga Esther. *La Economía de Frontera: El Caso de la Frontera Norte de México.* México, D.F.: Aries. 1979.

Ugalde, Antonio. "Regional Political Processes and Mexican Politics on the Border." In *Views Across the Border: The United States and Mexico,* edited by Stanley R. Ross. Albuquerque: University of New Mexico Press. 1978.

U.S. Department of Commerce, Bureau of the Census. *Statistical Abstract of the United States: 1981.* Washington, D.C.: U.S. Government Printing Office, 1981.

U.S. Department of Commerce, Bureau of the Census. *State and Metropolitan Area Data Book.* Washington, D.C.: U.S. Government Printing Office. 1982.

U.S. Department of Commerce, Bureau of the Census. *Summary Characteristics for Governmental Units and Standard Metropolitan Statistical Areas.* 1980 Census of Population and Housing, PHC 80-45. Washington, D.C.: U.S. Government Printing Office. 1982.

2
Interdependence in the U.S.-Mexico Borderlands: Irresistible Dynamic or Fragmented Reality?

Kevin F. McCarthy

Introduction

The growing American awareness of the interconnections binding the United States and Mexico are most keenly felt along the 2,000-mile border between the two countries. Indeed, one commentator, in light of what he views as the declining importance of traditional national and regional boundaries on the North American continent, heralds the emergence of "Mexamerica," a binational, bicultural, and bilingual regional complex in the borderland region of the United States and Mexico. He cites several developments as evidence of this phenomenon. First is the increasing intermingling of populations in the borderlands as evidenced by the tremendous growth of the Mexican-origin population on the U.S. side of the border. Second, Mexican food, fashion, and music are becoming increasingly pervasive north of the border as are American food, fashion, and music south of the border. Third, and particularly noteworthy, Spanish is now read and heard with increasing frequency not just in the barrios of the United States, but also in advertisements, businesses, and schools (Garreau, 1981).

Although the popular awareness and, perhaps, even the desirability of this phenomenon decline as one moves north from the border, the phenomenon itself is in fact a by-product of a long-standing series of interlocking economic, social, and cultural interests that are inextricably binding together the U.S.-Mexican borderlands. What is most

This chapter is a revised version of a presentation given at the Second Conference on Regional Impacts of U.S.-Mexican Economic Relations, May 25-27, 1983, Tucson, Arizona.

novel about this phenomenon is its discovery by the U.S. media. This discovery, which is no doubt tied to America's increasing sensitivity to conflicts in Central America, our need for a stable oil supply, and the large influx of immigrants during a period of high unemployment, must strike many Mexicans as ironic given the pervasive and long-standing influence of American business and culture in Mexico. However, the phenomenon of borderland interdependence is, by now, a familiar topic of discussion among scholars and policymakers in both countries who, depending on their perspective, debate the degree of equality or inequality of that relationship.

This paper re-examines the phenomenon of borderlands interdependence in an attempt to distinguish the rhetoric from the reality. Focusing on the exchange relationships (socio-cultural, economic, and political) that promote interdependence as well as the characteristics and motives of the parties to the exchange, it reviews the current situation in the borderlands and considers longer-range trends and their implications both for the border and for the wider range of bilateral U.S. and Mexican relations.

Interdependence and U.S.-Mexican Relations

The general phenomenon of interdependence has been fostered by international events and developments since World War II that have produced tremendous increases in the flows of information, technology, capital, people, and cultural influences across national boundaries. Although primarily originating as flows of capital and technology responding to international disparities in the supply and mix of production factors that allow their more productive use elsewhere, once underway, such flows foster increases in other flows. Global exchanges of goods and technology, for example, promote transportation improvements that make it easier and cheaper to increase other flows. Thus, the flow of information through communication satellites runs in two directions. As it projects the poverty of various regions of the world into American living rooms, it also provides the people of those regions with a glimpse of American affluence and hence a motive for migrating. Moreover, once started, such flows often become self-perpetuating and, as a result, difficult to control. We see this in the sociology of immigrants' destination choices, whereby people tend to congregate in places where their friends and relatives have led the way—so-called chain migration. Finally, such flows serve multiple purposes and involve multiple actors with the result that they often have unanticipated and unintended consequences.

The general characteristics of global flows have direct implications for the nations involved in such transactions—implications that are especially pronounced in the case of the U.S. and Mexico, given the long-standing and wide-ranging flows of people, capital, and goods between these two nations. First, such flows result from interdependence and, in turn, foster its growth because all parties have a stake in the system of exchange. Although those stakes are not always equal and that imbalance can sometimes be exploited to the stronger party's advantage, by its very nature interdependence reduces any one nation's ability to regulate the system of flows or restrict their effects. Second, because they serve multiple interests and purposes, global flows have wide-ranging effects that cannot be restricted to a single dimension. Thus, the apparent interpenetration of American and Mexican social and cultural influences within the border region can be seen as an inevitable result of the system of flows of people, goods, tourists, information, etc., between these two countries. Moreover, the wide-ranging objectives served by these flows make it unlikely that either nation, even if it wanted to, could limit those effects.

The Context of U.S.-Mexican Relations at the Border

These characteristics of global flows are most evident in the borderlands. Witness, for example, the diverse and mutually dependent character of economic relations along the border itself. Located in a terrain that is not well-suited for agriculture nor well-situated for industry, the borderlands have nurtured a vibrant system of economic exchange upon which residents on both sides have come to depend. The maquiladora plants, for example, provide jobs and incomes for Mexicans which, in turn, promote profits for American manufacturers and provide markets for American retailers. Characteristically, these twin plant arrangements, while established for one purpose, end up serving and promoting a much wider range of interests. Moreover, the transportation routes set up to foster these legitimate economic exchanges facilitate a much wider range of transactions, including U.S. contraband into Mexico and Mexican contraband and migrants into the U.S. Finally, efforts of both governments to restrict these respective flows have not been notably successful. Even when they are, they often trigger a response by the other government. For example, when the Mexican government's drastic devaluation of the peso severely curtailed retail trade in American border cities, pressure by economic interests on the U.S. side of the border prompted President Reagan to promise to study the impact of devaluation on American retailers.

Such exchange networks are rarely limited simply to economic transactions. Indeed, an important distinguishing element of borderland interdependence is its propensity to promote social and cultural interpenetration across national boundaries. During the 1970s, for example, the four U.S. metropolitan areas in the border region grew three times more rapidly than the total U.S. population and much of that growth was fueled by their higher-than-average Hispanic populations (U.S. Census, 1981). Similarly, the Mexican *municipios* along the border have consistently grown faster than the country as a whole for several decades (Stoddard, 1978; Hansen, 1982). Moreover, eight of the twelve largest U.S. cities in the borderlands have mayors with Hispanic surnames—a percentage far exceeding the national average (less than 8 percent of the U.S. population is of Hispanic origin). Even more important than such formal signs of interpenetration are the informal mixing of cultures such as businesses on both sides catering to nationals in both countries, the widespread use of both English and Spanish, and the casual familiarity displayed toward the social customs of both nationalities in the borderlands.

While such signs of familiarity and acceptance do not entirely mask underlying tensions and occasional hostility, they do signal an altogether different attitude than prevailed less than 20 years ago when Carey McWilliams could accurately report that the Mexican-origin population in the United States was a "group so old it has been forgotten and so new that it has not yet been discovered" (McWilliams, 1964).

These changes implicitly signal an awareness among American businessmen and politicians that Mexican-Americans and Mexico can no longer either be taken for granted or ignored. Indeed, the long-coming recognition of the U.S.-Mexican connection has reached the point that, even in the face of the highest unemployment rates since the Depression, no responsible politicians either along the border or in Washington have proposed anything like an "Operation Wetback." Instead, they have incorporated amnesty for the undocumented as an essential element of immigration reform.

Social and Cultural Aspects of Borderlands Interdependence

Despite the current blending of social and cultural influences in the borderlands, it remains to be seen whether this process will produce an organic binational, bicultural, and bilingual "Mexamerica" region. There are, for example, not two but at least three distinct cultures currently mixing in the border region: Mexican, Anglo, and Chicano. I use the modifier "at least" since none of the three can realistically be considered homogeneous. Given the multi-ethnic (and indeed multiracial) character of the non-Hispanic population of the United States, the notion of a homogeneous Anglo culture is obviously an abstraction. Similarly, there are notable differences between Hispanos in New Mexico, Chicanos in California, and Tejanos in Texas, who can, in turn, be differentiated from the Mexican population in each of those areas. The distinction between Chicanos and Mexicans is drawn here in terms of which nation is regarded as "home" (Browning and Rodriguez, 1982).

The distinction between Chicanos and Mexicans is particularly important because, as a population with a foot in both cultures,

Chicanos might be expected to provide a natural bridge between Anglos and Mexicans. However, as de la Garza (1980) has suggested, this possibility seems unlikely. For example, when asked to identify their high priority issues, Chicanos place little emphasis on Mexican-U.S. relations per se; rather they stress issues that relate directly to their acceptance by the dominant Anglo society. Thus, employment discrimination, access to education, and pressures to abandon their language and culture are their paramount concerns (de la Garza, 1980).

One issue that might be expected to transcend the apparent gap between Mexican-Americans and Mexican nationals is immigration. Indeed, most Hispanic groups have joined in opposition to the pending immigration legislation (the Simpson-Mazzoli bill). However, this opposition seems to stem less from a concern with Mexico per se than from Chicanos' concern with their access to jobs and political power in the United States. As Chicanos have become more adept in the ways of the American political system, for example, they have realized, as have numerous immigrant groups before them, that American politics is played by the numbers. The more successful they are in building an active electoral constituency, the more effective they will be in exercising political power. This goal is clearly served by continued immigration from Mexico, but only to the extent that these immigrants become part of the American political process—a transformation that *sui generis* requires renunciation of their Mexican citizenship. Similarly, the vocal opposition of American Hispanics to the worker identification provisions of the current legislation relates to fears that those provisions will be used to deny them employment rather than to concern for undocumented workers. Indeed, the position of Chicanos towards the employment of the undocumented worker has been decidedly ambivalent (de la Garza, 1979).

Hispanic Americans' opposition to the current immigration legislation is not solely based on political and economic considerations, since there are distinct social and cultural advantages to be reaped from a continuation of the status quo. As was true for prior immigrant groups in the United States, the ongoing replenishment of the existing immigrant stock serves a central role in the maintenance of a distinctive Mexican-American cultural and social identity. The clearest example of these advantages is the maintenance of the native language— traditionally a very important vehicle for the intergenerational transmission of basic cultural values. Among all the immigrant groups to the United States, for example, the Germans were perhaps the most successful in maintaining the use of their native language from their initial settlement (in the early eighteenth century) until early into the twentieth. Their success was in no small part attributable to the fact that Germany sent more immigrants to the United States during the nineteenth century than any other nation (Schlossman, 1982). As

German immigration tailed off, so did the use of German among German-Americans.

The Mexican-Americans enjoy, of course, an advantage not shared by other immigrant groups—geographic adjacency. However, the current immigration legislation could limit that advantage by limiting the access of Mexican immigrants to the U.S. labor market.[1]

While language maintenance is clearly a central concern among Mexican-Americans as reflected by their strong support for bilingual education, the motivation for that support focuses less on identification with their former motherland than on their desire to perpetuate what has become a distinctive Chicano culture. Although sharing a common ancestry and language with Mexicans, Chicanos have developed their own distinctive culture by blending their Mexican heritage with their American experience. Within certain border areas, for example, Chicanos have developed their own distinctive music and language patterns (Browning and Rodriguez, 1982), and as Octavio Paz (1961) has pointed out, the "pachuco" is a distinctively Chicano phenomenon.

The differences between Chicanos and Mexicans increase noticeably among second and third generation Mexican-Americans since assimilation to American society occurs relatively rapidly among later generation Mexican-Americans (Jaffe et al., 1980). For example, among monolingual Chicanos a far greater percentage speak English than Spanish (Lopez, 1976) and the fertility of American-born Chicanos is much closer to that of native-born Anglos than of Mexican-born women (Jaffe et al., 1980). Moreover, on several key dimensions (e.g., residential location and earnings) Chicanos appear better integrated into U.S. society than other American minorities (Massey and Mullen, 1982). Indeed, Stolzenberg (1982) finds that after controlling for language skills among second and succeeding generations, Hispanic Americans perform as well in the labor market as Anglos with the same level of human capital.

This assimilation pattern is rooted in the dominance of English and Anglo cultural practices in America's social, political, and economic life. As a result, Mexican migrants who come to the United States for upward mobility (as indeed most do) must adapt to Anglo patterns in order to advance. Such adaptation involves learning English as well as assuming the social mores of the dominant culture. This situation contrasts sharply with that of Cuban immigrants in Miami, where much of the commerce and the political power is dominated by Spanish-speaking Cubans, as well as with that of French Canadians in Quebec, where the dominant social and cultural institutions are French. Such differences help explain the sharply different assimilation patterns of Cubans and French Canadians to what are otherwise similar Anglo cultures and suggest that the analogy of Mexican-Americans in the borderlands to Cubans in Miami and French Canadians in Quebec—often cited by those who fear that a substantial influx of

Hispanics into the United States will threaten the national cohesion of what is already an ethnically diverse nation—is unlikely to hold in the borderlands.

The dominance of Anglo economic, political, and social institutions is, however, not the only factor creating ambivalence in the relationship between Chicanos and Mexicans. As Gutierriez (1973) has pointed out, Mexican officials have, in general, made little effort to cultivate a positive relationship between these two groups. Instead, for whatever reasons, the Mexican government has displayed what can be characterized as an essentially disparaging attitude towards Mexican-Americans. A clear example of this attitude was the reaction of Mexican officials and the Mexican press to former President Carter's appointment of a Hispanic, Dr. Julian Nava, to the ambassador's post in Mexico City.

In summary, while the Chicano population in the United States could serve to promote social-cultural understanding and acceptance in the border region by acting as a bridge between the Anglo and the Mexican national populations, the mutual ambivalence of Chicanos and Mexicans, combined with the Chicanos' need to assimilate, seems likely to inhibit that role. This point is especially important because the typical Anglo in the borderlands will come into much closer contact with Chicanos than with Mexican nationals. Those Chicanos are, of course, likely to speak English and to be more interested in making it economically than in promoting understanding between Anglos and Mexicans.

The typical contact between Anglos and Mexicans, even in the border region, is likely to be one of economic exchange (e.g., Mexicans dealing with Anglo tourists or Anglo businessmen catering to a growing Hispanic market). Such "gesellschaft" relationships are typically segmented and formalized and are unlikely to promote either a sense of community or a mutual understanding of alternative cultures except in the most narrow way. Furthermore, immigrants from Mexico, particularly the undocumented, often view themselves as sojourners, who enter the United States to earn, remit, and return and, as such, have little incentive to seek extensive contact with the Anglo population or culture. Indeed, with the proliferation of Spanish-language television and radio stations, movie theaters, newspapers, and the like along the border, the undocumented immigrant who intends to return to Mexico has little reason to interact with Anglos other than for economic reasons.

This situation could change if an increasing fraction of the undocumented population settles permanently in the United States—a phenomenon that already appears to be occurring. Cornēlius (1981) and Browning and Rodriguez (1982), for example, report an increasing percentage of families (who are likely to settle permanently) and a declining fraction of young single males (who are likely to return to

Mexico) within the undocumented population. Moreover, by raising the cost of entry, a stricter border enforcement policy will increase the incentive to remain in the United States for longer periods and, indirectly, the percentage of undocumented who settle permanently in the United States.

This apparent shift in the migration patterns of the undocumented is likely to continue for two certain and a third potential, reasons. First, it reflects a secular shift of undocumented workers out of seasonal agriculture work, well suited for circular migration, into year-round jobs in the urban service and manufacturing sectors. This shift reflects a long-run substitution of capital for labor which is likely to continue even without changes in immigration law. Second, rapid population growth combined with economic problems in Mexico will almost certainly continue to generate a labor surplus that cannot be effectively absorbed by the Mexican economy. Mexico's economy, for example, was unable to fully employ its growing labor force during the period of very rapid growth preceding the recent economic crisis and is unlikely to do so soon after the crisis has passed. The third and potentially the most important reason for assuming that settlement rates may increase is the distinct possibility of future labor shortages in the United States. Although United States labor markets are currently very loose, demographic factors could change this situation dramatically in the next decade (Butz et al., 1980).

The long-term effects of higher settlement rates for borderland interdependence are, however, uncertain. Traditionally, a large fraction of the undocumented migrants who eventually settle in the United States arrive with the intention of returning and thus make little effort either to learn English or to become familiar with Anglo culture. This limits their contact with the non-Hispanic population and helps, in part, explain the low naturalization rates even among legal permanent resident aliens from Mexico.[2] Indeed, as long as undocumented migrants face the possibility of deportation, they have little incentive to pursue a strategy of assimilation. Consequently, a higher settlement rate and even an explicit amnesty program will not of themselves facilitate the interaction among the Anglo and Mexican national population necessary to promote a socially and culturally integrated Mexamerica. Indeed, as long as Mexicans living in the United States are residentially and socially segregated from the non-Hispanic population, the result is more likely to be an increasing sense of distinction rather than communality between the two populations.

In summary, while the borderlands exhibit many features of interdependence, the dynamic underlying that phenomenon rests less on a shared sense of social and cultural community and more on an implicit recognition of mutual economic need. Furthermore, the recognition of that need declines markedly as one moves away from the border. Thus, while residents of San Ysidro or El Paso may be acutely aware of their dependence, those in Los Angeles and Dallas are less so, and those in Salt Lake City and Oklahoma City hardly at all. Thus, despite the obvious facets of interdependence in the borderland, the primary dynamic for interdependence remains economic; and until that changes, the notion of an emergent organic "Mexamerica" will be too simplisitc.

The Wider Context of Borderland Interdependence

While cities on both sides of the border have developed common ties that are in some ways stronger than their ties to their respective countries, the dynamic behind that interdependence can only partly be explained by events at the border itself. Decisions made by officials in Washington and Mexico City, as well as the actions of a wide variety of individuals and businessmen throughout both countries, have contributed to the evolution of the institutions and exchanges that have promoted interdependence in the borderlands.

From the United States perspective, economic, strategic, foreign-policy, and even domestic political considerations dictate an explicit recognition of the need for a special relationship with Mexico. The United States has historically relied on Mexico for a variety of economic purposes, e.g., as a source of goods and labor and as a market for trade and investments. Indeed, while increasing competition from Japan and Western Europe has reduced our once overwhelming dominance in trade with the rest of the Western Hemisphere, our trade and investment in Mexico have increased substantially. Similarly, the growing Soviet presence and general political instability in the hemisphere have made Washington increasingly aware of the importance of a stable and friendly neighbor on our southern border. Finally, a growing number of interest groups within the United States, including local officials, businessmen, and Hispanics, has added domestic political considerations to the policy equation. Similar, although not identical, considerations in Mexico have led policymakers in Mexico City to promote the continued development of their northern border region even though incomes and industrial development in that region surpass those in most of the rest of the country.

As a result, both governments have instituted policies, particularly with regard to trade and investment, that have increased the volume of flows between the two countries. These flows have in turn promoted the development of borderlands interdependence. Indeed, these policies are often cited as an example of the explicit recognition of the growing interdependence between the two countries.

However, it would be a mistake to equate the degree of interdependence in the borderlands with that of the federal level. By almost any measure, the extent and symmetry of the relations between the two countries are far greater at the border than elsewhere. For example, while trade with Mexican nationals in the border region constitutes a very important element of that region's economy, United States trade with Mexico as a whole, although increasing, still constitutes a relatively small share of total United States trade.

Moreover, United States–Mexican relations at the federal level are complicated by an array of considerations that simply do not come into play in borderland relations. Such foreign policy issues as United States policy in Central America, for example, often play an important role in bilateral United States–Mexican relations but are of little importance to the border. Similarly, the range of domestic political interests with a stake in relations between the two countries at the federal level is both greater and more diverse than in the border region. Indeed, despite differences between United States and Mexican nationals in the border region over such issues as water rights, pollution, and a host of other border-related issues, there is far more likely to be agreement about the mutual interests of both parties in the border than in the wider federal context. As a result, linking such broader issues to borderland problems can significantly complicate borderland relations.

The contrast between the border and the federal level exists not only in terms of the range of issues and interests involved, but also in terms of the goals of the parties. As Urquidi and Villarreal (1975) have pointed out, residents along the Mexican side of the border, in the face of their distance from the Federal District, the centralized pattern of decision-making in Mexico, and their superior income levels vis-à-vis the rest of the country, have far more reason to favor increased integration with United States border cities than do policymakers in Mexico City who already fear that the close connections between the northern border states and the United States threaten national integration. Correspondingly, United States residents in the borderlands have a vested interest in policies which increase the volume of trade between the two countries and thus promote the economic welfare of what has historically been among the poorest regions in the United States. Indeed, the continued economic development of the United States border region no doubt depends significantly on increased cross-border trade. These mutual interests in the border region are further strengthened by the frequent exchanges between business and political elites in border cities.

United States residents living outside the border area, in contrast, often feel that their economic interests are threatened by increased trade with Mexico. For example, United States labor unions frequently complain that the effect of such special arrangements as the in-bond industries is to take jobs from their members. Similarly, farmers often view Mexican agriculture as competitors for United States markets, just as non-Hispanic minority groups view the on-going flows of documented and undocumented immigrants as a direct threat to their jobs as well as their political aspirations.

Thus, the broader context of United States–Mexican relations has a decidedly ambivalent effect on borderland interdependence. While it fosters increasing interdependence in the border region by emphasizing the special character of binational relations, it also complicates and in some ways impedes that integration by introducing into cross-border relations a much wider and decidedly less manageable set of issues. Indeed, by linking regional and federal concerns and expanding the range of domestic interest groups whose concerns must be accommodated, bilateral relations at the federal level significantly complicate negotiations about specifically border issues. In sum, the broader context of United States–Mexican relations on balance probably limits the possibilities of an organic "Mexamerica."

Coming Trends and Their Implications for Borderland Interdependence

While the current state of interdependence in the borderland reflects less the significance of social and cultural factors than the priority of economic realities, what will the future hold? Any number of events and trends could profoundly affect interdependence in the borderlands; however, I will discuss two issues that I believe to be of special importance.

The first issue concerns the potential complementarity between longer-term demographic trends in both countries. Currently, unemployment rates in the United States are at their highest levels since 1940, and the prospect of continued large-scale immigration seems likely to pose additional problems for national economic recovery. In contrast, continued high fertility and slowing economic growth in Mexico will produce a labor surplus and thus a large pool of potential immigrants. However, this apparent incompatibility could well change, and a large influx of migrants may forestall a severe labor shortage in future decades. Specifically, the recent flows of immigrants into the United States, which rival the enormous waves at the turn of the century, have been only one of three demographic events that have strained the absorptive capacity of the American economy. At the same time that we were experiencing increased flows of immigrants, our labor market was also trying to create jobs for the maturing "baby boom" cohorts and to accommodate an unprecedented influx of women into the labor force. With the drop in the fertility rate, however, and the likely peaking of women's labor force participation, fewer and fewer native-born workers will be entering the labor force. Thus, what currently appears to be a labor surplus could well become a labor shortage by the end of the decade.

Whether this possible complementarity between the economic and demographic situations in the United States and Mexico will in fact serve to increase the mutual dependence of the two countries depends on factors whose future course is uncertain. Specifically, the pattern of future growth in the various sectors of the American economy and, correspondingly, the level of skills that will be needed in the next decade, will largely determine the types of immigrants the American economy will need.

If, as is certainly possible, the future supply of low-skilled labor fails to keep pace with demand, then the complementary demographic and economic situation in the United States and Mexico will almost certainly promote increasing interdependence—not just in the borderland but more generally throughout American society. For example, to the extent that tight labor markets raise wages and reduce unemployment, then the traditional opposition of American labor unions to wide-scale immigration may well abate. Moreover, unions could well view these new immigrants as a fertile ground for new recruits, with the result that their membership will contain significant numbers of Mexican-born and second generation Mexican-Americans (Butz et al., 1982). By facilitating a wider range of social contacts among Anglos and Mexican-Americans, such a development would certainly promote a better socio-cultural understanding between those two groups than currently exists.

If, on the other hand, the changing industrial composition of the U.S. economy creates a supply-demand imbalance in its high-skill service and so-called "high tech" industrial sectors, then the continuing economic and demographic situations in the United States and Mexico could well exacerbate tensions between the two countries. Historically, immigrants have concentrated in low-skill, low-wage jobs and industries, in particular in agriculture and basic manufacturing, for which plentiful cheap labor was vital. However, these industries are no longer growing. Their place in the American economy has been usurped by services and high-technology industries, which are widely expected to spur the nation's future economic growth. If, as many believe, these industries will require predominantly highly skilled workers, then a continuing large influx of low-skill immigrants from Mexico and elsewhere could well produce a situation of unacceptably high unemployment in some skills and industries with shortages in others. This possibility could well shift the traditional family reunification emphasis of U.S. immigration policy toward a policy favoring the importation of highly skilled labor. Such policies could induce a "brain drain" from the lesser developed countries (including Mexico) and thus exacerbate rather than alleviate their economic problems.

The second uncertainty concerns the future political role of Mexican-Americans in bilateral U.S.-Mexican relations. As we have already noted, the relationship between Chicanos and Mexicans can best be characterized as ambivalent, with neither group attaching a high priority to cooperation. Indeed, we have argued that Chicanos today place a much greater emphasis on gaining full access to the benefits, both economic and political, that American society has to offer than on rapprochement with Mexico.

This situation could change, however, as the Hispanic population continues to increase in size and political power. Although Hispanics comprise only 6 percent of the current U.S. population, their numbers are growing more rapidly than either the Anglo or the black population (the largest of the minority groups in the United States) and, given their currently higher immigration and fertility rates, should continue to do so for the foreseeable future. Indeed, Hispanics are already the dominant minority group in two of America's three largest states and, according to some projections, will surpass blacks as the dominant minority group in the country as a whole by early in the next century.

Although Hispanics, and Mexican-Americans in particular, have been unable to translate their increasing demographic importance into equivalent political power (primarily due to low naturalization and voting rates), there is considerable evidence that this situation may also be changing. Witness, for example, the growing number of political positions held by Hispanic Americans and the increasing political visibility attached to issues of special concern to Hispanics, e.g., bilingual education. Given their potential demographic and political importance, Mexican-Americans could well become a potent lobby for Mexican interests in bilateral U.S.-Mexican relations, much as Jewish Americans are in U.S.-Israel relations today. If this should occur, it would affect not just interdependence in the borderlands but the whole character of U.S.-Mexican relations by bringing the interest at the federal level in line with the U.S. borderlands' interests in strengthening U.S.-Mexican interdependence.

Notes

1. Interestingly, only one other non-English-speaking immigrant group—French Canadians—shares the same advantage of adjacency, not to mention many other similarities, and although their numbers are substantially smaller, their experiences are remarkably similar to those of Mexican-Americans.

2. Again, an interesting parallel can be made between Mexico and Canada, both of which send to the United States a large number of immigrants who enter with the intention of returning but eventually settle. Those immigrants are far more likely than others to emigrate later or, if they do decide to settle, to become United States citizens.

References

Browning, Harley L. and Nestor Rodriguez. "Mexico-U.S.A. Indocumentado Migration as a Settlement Process and Its Implications for Work," U.C.–Santa Barbara. 1982.

Butz, William, Kevin F. McCarthy, Peter A. Morrison, and Mary E. Vaiana. *Demographic Challenges in America's Future*. The Rand Corporation. Report R-2911-RC. 1982.

Cornelius, Wayne, et al. *Mexican Immigrants and Southern California: A Summary of Current Knowledge*, University of California, San Diego. 1981.

de la Garza, Rodolfo. "Chicano-Mexican Receptions: A Framework for Analysis," paper presented at Latin American Studies Association Meeting. 1980.

de la Garza, Rodolfo. "Public Policy Priorities of Chicano Political Elites," paper presented to Overseas Development Council, 1981.

Garreau, Joel. *The Nine Nations of North America*, Houghton Mifflin, Boston. 1981.

Gutierriez, G. "Illusion or Realism: The Rapprochement of Mexican America and Mexico," unpublished paper. 1973.

Hansen, Niles. "Transboundary Environmental Issues in the United States–Mexico Border Region," *Southwest Review of Management and Economics*. 1982.

Jaffe, A. J., et al. *The Changing Demography of Spanish Americans*. Academic Press, New York. 1980.

Lopez, David E. "The Social Consequences of Chicano Home/School Bilingualism," *Social Problems*, Vol. 24, No. 2. 1976.

Massey, Douglas, and Brendan Mullen. "Social Class and Hispanic Residential Succession," paper presented at Population Association of America Meetings, San Diego. 1982.

McCarthy, Kevin F., and David F. Ronfeldt. *U.S. Immigration Policy and Global Interdependence*, The Rand Corporation. Report R-2887-FF/RF/RC/NICHD. 1982.

McWilliams, Carey. *Brothers Under the Skin*. Little, Brown, Boston. 1964.

Paz, Octavio. *The Labyrinth of Solitude*. Grove Press, New York. 1961.

Schlossman, Stephen. "Is There an American Tradition of Bilingual Education? Germans in the 19th Century Public Elementary," *American Journal of Education*, Vol. 91, No. 2, pp. 139–186. 1983.

Stoddard, Ellwyn R. "Selected Impacts of Mexican Migration on the U.S.-Mexico Border," paper presented at State Department conference. 1978.

Stolzenberg, Ross M. *Occupational Differences Between Hispanics and Non-Hispanics*, The Rand Corporation. Note N-1889-NCEP.

U.S. Bureau of the Census. Standard Metropolitan Statistical Areas: 1980, PC80-S2-5, U.S.G.P.O., Washington, D.C. 1981.

Ugaldo, Antonio. "Regional Political Processes and Mexican Politics on the Border," in *Views Across the Border*, Stanley Ross (ed.), Albuquerque, University of New Mexico Press. 1975.

Urquidi, Victor, and Sofia Mandez Villarreal. "The Economic Importance of Mexico's Northern Border Region," in *Views Across the Border*, Stanley Ross (ed.), Albuquerque, University of New Mexico Press. 1975.

3
National Identity Along Mexico's Northern Border: Report of Preliminary Findings

Jorge A. Bustamante

Introduction

The relationship which exists between national identity and the use of anglicisms in everyday Spanish speech has been the focus of many heated discussions but of few efforts at scientific verification. The presence of foreign words in advertisements for consumer products in Mexico, the "Spanish-ization" of English words, and the scattered appearance of words taken directly from English can easily lead one to envision a gradual deterioration in the everyday Spanish spoken by many persons in Mexico.

When we observe the modifications, alterations, or distortions in the Spanish language which result from the influence of English, we are observing not only usage problems in Spanish but also their point of origin. Changes occurring in Spanish under the impact of the English influence have been interpreted as a process by which intro-duced elements from another language are substituted for "correct" Spanish speech. Implicit in this view is the assumption of a loss of something national, provoked by the introduction of something foreign. It is as easy as it is erroneous to deduce from this supposition that if language is an element of national identity, the "loss" of language is identical to the loss of national identity. It is equally erroneous to deduce that if the loss of language is due to the introduction of elements from the United States, those areas of Mexico closest to the United States will be at greatest risk of losing their national identity through the loss of "correct usage" of the Spanish language.

Following this logic, one arrives at the fallacious hypothesis that closer geographic ties with the United States imply a stronger influence of English on Spanish and a weakening of national identity. Although this hypothesis has never received scientific support, it survives as a misconception which distorts our understanding of the cultural dynamic along Mexico's northern frontier and blocks communication between those who accept this misconception as fact *a priori* and those who experience a different reality along the border, not only distant from the underlying premises of this misconception, but also, as we will demonstrate shortly, in a situation diametrically opposed to that which is accepted as underlying this mistaken view.

In any discussion of national identity there is a risk of oversimplification, to the point of making Manichean accusations based on a simplistic nationalized-denationalized dichotomy. The risk of Manicheanism is even greater when generalizing from specific regions of the country to the nation as a whole. Overgeneralizations regarding national identity in border areas are common, both in Mexico and elsewhere. Such generalizations frequently contain an element of ethnocentrism deriving from the belief that national identity, or nationalism, is stronger in the center than on the periphery. This in turn has political implications in terms of discriminatory attitudes, interregional divisionism, and the breakdown of national solidarity. Because of the seriousness of these outcomes, such ethnocentrism must be resisted. The most logical manner of resistance is to attempt to verify scientifically the degree of truth or falsity to be found in the hypothesis that the greater the geographic proximity to a foreign country, the weaker will be the sense of national identity. This was the primary objective of a research project undertaken by the Centro de Estudios Fronterizos del Norte de Mexico (CEFNOMEX), located in Tijuana.

Methodology

The following working hypothesis directed this research: with greater geographic proximity to the United States, the use of anglicisms in daily Spanish speech will increase and national identity will decrease.

The alternative hypothesis stated: differing levels in the use of anglicisms and in the measures of national identity are associated more with the socioeconomic levels of the population than with greater or lesser geographic proximity to the United States.

The principal variables were operationally defined as follows:

Use of Anglicisms. For the purposes of this research, Dr. Luis Fernando Lara, a linguist from the Colegio de México, defined "anglicisms" not only as a series of words originating in the English language which are frequently incorporated into Spanish, but as expressions, syntactic forms, and intonation patterns derived from the influence of the English language on the Spanish. Measures were taken of the frequency with which these anglicisms appeared in recordings of spoken Spanish taped in a representative sample of neighborhoods in seven Mexican cities: Tijuana, Ciudad Juarez, Matamoros, Acapulco, Uruapan, Zacatecas, and Mexico City. A total of 3,180 persons were interviewed, with each subject being asked to discuss his activities during the week prior to the interview: economic activities, recreational activities, and family interactions, including the recounting of a conversation with a family member which took place during that week. Interviews lasted between five and ten minutes. The frequency of anglicism usage was then calculated for each interview.

National Identity. Because time and material limitations did not allow us to construct and test a scale of national identity which would measure an individual's perception of himself as Mexican in terms of his values, beliefs, national history, national symbols, cultural traditions, artistic accomplishments and craft production, language, etc., we employed a psycho-sociological test developed by Dr. Rogelio Diaz Guerrero. This test, a measure of "sociocultural" premises, was designed to measure "national character," understood as an individual's alienation from or acceptance of the distinctive traditional values of the Mexican culture. While Dr. Diaz Guerrero's test cannot be considered a thorough measure of national identity, it does include elements which are essential in its definition. Following the application of this test of "sociocultural premises," each of the 3,180 interviews was scored, and from these scores we were able to operationalize the levels of "national identity" present among individuals included in the interview sample.

Geographic Proximity to the United States. For comparative purposes, we selected three northern border cities (Tijuana, Ciudad Juarez, and Matamoros) and four cities in the interior of Mexico (Uruapan, Zacatecas, Acapulco, and Mexico City).

Socioeconomic Levels. Two population sectors were defined in the sample design: Sector 1 comprises individuals living in upper-income residential areas of each of the cities selected. Sector 2 includes people of middle and low-income levels residing in the urban areas of these cities. Relying on statistical probability procedures, maps, and census data, a method was designed for randomly selecting residences within each sector for interview purposes. Within each residence, interviews were conducted with individuals over 15 years of age. Conventional interviewing procedures were followed in which interviewers trained for fieldwork in this research project completed the questionnaires, recording the information elicited during the interviews.

Preliminary Findings

A principal finding of this research is presented in Graph 1. A regression analysis between the variables "use of anglicisms," or language usage, and "national identity" did not provide any statistical support for the central working hypothesis (that is, the greater the use of anglicisms, the lower the level of national identity). However, significant differences appeared in this analysis between the two

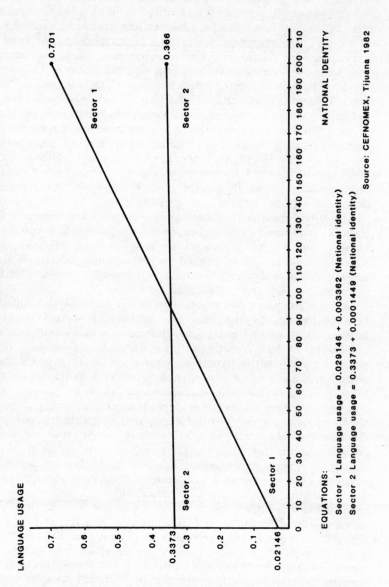

GRAPH 1

Relationship between Language Usage and National Identity

LANGUAGE USAGE

NATIONAL IDENTITY

EQUATIONS:

Sector 1 Language usage = 0.029146 + 0.003362 (National identity)

Sector 2 Language usage = 0.3373 + 0.0001449 (National identity)

Source: CEFNOMEX, Tijuana 1982

population sectors equated with socioeconomic levels within the population of each city included in the sampling design. Graph 1 indicates that no statistically significant relationship exists between "language usage" and "national identity" in Sector 2 of the population, representing the lower- and middle-income groups of each city. But in Sector 1 (the population of upper-income residential areas of each city) an inverse relationship was found between these two variables; this is the opposite of what would be expected if the central working hypothesis (greater use of anglicisms, or "language usage," lesser national identity) held true. This inverse relationship which appears in Graph 1 would seem to prove overwhelmingly the inappropriateness of the central working hypothesis. However, we must remember that residents of these zones tend to have a higher level of education, and thus greater familiarity with the English language. This fact could well explain the more frequent use of anglicisms among this population; but this usage is totally unrelated statistically with their measured degree of national identity.

The single most important finding represented in Graph 1 is the absence, in all seven cities studied, of any relationship between national identity and the use of anglicisms by individuals in either of the socioeconomic categories defined in the sampling design. With this absence of any statistically significant relationship between variables in mind, we may proceed to examine Graph 2.

When examining each variable individually and analyzing differences between the various cities selected, and between sectors within each of these cities, we find unexpected differences which clearly contradict our central working hypothesis. These differences, moreover, strongly support the alternative hypothesis (that different levels in the "use of anglicisms" and in "national identity" result to an important extent from differences between socioeconomic levels as defined by the residential sectors of the individuals interviewed, rather than from the geographic proximity of these populations to the United States). A close examination of Graph 2, which presents the mean scores recorded on the "sociocultural premises" scale, by sector and by city, reveals some startling findings. Given that in this test of sociocultural premises a higher score indicates greater acceptance of Mexico's cultural values, and thus a higher degree of national identity, it is very important to note that the highest average score for Sector 2 (lower and middle income groups) is found in Ciudad Juarez, and this is followed by the second highest score, recorded in Matamoros. That is, the two highest scores for national identity are found in two of the three border cities studied. Moreover, continuing our examination of national identity scores in Sector 2, we find Tijuana in fourth place, immediately behind Acapulco, whose population stands out for its heavy use of anglicisms in daily speech.

These findings clearly contradict the working hypothesis which states that border cities, because of their proximity to the United States,

GRAPH 2

Socioeconomic characteristics of the populations of seven Mexican cities in July 1982 (mean scores in language usage,[1] and national identity,[2] by city and by population sector[3]).

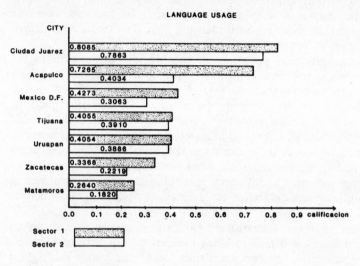

LANGUAGE USAGE

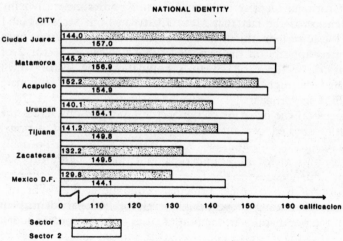

NATIONAL IDENTITY

1 Frequency of linguistic expressions displaying English-language influence.

2 Degree of proximity to the "sociocultural premises" of the national character.

3 Each sector represents a statistically valid sample in terms of place of residence of the respective population of each city. Sector 1 residential areas; Sector 2 the remainder of the urban area.

Source: CEFNOMEX, Tijuana, 1982

display a higher degree of incorporation of anglicisms into everyday Spanish speech and, consequently, a lower degree of national identity. Our findings indicate that the opposite is true. Graph 2, which indicates that the populations of Ciudad Juarez and Acapulco commonly use anglicisms in daily Spanish speech, also indicates that these same populations display a very high level of what we have operationally defined in this study as national identity. This allows us a high degree of confidence in concluding that:

1. The geographical proximity of the Mexican population to the United States is not the determinant variable in the extent to which anglicisms are incorporated into everyday Spanish speech. Even though Ciudad Juarez appears the leader in terms of the use of anglicisms, it is followed very closely by two cities located far from the border, Acapulco and Mexico City. And in terms of Sector 2 of the population, Tijuana and Zacatecas are measured at the same level. Our conclusion receives additional confirmation when we examine the position of Matamoros in Graph 2. Although it is a border city, the two sectors of its population register the lowest levels of incorporation of anglicisms into daily Spanish speech uncovered in this study.

2. In terms of our operational definition, geographic proximity to the United States also fails to affect the national identity of Mexico's border populations. The two populations in Sector 2 with the highest degrees of national identity are found in two border cities. Worthy of our attention is the fact that Mexico City, in both Sectors 1 and 2, scored the lowest on this measure of national identity. And, once again, Tijuana appears on the same level as Zacatecas in Sector 2 of its population; Sector 1 of Tijuana's population, the sector which demonstrated the higher level of national identity, is seen to equate with Sector 1 in Uruapan.

If we focus on the behavior of the Sector 1 populations across the various cities studied, we find the highest mean level of national identity in Acapulco. This finding is very surprising, since one normally assumes that this sector of Acapulco's population is highly exposed to foreign influences, especially from the United States, because of the international nature of its principal economic activity. For this same reason the finding of very high levels of national identity in Sector 1 of the populations in the border cities of Matamoros, Ciudad Juarez, and Tijuana was also unexpected. It appears that, contrary to our working hypothesis, those populations in Mexico which are closest to the United States, and which have the closest contact with U.S. tourism in Mexico, demonstrate higher levels of acceptance of traditional Mexican cultural values than do populations which have less contact with U.S. tourism, or with the U.S. population in general. It appears that those cultural traditions which identify value sets for the Mexican population are reinforced precisely in those areas where there is greatest contact with foreign influences. Our findings did not support the supposition that border populations along Mexico's northern frontier are undergoing a process of cultural denationalization. If such a process does indeed occur, it would appear that Mexico City is most likely to suffer its effects.

4
Sectoral and Territorial Implications of Industrialization in the U.S.-Mexico Borderlands

Luis Suarez-Villa

Introduction

One potentially important but as yet little realized area of research on industrialization lies in the analysis of rapidly expanding manufacturing export zones. The increasing internationalization of capital and of western industrial economies has made such zones, and the related plant closings and relocations in advanced nations, a major concern of our time (Fröbel et al. 1980, Bluestone and Harrison 1982, Grunwald 1984). The Mexican Border Industrialization Program (hereinafter BIP) has become one of the most dynamic industrial export enclaves today, growing to include over 620 plants and 120,000 workers in little more than a decade's time (Secretaría de Programación y Presupuesto 1981). The proximity of Mexico's BIP to United States markets, and the fact that the vast majority of BIP plants are U.S.-owned, have strengthened the assumption that the Mexican border has become a favored location for many U.S. industries that seek to relocate operations abroad while continuing to serve U.S. markets (e.g., Baird and McCaughan 1979). Unfortunately, with the exception of Ayer and Layton (1974), Hansen (1981), Suarez-Villa (1981, 1982), and Seligson and Williams (1982) almost no empirical research on U.S.-Mexico border industrialization has been undertaken. The unavailability of data on Mexican border industries and of sufficient and compatible U.S. manufacturing census year data has, until recently, been a major obstacle to research in this area.

This paper assumes the existence of an evolutionary process of manufacturing locational change. Industries are assumed to shift their location to more labor-abundant and wage-competitive regions as their manufacturing processes mature. In this respect, therefore, industries that were very important in U.S. industrial heartland regions three or more decades ago can be expected to exhibit significant patterns of decline. Those same industries may, on the other hand, be expected to become increasingly important in "peripheral" regions such as the U.S.-Mexico border area. Time-series data for eight selected 3- and 4-digit industries from U.S. industrial heartland regions and border states, as well as from Mexico's BIP, will be analyzed to determine trends and contrasts in both sectoral and regional industrialization performance.

Sectoral Evolution in Manufacturing

Various evolutionary phases may be distinguished in the development of any given manufacturing activity. These phases are related to the evolutionary characteristics of manufacturing processes within the general framework of the manufacturing process cycle (see Suarez-Villa 1983, 1984). This conceptual framework will be generally related to the data analysis of the following section. In the first stage of the process cycle, *Phase A*, it may be expected that research and development activities (hereinafter R&D) will be the major concern of the firm. It is therefore anticipated that R&D productivity maximization will be the most important priority of the firm, partnership, or other organizational unit engaged in product innovation in this phase. This strategy may be translated into action through hiring uniquely qualified technical personnel, providing an appropriate working environment, and establishing strong informal links with major university or research center activities and personnel. Other activities may also include the analysis of other innovations in related fields that could provide breakthroughs, the internal streamlining of the patent-filing process and the careful organization of any activities that may accelerate the productive application of innovations. Profits during this phase are nonexistent since there is neither regular productive output nor a market, and the firm or partnership may be operating with out-of-pocket funds or savings. It is difficult to specify any systematic locational preference for this phase, but it may be anticipated that there will be greater possibilities for location in the areas where major research institutions are found.

If useful innovations are produced in the first phase of the process cycle, the productive unit may move on to a second stage, *Phase B*, in which the firm may enjoy a short-term monopoly situation over the product's growing market. In this situation, it may be anticipated that the firm's primary objective may be to maximize its market outreach before other firms are able to enter the same market. This may therefore be considered a "high profits" phase. The profit-making drive will tend to emphasize the revenue side of the profits equation and may be more accurately termed revenue-side profit satisfying. In this phase, the firm's top priority will be translated into action primarily through the installation and rapid expansion of productive capacity.

The work force will tend to consist mostly of professional and technical personnel with a growing proportion of skilled labor. In terms of locational preferences, the firm may still be located where it originated, which may be a major population center.

Phase C may be characterized as one where the firm's major priority becomes one of domestic market share maximization. Revenue-side profit satisfying will continue, although profit rates will drop as a few firms enter the market and an oligopolistic market situation develops. Market share maximization may be implemented through such actions as aggressive advertising and temporary price-cutting, or through the application of marketing gimmicks such as cash rebates. The labor force continues to grow throughout this phase, finding greater balance between professional/technical and blue-collar occupations. Spatial tendencies will begin to vary significantly, with the establishment of major plants in several locations in, or close to, major cities.

With *Phase D*, product market competition develops and, along with it, major transformations occur in corporate strategies and organizational structure. The firm turns to mass production efficiency maximization as markets become more saturated and the potential for revenue increases through market share expansion becomes very limited. Cost-side profit maximization therefore becomes the norm. Product differentiation may provide firms with some respite from competition and a possible short-term regression to Phase C. International subsidiaries that enjoy a monopoly or near-monopoly situation may be established abroad in an effort to enjoy a partial regression to Phases B or C. Spatial decentralization may be characteristic of this stage, with numerous branch plants dispersing the productive structure of firms toward the various regional markets. The blue-collar labor force becomes proportionately most important and unionization may become widespread. Some deskilling of the labor force may start, through task division. In this phase the firm's most important priority may be translated into action through greater mechanization of the productive process to increase labor productivity, through the subcontracting of activities which may not be efficiently performed in-house due to suboptimal scale economies, or by implementing multiple shift work.

In *Phase E*, cost-side profit maximization may turn to labor-cost minimization as the most feasible possibility of achieving a profitable situation. With highly saturated markets and much competition, profit levels can be expected to be lower than at previous phases. Efforts at product differentiation may be intensified in this phase and, if successful, may allow a short- or perhaps medium-term regression to a previous phase (C or D) where less competition or a more oligopolistic situation may be found. The firm's major priority in this phase may be reflected through the hiring of less skilled, lower-wage labor, attempting to speed up work tasks and the hiring of nonunion labor, and increasing automation insofar as profits and capital availability allow. Product markets will generally be very competitive. Locational tendencies will reflect the need for the firm to reduce labor costs substantially by relocating in industrial export zones abroad, from where its products can be shipped back into the original home market.

A final, declining stage is found in *Phase F*, where intense efforts to reduce losses may induce management to engage in outright liquidation of productive capacity. Curtailment of production, selective at first but more extensive later on, will therefore reflect the major priority of overall cost minimization. Extensive deskilling may be more characteristic of the labor force in this phase, and its vast composition will be made up of low-wage blue collar workers with a high turnover rate. Curtailment of productive activities in previously established locations will cause unemployment and community concern. Plant closings will be a common occurrence throughout this phase. At this final stage, some firms may look at the relocation in export zones abroad as the only possibility to continue operations, while others may simply be too advanced in their decline to consider this alternative.

Data Analysis: Selected Industries

This section will evaluate, within fairly general parameters, the sectoral and spatial performances of the various industries selected for the study and their consistency with the overall expectations for the late phases of the process cycle. It is expected that industry performance trends will exhibit significant spatial variations between the older, established industrial heartland regions of the U.S. (Northeast, Midwest) and the growing sunbelt states that border Mexico and the Mexican border zone. Time-series data for a 30-year period (1947–1977) from the U.S. Census of Manufactures will be analyzed, along with annual data for an eight-year period (1974–1981) for selected industries in the Mexican Border Industrialization Program (BIP). The U.S. industries surveyed are those which most closely approximate the manufacturing categories that have grown fastest in the Mexican BIP and which also account for the bulk of employment in BIP industries. The production processes of these industries involve much assembly-type work with the vast majority of their output exported to U.S. markets.

The selection of industries instead of product categories responds to the conceptual perspective of the process cycle and its emphasis on productive processes rather than on products or output. This corresponds to one of the important conceptual differences between the product and the process cycle (Suarez-Villa 1983, 1984, Vernon 1966, 1979). Manufacturing conditions, suitably disaggregated, are therefore assumed to cluster around distinct production processes. Another consideration is the fact that spatial disaggregation is provided only for industry groups by the U.S. Census of Manufactures. Curiously enough, recent research updating Hirsch's (1967, 1975) work on the product cycle found that its assumptions were better verified when industry-group instead of individual product data were utilized (Mullor-Sebastián 1981).

Three- and four-digit data for eight industries (see Table 1) were chosen for this study. Although it would have been desirable to have greater levels of disaggregation, the limitations imposed by the censuses' nondisclosure requirements and level of spatial disaggregation are binding. In any case, greater dissaggregation beyond the four-digit level would have suffered compatibility problems in several of the census years due to restructuring of the more disaggregated categories because of the 30-year time span in question. Three-digit textiles-industry groups (232, 233) were selected rather than four-digit groupings, because the productive processes of the latter were considered to be homogeneous enough, and because a relatively greater incidence of multi-product fabrication occurs in those categories in this group. The three-digit electronics category (367) was not disaggregated because of the extensive restructuring of the more detailed categories in recent censuses. Mexican BIP industry data, although less disaggregated than the equivalent U.S. data, may nevertheless be considered to be relatively homogeneous in terms of the production processes utilized, given the universal assembly-type character of these operations.

The general limitations of using Census of Manufactures data are those which would apply to any other study of industries using this source of information. The limited number of years that can be used as observations is a shortcoming that may lend the data some conjunctural character. It is therefore difficult to assess to what extent recessionary periods, or such events as the occurrence of product substitution, may distort the various indexes utilized. The product mix may also be another problem with the S.I.C. classification system utilized by the U.S. Census of Manufactures. Its impact may nevertheless be reduced somewhat by the fact that four-digit and relatively homogeneous three-digit industry groups have been selected.

Seven indexes were constructed to analyze U.S. industry data. The choice of indexes was limited by the type of information provided by the Census of Manufactures. The spatial performance of the various industries in two major geographical/territorial areas is considered: the established U.S. industrial heartland (Northeast, Midwest) and the U.S.-Mexico border region (Arizona, California, Texas and BIP industries in Mexican border municipalities). New Mexico was excluded from the study because of its relatively low level of industrialization in the industry groups considered.

TABLE 1:   Typologies of Trends in Selected U.S. Industries, 1947-1977

Industry 232 - Men's and Boys' Furnishings

Index	North- U.S.	Mid- east	west	Ariz.	Calif.	Texas
N<20	4	1	1	5	5	7
N>20	6	1	1	8	7	8
E	9	1	1	9	7	9
L/N	7	8	8	8	5	9
L/E	3	2	2	3	3	5
C/VA	(2)	(5)	(2)	(2)	(6)	(4)
I/VA	6	6	6	(6)	6	9

Industry 233 - Women's and Misses' Outerwear

Index	U.S.	east	west	Ariz.	Calif.	Texas
N<20	6	2	2	6	9	9
N>20	7	4	1	7	9	9
E	8	4	1	8	9	9
L/N	8	8	5	9	2	5
L/E	3	3	2	4	3	2
C/VA	(2)	(2)	(5)	(2)	(2)	(2)
I/VA	8	8	5	8	(6)	7

(continued)

TABLE 1 (continued)

Index	North- U.S.	Mid- east	west	Ariz.	Calif.	Texas

Industry 2511 - Wood Furniture, not Upholstered

Index	North- U.S.	Mid- east	west	Ariz.	Calif.	Texas
N<20 9	4	4	(8)	9	8	
N>20 3	1	1	(8)	9	8	
E 5	3	2	(7)	9	8	
L/N 3	3	3	(3)	5	7	
L/E 5	3	3	(4)	6	5	
C/VA 2	7	3	(2)	(7)	(7)	
I/VA 3	5	3	(5)	7	7	

Industry 2512 - Upholstered Household Furniture

Index						
N<20 4	1	1	(5)	4	7	
N>20 8	3	4	(8)	8	8	
E 8	4	3	(8)	8	8	
L/N 8	7	7	(2)	7	7	
L/E 3	3	3	(2)	3	3	
C/VA 5	3	3	(7)	(8)	(8)	
I/VA 3	3	6	(2)	3	3	

(continued)

TABLE 1 (continued)

Industry 2521 - Wood Office Furniture

Index	North- Mid- U.S.	east	west	Ariz.	Calif.	Texas
N<20 9	4	7	-	(9)	(8)	
N>20 9	4	5	-	(9)	(8)	
E 7	5	(5)	-	(8)	-	
L/N 3	3	(6)	-	(7)	-	
L/E 3	3	(3)	-	(3)	-	
C/VA 2	3	(3)	-	(8)	-	
I/VA 6	3	(7)	-	(6)	-	

Industry 2522 - Metal Office Furniture

N<20 8	5	4	-	(8)	-	
N>20 8	4	4	-	(5)	-	
E 8	8	(2)	-	(8)	-	
L/N 5	5	(3)	-	(8)	-	
L/E 3	3	(3)	-	(8)	-	
C/VA 5	7	(7)	-	(2)	-	
I/VA 5	5	(2)	-	-	-	

(continued)

TABLE 1   (continued)

Industry 367 - Electronic Components and Accessories

Index	U.S.	North-east	Mid-west	Ariz.	Calif.	Texas
N<20 9	7	7	9	9	9	
N>20 9	8	7	8	9	8	
E 7	4	4	9	9	(9)	
L/N 3	3	3	4	4	(2)	
L/E 2	2	3	5	3	(2)	
C/VA (2)	(3)	(3)	(7)	(7)	-	
I/VA 7	7	4	7	(8)	(8)	

Industry 3714 - Motor Vehicle Parts and Accessories

Index	U.S.	North-east	Mid-west	Ariz.	Calif.	Texas
N<20 (9)	(8)	(8)	(8)	(9)	(8)	
N>20 (8)	(4)	(8)	(8)	(8)	(8)	
E (8)	(2)	(2)	(8)	(8)	(8)	
L/N (2)	(1)	(6)	(8)	(7)	(3)	
L/E (5)	(4)	(8)	(8)	(4)	(4)	
C/VA (6)	(4)	(6)	(8)	(6)	(6)	
I/VA (4)	(4)	(7)	-	(2)	(2)	

(continued)

TABLE 1   (continued)

Typologies:

  1: outright decline (1.33% average annual rate or more, 1947-1977).

  2: declining trend (less than 1.33% average annual rate, 1947-1977).

  3: generally declining, with fluctuations (total decline less than 1.33%
      average annual rate, 1947-1977).

  4: declining in later years (convex pattern, total decline less than 1.33%
      average annual rate, 1947-1977).

  5: approximately constant, with or without fluctuations.

  6: increasing in later years (concave pattern, total increase less than
      1.33% average annual rate, 1947-1977).

  7: generally increasing, with fluctuations (total increase less than 1.33%
      average annual rate, 1947-1977).

  8: increasing trend (less than 1.33% average annual rate, 1947-1977).

  9: outright increase (1.33% average annual rate or more, 1947-1977).

Figures in parenthesis ( ) indicate estimate of trends based on limited number
of observations (more than two census years missing).

Indexes:

  N<20: number of plants with less than 20 employees.

  N>20: number of plants with 20 or more employees.

  E: total employment.

  L/N: production labor per plant.

  L/E: production labor's share of total employment.

  C/VA: production costs per unit of value-added.

  I/VA: investment per unit of value-added.

Estimates for industry 367 based on data from 1958, 1963, 1967, 1972 and 1977;
estimates for industry 3714 based on data from 1967, 1972 and 1977.

Regions:

Northeast includes New England and Middle Atlantic U.S. census divisions.
Midwest equivalent to East North Central U.S. census division.

All estimates are based on data obtained from U.S. Bureau of the Census,
Census of Manufactures, Washington, DC: U.S. Government Printing Office
(for 1947, 1954, 1958, 1963, 1967, 1972 and 1977).

Number of Plants with Fewer than 20 Employees. In terms of the process cycle and of industries in its late phases, this index may be expected to be declining in the industrial heartland regions. A declining index will reflect a tendency toward higher concentration of productive capacity where firm exit is more frequent than entry. Product substitution may accelerate firm exit. Such decline may also reflect the possibility of achieving greater scale economies in production. In peripheral regions such as the U.S.-Mexico border area, this index may be expected to be increasing. The trends shown in Table 1 confirm these expectations: in the Northwest, this index is declining in all industries but two (367, 3714), while in the Midwest it is also declining in all but three industries (2521, 367, 3714). A more mixed performance in the Midwest may be attributed to an increase in the number of smaller operators. In contrast, the border states surveyed show increasing trends for this index in all industries considered (2512 in California). Increasing trends may reflect the possibility that production can be economically undertaken in smaller units in peripheral regions as locational advantages allow.

Number of Plants with 20 or More Employees. This index may also be expected to be declining for industries in late phases of the process cycle in industrial heartland regions. In the border area this index may be expected to be increasing, given moderate-to-high growth rates as comparative advantages favor location in these areas. These assumptions are also mostly verified by the data of Table 1: in the Northeast this index is declining in all industries but one (367) while in the Midwest it is also declining in all but two (367, 3714). In the U.S. border states surveyed, this index is increasing in all industries. A comparable index, *total number of plants* for Mexican BIP industries, also shows increasing trends in all but one industry (the apparel category) which has remained relatively stagnant in terms of plant growth yet shows an increasing trend in employment. This may reflect efforts to take advantage of scale economies in those industries.

Overall Employment. This index may be expected to be declining in heartland regions in industries in the late phases of the process cycle. Taken together with some of the other indexes, overall employment may be a good indicator of interregional industry shifts and of the overall growth and decline of industrial activities. Table 1 also provides verification for the assumptions on this index. In the Northeast all but one (2522) of the industries surveyed are declining while in the Midwest all industries show declining trends, without exception. In the U.S. border states surveyed, all industries show increasing employment trends, without exception, and therefore conform to the expectations of the process cycle. This situation also applies to all Mexican BIP industries (Table 2).

Production Labor Per Plant. The performances represented by this index will depend greatly on tendencies related to concentration of

TABLE 2:   Typologies of Trends in

Selected Mexican Border Industries, 1974-1981

U.S. S.I.C. equivalence	Indexes						
	N	E	L/N	L/E	C/VA	D/VA	M/VA
232, 233	5	8	8	5	6	6	7
2511, 2512, 2521, 2511	6	8	5	5	3	4	7
367	7	6	9	3	7	3	7
3714	7	7	7	4	4	5	5

Typology categories as in Table 1.

Indexes:

  N: number of plants.

  D/VA: domestic (Mexican) inputs' share of value-added.

  M/VA: imported inputs' share of value-added.

  All other indexes as in Table 1.

All estimates refer to Border Industrialization Program (BIP) industries in
Mexican border municipalities and are based on data obtained from Secretaría
de Programación y Presupuesto, Estadística de la industria maquiladora de
exportación 1974-1980, Mexico City: S.P.P. (1981 data also obtained from
S.P.P.).

productive capacity and the composition of employment in each
industry. Underlying these manifestations will be questions related
to the comparative advantages offered by each geographical area and
the potential to achieve greater scale economies. It may be expected
that if increasing automation is occurring in heartland regions, this
will cause this index to show declining trends. If, on the other hand,
increasing concentration of productive capacity is occurring, then this
index may be increasing in those regions. Given the lack of accessory
data, it is therefore very difficult to predict a clear-cut performance
for this index. Labor force composition may also be "inherited" by
industries in peripheral regions if substantial standardization of processes occurs through the establishment of branch plants. The analysis
of trends for this index (Table 1) shows very mixed performances:

in the Northeast, increasing trends are found for three industries (232, 233, 2512), while four industries are declining (2511, 2521, 367, 3714). In the Midwest, three industries are declining (2511, 2522, 367) while four other industries (232, 2512, 2521, 3714) show increasing trends. A similar mixed performance is found in Arizona, with four industries increasing (232, 233, 2521, 3714) while three others are declining (2511, 2512, 367). The two remaining U.S. border states (California, Texas) show increasing trends in all but two industries (233, 367, California) and all but one industry (367, Texas). The Mexican BIP industries follow California and Texas performance closely, showing increasing trends in all but one industry (furniture group).

Production Labor as a Share of Total Employment. This index may be expected to show declining trends in heartland regions if automation of productive processes increases or if greater concentration of productive capacity occurs. Both of these possibilities are consistent with the expectations of the process cycle in the late phases, particularly Phase E. In peripheral regions, it becomes more difficult to predict the performance of this index. If substantial standardization has occurred in production processes and this has diffused through the establishment of branch plants, then such industries in peripheral regions may exhibit characteristics similar to those of the heartland areas. Conversely, if such industries benefit from comparative advantages, such as lower-wage labor, this indicator may be expected to rise. In Table 1, declining trends are shown for all industries in the Northeast and for all but one industry (3714) in the Midwest. In the U.S. border states, declining trends are shown in all but one industry (3714, Arizona), in all but two (2511, 2522, California), and in all industries without exception (Texas). In the Mexican BIP industries, this index has remained relatively stable throughout the various years surveyed. This may be due to the relatively short period of time covered in the analysis and possibly also to the absence of any significant degree of automation in these industries.

Production Costs Per Unit of Value-Added. The various cost components which this index incorporates make it more difficult to predict the possible trends that may occur. Nevertheless, it may be expected that, if the general assumptions of the process cycle are followed, this index may show declining trends in the heartland regions. This may be a result of increasing automation, or of increases in productive capacity concentration that provide greater scale economies. This assumption is verified by the data of Table 1 where, in the Northeast and Midwest, all but two industries exhibit declining trends (2511 and 2522 in Northeast, 2522 and 3714 in Midwest). In the U.S. border states, the results are more mixed for Arizona (2512, 367, 3714 increasing; all others declining) and Texas (2511, 2512, 3714 increasing; 232, 233 declining). In California, all but two industries

(2512, 3714) exhibit increasing performances. Mexican BIP industries also exhibit a mixed performance, with one half of all industries surveyed showing increasing trends.

Investment Per Unit of Value-Added. It may be expected that, if the assumptions of the process cycle are verified, this index may exhibit declining trends for the industrial heartland regions. Conversely, increasing trends may occur if significant investment in automation is occurring. This is less likely in the late phases of the cycle but is perhaps still a possibility insofar as Phase E is concerned. In peripheral regions it may be expected that this index may be increasing along with the growth of industrial activity. Unfortunately, the very limited number of observations available may lend this index a very conjectural character. The performances of the various industries are very mixed in the northeastern and midwestern regions (Table 1). Three industries show increasing trends (232, 233, 367 in Northeast; 2511, 2522, 367 in Midwest), while the remainder are either declining or stagnant in both the Northeast and the Midwest. In the U.S. border states surveyed, industry performances are much more clear-cut. In Arizona this index increases in all but one industry (2512), and in California and Texas in all but two (2512, 3714). Unfortunately, no investment data are available for Mexican BIP industries.

Two other indexes were constructed for Mexican BIP industries: *domestic inputs per unit of value-added* and *imported inputs per unit of value-added* (Table 2). These two indexes provide some indications of the development of Mexican BIP links with both domestic Mexican and foreign suppliers. Its performance is of interest in connection with the current debate on the vulnerability of Mexican BIP industrialization to U.S. economic conditions, and on the possibility of eventual BIP integration with Mexican domestic industries. Domestic inputs per unit of value-added show an increasing trend in only one industry (apparel group) and even there this increase comes after a relatively sharp pattern of decline. In contrast, imported inputs per unit of value-added increases in all but one industry (motor vehicle parts group) where it remains relatively constant.

Conclusions

The analysis of the manufacturing data utilized shows that, for the majority of selected industries and indexes surveyed, their performances conform, within general parameters, to the evolutionary expectations of the study. The fairly constant performance of selected industries in the U.S. industrial heartland regions (Northeast, Midwest) is important in this respect, given that industries in the late phases of the process cycle may be expected to show their characteristics more obviously in those regions. Still, data limitations place serious restrictions on the possibility of determining individual phase characteristics with greater precision. Only two of the various indexes tested, production labor per plant and investment per unit of value-added, show mixed performances in the U.S. heartland regions. On the first, its performance may be related to the characteristics of the individual production processes considered, as higher productive capacity concentration and automation may occur to take advantage of scale economies or raise labor productivity (increasing trends). Declining trends in this index may, on the other hand, be due to limited possibilities of achieving greater scale economies through greater productive capacity concentration or because of limited possibilities to further automate, given endogenous limitations (management, profitability) or exogenous factors (capital availability). Unfortunately, the lack of accessory data on these factors makes it very difficult to pinpoint the possible causes in any precise way. For this index, therefore, both increasing and declining trends may be considered to be consistent with the assumptions of the process cycle. Unfortunately, the limited number of observations available for the second index (investment per unit of value-added) gives a very tentative character to any possible conclusions or observations on its performance. Beyond this limitation, the possibly conjectural character of investment data for any of the years evaluated is another serious constraint.

In the U.S. border states surveyed, as well as in the Mexican Border Industrialization Program (BIP), the performance of all indexes is more predictable. Only one index, production costs per unit of value-added, shows mixed performances in two states (Arizona, Texas) and in the Mexican BIP. Again, the lack of accessory data makes it very difficult to pinpoint the causes with any precision. Here, it may be observed that declining trends may be due to increasing automation which could perhaps be "inherited" through the standardization of production processes and the proliferation of branch plants. Alternatively, a declining trend may also be due to increases in productive capacity concentration made to take advantage of greater scale economies. Increasing trends in this index may result from decreases in productive capacity concentration as industries decentralize. In any case, it is difficult to establish the possible causes with any precision without accessory spatial data for each component of the production costs variable.

Two indexes tested with Mexican BIP data, domestic inputs per unit of value-added and imported inputs per unit of value-added, reveal interesting results regarding the reliance of BIP industries on foreign (mostly U.S.) inputs. The trends indicated by these two indexes for the years surveyed (1974–1981) show increasing patterns in the utilization of imported inputs per unit of value-added. As far as the utilization of domestic inputs in BIP manufacturing is concerned, only one industry shows an increasing trend, and a very recent and modest one at that. The continuation of these trends over the medium-

or long-term may severely limit any hopes that Mexican BIP industries will become better integrated with the Mexican economy. The fact that the industries surveyed appear to be in the late phases of the process cycle and also, that they account for the majority of BIP employment, may present uncertain prospects for the permanence and sustained economic impact of these industries on the Mexican border economy. If so, the propensity of these industries to move to other locations may be relatively high if or when any of the most attractive location factors change. Important changes in this respect may be, for example, increases in labor costs due to eventual revaluation of the Mexican currency or to increasing unionization or labor strife.

SUMMARY

This paper considers sectoral and spatial evolutionary change in various manufacturing industries that have experienced significant growth in the U.S. and Mexican border areas. Seven indexes and selected three- and four-digit industry data from U.S. heartland regions and border states (1947–1977) and from Mexico's Border Industrialization Program (1974–1981) are analyzed to provide indications of temporal and spatial changes in selected border industries. The analysis concludes that, within general parameters, the performances of the majority of the various industries surveyed conform to the evolutionary assumptions of the paper.

References

Ayer, H., and M. R. Layton. "The Border Industry Program and the Impacts of Expenditures by Mexican Border Industry Employees on a U.S. Border Community: An Empirical Study of Nogales," *Annals of Regional Science*, 8:105–117. 1974.

Baerresen, D. *The Border Industrialization Program of Mexico*. Lexington, Mass.: Lexington Books. 1971.

Baird, P., and E. McCaughan. *Beyond the Border: Mexico and the U.S. Today*. New York: North American Congress on Latin America. 1979.

Bluestone, B., and B. Harrison. *The Deindustrialization of America*. New York: Basic Books. 1982.

Fröbel, F., J. Heinrichs, and O. Kreye. *The New International Division of Labour*. Cambridge, England: Cambridge University Press. 1980.

Grunwald, J. *The Internationalization of Industry*. Washington, D.C.: The Brookings Institution (in press). 1984.

Hansen, N. "The New International Division of Labor and Manufacturing Decentralization in the United States," *Review of Regional Studies*, 9:1–11. 1979.

_____ . "Dualism, Capital-Labor Ratios and the Regions of the U.S.: A Comment," *Journal of Regional Science*, 20;401–403. 1980.

_____ . "Mexico's Border Industry and the International Division of Labor," *Annals of Regional Science*, 25:1–12. 1981.

Hirsch, S. *Location of Industry and International Competitiveness*. London: Oxford University Press. 1967.

———. "The Product Cycle Model of International Trade: A Multi-Country Cross Section Analysis," *Oxford Bulletin of Economics and Statistics*, 37:305–317. 1975.

Mullor-Sebastián, A. "The Product Cycle Theory: Empirical Evidence." Paper presented at the 94th Annual Meeting of the American Economic Association, Washington, D.C. 1981.

Secretaría de Programación y Presupuesto. *Estadística de la Industria Maquiladora de Exportación 1974-1980*. Mexico City: Secretaría de Programación y Presupuesto. 1981.

Seligson, M. A., and E. J. Williams. *Maquiladoras and Migration*. Austin: University of Texas Press. 1982.

Suarez-Villa, L. "Technological Dualism, the Sunbelt, and Mexico's Border Area Industrialization." Paper presented at the First Conference on Regional Impacts of U.S.-Mexico Economic Relations, Guanajuato, Mexico. 1981.

———. "Factor Utilization in Mexico's Border Industrialization Program," *Annals of Regional Science*, 16:48–56. 1982.

———. "Industrial Export Enclaves and Manufacturing Change." Paper presented at the 30th North American Meetings of the Regional Science Association, Chicago. 1983.

———. "Industrialization in the Developing World, Process Cycles, and the New Global Division of Labor," *Canadian Journal of Regional Science*, 7, in press. 1984.

Vernon, R. "International Investment and International Trade in the Product Cycle," *Quarterly Journal of Economics*, 80:190–207. 1966.

———. "The Product Cycle Hypothesis in a New International Environment," *Oxford Bulletin of Economics and Statistics*, 41:255–267. 1979.

5
Income Distribution in the U.S.-Mexico Borderlands

James T. Peach

I. Introduction

This paper contains an analysis of the distribution of income in the 25 counties along the U.S. side of the U.S.-Mexico border. Throughout this paper, the term "income distribution" will refer to the "size distribution of income" rather than the "functional distribution of income."[1] Several alternative measures of income distribution will be used in order to address the question of whether or not income distribution in the 25 border counties is different from the distribution of income in (a) the four border states, and (b) the United States as a whole. The answer to this question has a number of significant policy implications as well as implications for the analysis of other "border problems."

The 25 border counties examined in this paper include the 23 U.S. counties which share a border with Mexico plus Culberson and Dimmit counties in Texas, which are located so close to the border as to be indistinguishable from the others. The selection of these particular counties is somewhat arbitrary. Others engaged in the study of the border region have defined the borderlands to include a much wider geographic region.[2] While the influence of the border no doubt extends far beyond the counties immediately adjacent to the border, the influence of the border should be felt most strongly in those counties.[3]

The organization of the paper is as follows. Section II contains a discussion of the data used throughout the study. Section III contains a discussion of the selection of measures of income distribution. Section IV contains a brief examination of levels of income in the border region. Section V contains an analysis of the distribution of family income in the 25 border counties and the four border states. Section VI contains some speculation on the causes and consequences of the distribution of income in the border region described in Section V.

II. The Data

The 1979–1980 data used in this study were obtained from the U.S. Bureau of the Census Summary Tape File 3C (STF3C) and related published documents. This computer tape contains both 100 percent and sample data from the 1980 Census of Population and Housing for the entire United States at the county and city level as well as higher levels of aggregation.

It should be pointed out that the income data contained in the census were obtained on a sample basis. The sample, however, is a large one. For most of the United States, one in every six households received the sample questionnaire. In areas estimated to have fewer than 2,500 inhabitants, 50 percent of all households received the sample questionnaire. Thus, the income data collected during the census provide the most comprehensive and efficient estimates of income available. The only serious drawback of the income data is the way in which the data are reported. Income data are reported only by groups. Thus, income distribution measures which are sensitive to the grouping of the data may show some distortion.

The data on income from the 1980 Census of Population and Housing refer to money income received during calendar year 1979. Population and household characteristics reported by the Bureau of the Census, however, were collected as of April 1, 1980. Therefore, slight discrepancies may exist when the data are used to calculate figures such as per capita income and median income.

Further, it should be pointed out that the census definition of income excludes certain types of income. In particular:

> Receipts from the following sources were not included as income: money received from the sale of property (unless the recipient was engaged in the business of selling such property); the value of income from "in kind" sources such as food stamps, public housing subsidies, medical care, and employee contributions for pensions, etc.; withdrawal of bank deposits; money borrowed; tax refunds; exchange of money between relatives in the same household; gifts and lump-sum inheritances, insurance payments, and other types of lump-sum receipts.[4]

While the inclusion of some of these "excluded sources" of money income might significantly affect measures of income inequality, there is no feasible method of estimating the impact of these exclusions at present.

The 1970 census data on income were also collected via a sampling procedure and refer to total money income for the calendar year 1969. The sample size was approximately 15 percent of all households.[5] Thus, in terms of sampling procedure and reference dates, the data from the two census years are roughly comparable. However, it is not clear from Census Bureau definitions that the concept of family income is identical in the two years. In particular, a category of income used in the 1970 census was labelled "other money income." This category appears to include some of the sources of money income that were excluded from the 1980 data as discussed above. Therefore, conclusions concerning the changes in the distribution of income over time will not be a central issue in this paper.

III. Alternative Measures of Income Distribution

Unfortunately, no study of income distribution can avoid a discussion of the many alternative measures of income distribution which are now in common use. The fundamental problem is, of course, that alternative measures of income distribution frequently lead to alternative rankings in inequality—even when applied to the same data sets.[6] Additional difficulties with alternative measures of income distribution arise because of ambiguities in interpreting specific measures and computational problems associated most frequently with grouped data.

One approach to solving this problem is to establish a set of properties or characteristics of "ideal" measures of income distribution and to use only those measures that closely approximate these properties. Fossett and South (F-S) have recently provided a set of principles or guidelines designed to make the selection of a measure of income distribution somewhat easier.[7] The F-S set of guidelines include:

1. The principle of *directionality*—a measure of inequality should indicate the direction of group advantage.
2. The principle of *transitivity*—any measure that is not transitive will fail to yield an unambiguous ordering of inequality comparisons.
3. The principle of *transfers*—essentially this principle is a requirement that a transfer of income from one group to another should be reflected in any measure of income inequality.
4. The principle of *scale invariance*—this requirement implies that a measure of income distribution should not change if all incomes are multiplied by a positive constant.
5. The principle of *equal additions*—this principle states that absolute differences in income should become less important as the level of income increases.
6. The principle of *symmetry*—this requirement means that if two groups were to exchange income distributions, then the absolute value of the measure should not change, but the sign of the measure should be reversed.

Fossett and South point out that this set of guidelines does not yield an unambiguous ordering of inequality comparisons. In other

words, it is possible for several measures of income distribution to
meet all of the above requirements and still lead to different rankings
of inequality. Further, there is still a computational problem that is
ignored in the F-S guidelines. The simple fact is that some measures
of inequality are sensitive to the number of groups when applied to
grouped data. For these reasons, the two principal measures of income
distribution used in this study will be (1) the Gini coefficient and
(2) an index of dissimilarity.

The Gini coefficient is perhaps the most commonly used measure
of income distribution. The Gini coefficient may be defined as

$$\text{Gini} = 1 = \frac{1}{2} \int_0^1 f(x)dx$$

where, $f(x)$ represents an equation for the Lorenz curve. In other
words, the Gini coefficient is the ratio of the shaded area to the area
of triangle ABC in Figure 1.

Of course, when the data are presented in the form of groups
rather than individual observations, approximation methods must be
used to calculate the area. The number of categories is the primary
variable affecting the accuracy of the approximation method used. The
family income data used in this study for 1969 contained 15 groups,
the data for 1979 contained 17 groups. It is generally argued that
nine or ten groups are sufficient to insure minimal distortion in
calculated Ginis due to approximation error.[8]

The Gini coefficient also has an easy interpretation. Since the diagonal
line forming the upper boundary of the shaded area in Figure 1
represents a line of "perfect equality" and the Lorenz curve represents
the actual distribution, a Gini coefficient of zero indicates perfect
equality in the distribution of income and a Gini coefficient of one
indicates that one individual receives all of the income in the area
being studied.

The Gini coefficient, however, does *not* satisfy the Fossett-South
principles of directionality, transitivity, or symmetry. Thus, though
widely used and easily understood, the Gini coefficient has been
severely criticized as a measure of income distribution.

Another popular measure of income distribution is the index of
dissimilarity. This index may be defined as:

$$\text{INDEX} = \sum_{i-2}^{K} \frac{P_{1i}-P_{2i}}{}$$

where P_{1i} represents the proportion of individuals (families) in category
i of distribution 1, and P_{2i} represents the proportion of individuals
(families) in category i of distribution 2. Thus, the index of dissimilarity
is based upon a comparison of one distribution with another. In
particular, if all categories or groups in both distributions contain

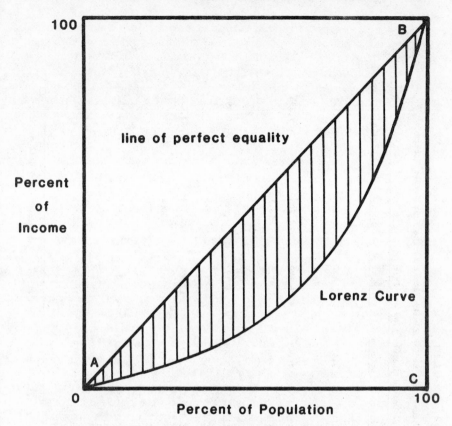

FIGURE 1   Sample Lorenz Curve

the same proportion of individuals or families, then the index of dissimilarity will take on the value zero. The upper bound on the index of dissimilarity is, of course, 1.

The interpretation of the index of dissimilarity is also appealing. The value of the index indicates the proportion of individuals in either of the two distributions that would be required to change categories in order to make the two distributions identical. Another interpretation of the index of dissimilarity is that it represents the maximum vertical distance between the line of perfect equality and the Lorenz curve.

IV. Income Levels in the Border Region

This section contains a brief examination of income levels in the border region. According to the data presented in Table 1, per capita

TABLE 1

Per Capita Income, Mean Family Income, and Median Family Income in the Four Border States
and the United States, 1969 and 1979

	California	Arizona	New Mexico	Texas	United States
Per Capita Income					
1969	3,614	2,937	2,437	2,792	3,119
(as percent of United States)	115.9	94.2	78.1	89.5	
1979	8,303	7,043	6,120	7,206	7,298
(as percent of United States)	113.8	96.5	83.9	98.7	
Mean Family Income					
1969	12,227	10,501	9,193	9,995	10,999
(as percent of United States)	111.2	95.5	83.6	90.9	
1979	25,563	22,123	19,926	23,192	23,092
(as percent of United States)	110.7	95.8	86.3	100.4	
Median Family Income					
1969	10,732	9,185	7,849	8,486	9,586
(as percent of United States)	111.9	95.8	81.9	88.5	
1979	21,541	19,019	16,930	19,619	19,917
(as percent of United States)	108.2	95.5	85.0	98.5	

SOURCE: 1979 data are from Summary Type File 3C, 1980 Census of Population and Housing. 1969 data are from
various volumes of the 1970 Census of Population and Housing.

income in three of the four border states (California being the only exception) was lower in both 1979 and 1969 than in the United States as a whole. In both 1969 and 1979 New Mexico had the lowest per capita income of the four border states. In both 1969 and 1979 California had the highest levels of per capita income of any of the four border states. This same pattern holds when median family income is compared for 1969 and 1979.

Between 1969 and 1979 the three border states with per capita incomes below the national level of per capita income in 1969 improved relative to the nation. Per capita income in California was 115.9 percent of the national average in 1969 and only slightly lower (113.8 percent) in 1979. In Arizona, per capita income was 94.2 percent of the national figure in 1969 and 96.5 percent of the national level in 1979. Per capita income in New Mexico in 1969 was only 78.1 percent of the national figure, but had reached 83.9 percent of the national figure by 1979. In 1969 per capita income in Texas was only 89.5 percent of the national average, but had reached 98.7 percent of the national average by 1979. Thus, it would appear that the border states are gaining, relative to the nation, in terms of per capita income.

When per capita incomes in the 25 border counties are examined in 1969 and 1979, there are some even more striking changes. In both 1969 and 1979 San Diego County, California, was the only one of the 25 border counties with per capita income exceeding the national average. However, between 1969 and 1979 the remaining 24 counties along the border all exhibited increases in per capita income as a percent of the national figures. As can be seen in Table 2, some of these changes were dramatic.

Hansen has indicated that ". . . there is a pronounced tendency for per capita income to decline from west to east along the border."[9] Although Hansen's analysis was in terms of Bureau of Economic Analysis economic regions which are larger than the border counties alone, the same tendency may be observed in the county-level census data. Indeed, the simple correlation coefficient between per capita income in 1979 and the rank order of the 25 border counties from west to east is −0.709. This correlation coefficient is significant at the 0.01 level.

Tables 3 and 4 display both mean and median family incomes in the 25 border counties in both 1969 and 1979. The data on both mean and median family incomes exhibit the same general tendencies described earlier in the discussion on per capita income. Thus, it would appear that no matter which measure of income is used: (1) income levels generally decline along the border from west to east, (2) the level of income in the border region is lower than in the nation as a whole, and (3) between 1969 and 1979 the level of income in the border region increased relative to the level of income in the United States.

TABLE 2

Per Capita Income in the 25 Border Counties, 1969 and 1979

	Per Capita Income 1969	Per Capita Income 1969 as Percent of U.S.	Per Capita Income 1979	Per Capita Income 1979 as Percent of U.S.
California				
San Diego	3392	108.8	7969	109.2
Imperial	2459	78.8	5809	79.6
Arizona				
Cochise	1709	54.8	5738	78.6
Santa Cruz	1782	57.1	5447	74.6
Pima	1892	60.7	7149	98.0
Yuma	1761	56.5	5681	77.8
New Mexico				
Hidalgo	1369	43.9	5242	71.8
Luna	1256	40.3	4790	65.6
Dona Ana	1487	47.7	5284	72.4
Texas				
El Paso	1594	51.1	5306	72.7
Hudspeth	1046	33.5	4480	61.4
Culberson	1174	37.6	4290	58.8
Jeff Davis	1425	45.7	5675	77.8
Presidio	1071	34.3	3751	51.4
Brewster	1181	37.9	4837	66.3
Terrell	1281	41.1	7069	96.9

(continued)

TABLE 2   (continued)

	Per Capita Income 1969	Per Capita Income 1969 as Percent of U.S.	Per Capita Income 1979	Per Capita Income 1979 as Percent of U.S.
Texas (continued)				
Val Verde	1250	40.1	4542	62.2
Kinney	799	25.6	4146	56.8
Maverick	1037	33.2	3100	42.5
Dimmit	871	27.9	3922	53.7
Webb	1352	43.3	3980	54.5
Zapata	1121	35.9	4395	60.2
Starr	1102	35.3	2668	36.6
Hidalgo	1006	32.3	4040	55.4
Cameron	1091	35.0	4336	59.4
United States	3,119		7,298	

SOURCE: U.S. Bureau of the Census.

V. The Distribution of Family Income

Tables 5 and 6 contain alternative measures of income distribution for the four border states and the United States in 1969 and 1979, respectively. As measured by the Gini coefficient, the distribution of family income in the four border states is not much different from the distribution of income in the United States as a whole. In 1969, for example, the Gini coefficient for the United States was 0.343. In the four border states the Gini coefficients were California (0.341), Arizona (0.351), New Mexico (0.378), and Texas (0.375). Although there is no formal statistical test for differences among Gini coefficients, the differences between the U.S. Gini coefficient and those for California and Arizona do not appear to be large. While the Gini coefficients for New Mexico and Texas are somewhat higher, the differences again do not appear to be large.

TABLE 3

Mean Family Income in the 25 Border Counties, 1969 and 1979

	1969		1979	
	Mean Family Income	As Percent of United States	Mean Family Income	As Percent of United States
California				
San Diego	8,335	75.8	24,202	104.8
Imperial	8,322	75.7	20,889	90.5
Arizona				
Cochise	7,390	67.2	18,118	78.5
Santa Cruz	8,396	76.3	20,174	87.4
Pima	8,346	75.9	22,117	95.8
Yuma	7,542	68.6	18,005	78.0
New Mexico				
Hidalgo	6,554	59.6	18,165	78.7
Luna	6,661	60.6	14,928	64.6
Dona Ana	7,072	64.3	18,365	79.5
Texas				
El Paso	7,838	71.3	19,012	82.3
Hudspeth	5,700	51.8	15,570	67.4
Culberson	7,515	68.3	15,123	65.5
Jeff Davis	5,886	53.5	17,325	75.0
Presidio	5,562	50.6	13,283	57.5
Brewster	4,834	43.9	15,704	68.0
Terrell	6,751	61.4	22,728	98.4

(continued)

TABLE 3   (continued)

	1969		1979	
	Mean Family Income	As Percent of United States	Mean Family Income	As Percent of United States
Texas (continued)				
Val Verde	6,512	59.2	16,220	70.2
Kinney	4,676	42.5	13,727	59.4
Maverick	5,252	47.7	13,248	57.4
Dimmit	5,043	45.8	15,181	65.7
Webb	5,922	53.8	16,122	69.8
Zapata	4,407	40.1	15,042	65.1
Starr	4,636	42.1	11,544	50.0
Hidalgo	6,054	55.0	15,920	68.9
Cameron	5,964	54.2	16,545	71.6

SOURCE: U.S. Bureau of the Census.

The conclusion that the distribution of income in the four border states is not much different from the distribution in the entire United States also is supported by the relatively low values of the index of dissimilarity (also displayed in Table 5). In calculating the index of dissimilarity for each state, the distribution of family income in the United States has been used as the "second" distribution. The values of this index based on the 1969 data indicate that only 2.9 percent of the families in Arizona would have been required to change income groups in order for the distribution of family income in Arizona to be identical to the U.S. distribution. At the same time, 12.2 percent of the families in New Mexico would have been required to change income groups for the two distributions to become identical. California and Texas would have needed about 7.5 percent of families to change income groups. If we consider the likelihood of purely random differences in the distribution of income between states and regions, the differences in income distribution between the four border states and the United States as a whole appear to be relatively minor in 1969.

TABLE 4

Median Family Income in the 25 Border Counties, 1969 and 1979

	1969		1979	
	Median Family Income	As Percent of United States	Median Family Income	As Percent of United States
California				
San Diego	6,595	68.8	20,306	102.0
Imperial	6,972	72.7	16,658	83.6
Arizona				
Cochise	6,396	66.7	15,484	77.7
Santa Cruz	6,747	70.4	16,155	81.1
Pima	6,983	72.8	19,000	95.4
Yuma	6,348	66.2	15,022	75.4
New Mexico				
Hidalgo	5,875	61.3	16,166	81.2
Luna	5,518	57.6	11,555	58.0
Dona Ana	5,414	56.5	14,914	74.9
Texas				
El Paso	6,413	66.9	15,366	77.2
Hudspeth	4,813	50.2	11,204	56.3
Culberson	6,455	67.3	12,894	64.7
Jeff Davis	4,919	51.3	11,365	57.1
Presidio	3,671	38.3	10,394	52.2
Brewster	3,039	31.7	13,147	66.0
Terrell	5,669	59.1	18,750	94.1

(continued)

TABLE 4 (continued)

	1969		1979	
	Median Family Income	As Percent of United States	Median Family Income	As Percent of United States
Texas (continued)				
Val Verde	5,488	57.3	12,274	61.6
Kinney	3,318	34.6	11,483	57.7
Maverick	3,860	40.3	10,623	53.3
Dimmit	3,719	38.8	11,301	56.7
Webb	4,262	44.5	12,181	61.2
Zapata	3,201	33.4	11,523	57.9
Starr	3,089	32.2	8,627	43.3
Hidalgo	4,184	43.6	12,083	60.7
Cameron	4,359	45.5	12,931	64.9

SOURCE: U.S. Bureau of the Census.

When the measures of income distribution for 1979 are examined (Table 6), the same general conclusion that the distribution of family income in the four border states is not much different from the distribution in the entire United States still holds. The Gini coefficient for the United States in 1979 was 0.376—an increase from the Gini coefficient of 0.343 observed in 1969. The Gini coefficients for the individual border states were California (0.385), New Mexico (0.372), Arizona (0.385), and Texas (0.393). As in 1969, three of the four border states had Gini coefficients slightly higher than the coefficient for the United States. However, the differences between the individual border states' Gini coefficients and the coefficient for the United States are relatively small.

Again, the values of the index of dissimilarity calculated for each of the four border states using the U.S. distribution as the standard of comparison tend to support the conclusion that the differences in income distribution between each of the border states and the United States are not great. In 1979 only 1.7 percent of Texas families would have needed to change income groups in order to make the two distributions identical. Nearly 9 percent of New Mexico's families

TABLE 5

Measures of Income Distribution in the Four Border States

and the United States, 1969

	Number of Families	Gini Coefficient	Index of Dissimilarity	Median Family Income
California	5,001,255	0.341	0.075	10,732
Arizona	438,389	0.351	0.029	9,185
New Mexico	242,740	0.378	0.122	7,849
Texas	2,818,123	0.375	0.076	8,486
United States	51,168,599	0.343	--	9,586

SOURCE: Number of families and family income in 1969 obtained from U.S.
Bureau of the Census, 1970 Census of Population and Housing. Gini
coefficients and index of dissimilarity calculated by the author.

would have been required to change income groups for the distributions
to be identical. This was a slight decrease from the 12.2 percent of
the families that would have been required to change income groups
in 1979. In 1979 California and Arizona were the intermediate cases
at 5.8 percent and 3.2 percent, respectively.

A similar conclusion may be reached by examining the percent of
families with incomes below $5,000 in 1979 in each of the four
states. In the United States as a whole, 7.3 percent of all families
reported incomes in 1979 below $5,000. Table 6 indicates that two
of the border states (California and Arizona) had a smaller percentage
of families in this low income category, while both Texas and New
Mexico had higher percentages of families in the low income category
in 1979. New Mexico had the highest percentage of families in 1979
with incomes below $5,000.

At the upper end of the income distribution, both California and
Texas had higher percentages of families with incomes above $50,000
than the comparable percentage of the nation. Both Arizona and New
Mexico had smaller percentages of families in this high income category
in 1979.

TABLE 6

Measures of Income Distribution in the Four Border States
and the United States, 1979

	Number of Families	Median Family Income	Gini Coefficient	Index of Dissimilarity	Percent Below $5,000	Percent Above $50,000
California	5,978,084	21,541	0.385	.058	6.3	7.9
Arizona	709,912	19,019	0.372	.032	7.1	4.8
New Mexico	334,069	16,930	0.385	.089	10.1	4.0
Texas	3,696,656	19,619	0.393	.017	8.2	5.9
United States	59,190,133	19,917	0.376	---	7.3	5.6

SOURCE: U.S. Bureau of the Census, Summary Tape File 3C, 1980 Census of Population and Housing. Computations performed by the author.

TABLE 7

Measures of Income Distribution in the 25

Border Counties, 1969

County	Number of Families	Gini Coefficient	Index of Dissimilarity
San Diego	326707.	0.340	0.043
Imperial	17261.	0.354	0.095
Cochise	14866.	0.332	0.092
Santa Cruz	3032.	0.382	0.131
Pima	87856.	0.351	0.047
Yuma	14784.	0.338	0.105
Hidalgo	1127.	0.361	0.239
Luna	2863.	0.355	0.238
Dona Ana	15607.	0.381	0.155
El Paso	81771.	0.369	0.128
Hudspeth	518.	0.362	0.323
Culberson	812.	0.349	0.195
Jeff Davis	404.	0.366	0.333
Presidio	1205.	0.475	0.411
Brewster	1769.	0.417	0.282
Terrell	537.	0.385	0.229
Val Verde	6422.	0.361	0.248
Kinney	505.	0.422	0.461
Maverick	3595.	0.422	0.364
Dimmit	1959.	0.439	0.418
Webb	15420.	0.436	0.340

(Continued)

TABLE 7   (continued)

County	Number of Families	Gini Coefficient	Index of Dissimilarity
Zapata	1054.	0.409	0.436
Starr	3654.	0.451	0.427
Hidalgo	38122.	0.459	0.351
Cameron	30317.	0.433	0.320

SOURCE: U.S. Bureau of the Census, 1970 Census of Population and Housing, 1970.   Computations by the author.

The conclusion that income distribution along the U.S.-Mexico border is not much different than the distribution of income in the U.S. generally must be modified somewhat when the 25 border counties are examined. Tables 7 and 8 contain measures of the distribution of family income in the 25 border counties in both 1969 and 1979. In 1969 only three of the 25 border counties had Gini coefficients that were smaller than the U.S. Gini coefficient of 0.343. These three counties were San Diego in California and Cochise and Yuma in Arizona. In 1969 Cochise County had the lowest Gini coefficient of any of the border counties (0.332), while Presidio County, Texas, had the highest Gini coefficient of 0.475.

In general, the Gini coefficients of the individual border counties tend to become larger from west to east along the border. This generally conforms to the pattern of lower per capita incomes observed from west to east in the border region. Thus, the general pattern in the distribution of family income along the border in 1969 is that: (1) the border counties in the western border states tend to have Gini coefficients approximately the same as the Gini coefficients in their respective states and the nation, (2) the border counties in Texas tend to have larger Gini coefficients than either the State of Texas or the nation, and (3) the New Mexico border counties have Gini coefficients either slightly lower or slightly higher than the statewide Gini coefficient, which in turn is higher than the Gini coefficient for the nation.

The 1969 values of the index of dissimilarity offer additional evidence for this pattern. In the two farthest western border states,

TABLE 8

Measures of Income Distribution for the 25 Border Counties, 1979

County	Number of Families	Gini Coefficient	Index of Dissimilarity	Percent Below $5,000	Percent Above $50,000
San Diego	461788.	0.382	.032	6.2	6.7
Imperial	22438.	0.396	.107	7.7	4.5
Cochise	22345.	0.355	.140	8.0	2.1
Santa Cruz	5073.	0.388	.128	6.6	4.7
Pima	137536.	0.370	.034	6.9	4.9
Yuma	23881.	0.364	.157	8.0	2.4
Hidalgo	1565.	0.355	.173	9.5	1.1
Luna	4359.	0.413	.272	15.5	2.4
Dona Ana	23431.	0.406	.159	12.0	3.9
El Paso	114045.	0.407	.140	10.9	3.4
Hudspeth	692.	0.442	.300	15.5	2.7
Culberson	861.	0.372	.251	12.2	1.9
Jeff Davis	469.	0.493	.295	14.7	3.4
Presidio	1282.	0.443	.336	26.0	1.9
Brewster	1832.	0.377	.242	11.7	1.2
Terrell	446.	0.432	.119	13.2	7.2

(continued)

TABLE 8 (continued)

County	Number of Families	Gini Coefficient	Index of Dissimilarity	Percent Below $5,000	Percent Above $50,000
Val Verde	8876.	0.424	.254	14.4	2.4
Kinney	596.	0.402	.324	20.0	1.2
Maverick	6775.	0.413	.330	19.1	1.6
Dimmit	2732.	0.452	.275	21.4	3.6
Webb	22067.	0.444	.237	17.5	3.1
Zapata	1804.	0.422	.278	16.6	2.3
Starr	5965.	0.446	.393	28.9	1.2
Hidalgo	65139.	0.435	.248	17.1	2.6
Cameron	49251.	0.429	.222	15.6	2.8
THE BORDER	986248.	0.400		9.0	5.0
THE U.S.	59190133.	0.376		7.3	5.6

SOURCE: U.S. Bureau of the Census, Summary Tape File 3C, 1980 Census of Population and Housing. Calculations by the author.

the county-level index of dissimilarity ranges from 4.3 percent in San Diego to 13.1 percent in Santa Cruz County, Arizona. In the Texas border counties, the index of dissimilarity ranges from a low of 12.8 percent in El Paso County to a high value of 46.1 percent in Kinney County. In the lower Rio Grande Valley of Texas from Kinney County to Cameron County none of the eight counties has a value of the index of dissimilarity less than 30 percent. Again, the data for 1969 indicate a trend toward increasing inequality in the distribution of income in the border counties from west to east along the border.

The measures of income distribution calculated using the data for 1979 exhibit a similar though by no means identical pattern. In 1979 five of the 25 border counties had Gini coefficients lower than the U.S. Gini coefficient of 0.376. No county to the east of Culberson County, Texas, was in this category. Culberson County had a Gini coefficient of 0.372, which is only slightly lower than the U.S. Gini coefficient.

As in 1969, the 1979 Gini coefficients of the border counties in the two most western states were not much different from the Gini coefficients observed in their respective states or the Gini coefficient for the United States. The 1979 Gini coefficients of the border counties in California and Arizona ranged from a low of 0.355 in Cochise County, Arizona, to a high of 0.396 in Imperial County, California.

In 1979 the lowest value of the individual county Gini coefficients was 0.355—observed in both Cochise County, Arizona, and Hidalgo County, New Mexico. The highest value of the county level Gini coefficients in 1979 was found in Jeff Davis County, Texas (0.493). However, perhaps not too much significance should be attached to this fact since Jeff Davis County in 1979 contained only 469 families. Nevertheless, the general pattern of higher values of the Gini coefficient found in the more eastern Rio Grande Valley counties of Texas is apparent.

Using the data for 1979, a Gini coefficient for the combined 25 border counties has been calculated to be 0.400. This value is somewhat higher than the U.S. Gini coefficient for 1979 of 0.376. It should be noted, however, that this "border" Gini coefficient is heavily weighted by the presence of San Diego County, California, which contained nearly 47 percent of all the families in the 25 border counties in 1979.

Also as in 1969, the values of the index of dissimilarity calculated for the individual border counties in 1979 tend to be lower in the border counties of the two western border states and higher for the more eastern border counties. In California and Arizona, the value of the index of dissimilarity ranged from 3.2 percent in San Diego County, California, to 15.7 percent in Yuma County, Arizona. Again, these values of the index are not particularly large. The highest of the 1979 values of the index was 0.393 in Starr County, Texas. Again, the values of the index of dissimilarity tend to support the conclusion that family incomes are more unequally distributed toward the eastern part of the U.S.-Mexico border.

Table 8 also contains the percent of families with incomes below $5,000 in 1979 and the percent of families with incomes above $50,000 in 1979 for each of the 25 border counties, the border counties combined and the United States. Not surprisingly, these percentages reflect the pattern of income distribution along the border indicated by the Gini coefficients and the index of dissimilarity.

In brief, the general pattern of the distribution of income along the U.S. side of the U.S.-Mexico border region may be summarized as follows. When the four border states are compared with the United States as a whole, no large differences in the distribution of income are apparent in either 1969 or 1979. However, when the 25 border counties are examined individually, a trend toward increasing inequality in the distribution of income appears to exist as one travels from west to east along the border. Further, this pattern generally follows the pattern of declining per capita incomes in the same easterly direction.

VI. Speculation

In recent studies of income distribution, the number of variables used to explain a particular distribution or changes in the distribution of income is large and growing.[10] The general rule seems to be: if a variable has any significant social or economic importance, then that variable will also be of importance in determining the distribution of income in any given area or region. While at first glance the previous statement may seem to be an exaggeration, a few examples are sufficient to indicate both the complexity and the diversity of the variables now being related to the distribution of income.

Demographic variables have become especially prominent and include the age-sex distribution of the population, migration rates, the natural rate of increase in the population, the absolute size of the population, family and household size and composition, and the racial and ethnic composition of the population.[11] Economic variables frequently cited as influencing the distribution of income include both the level and rate of economic growth, the structure of industry, labor force participation rates, methods of taxation, changes in the productivity of both capital and labor, and a host of others.[12]

In a border region the problem of explaining the distribution of income becomes even more complex. Along the U.S.-Mexico border many citizens of Mexico work in the United States, yet maintain their residences in Mexico. It seems reasonable that this phenomenon will influence the distribution of income on both sides of the border.

Due to the complexities described above, the approach taken here to "explain" the distribution of family income along the border will be a highly simplified one. Several variables that might have an influence on the distribution of income have been selected. A simple correlation coefficient between the 1979 Gini coefficients for the 25 border counties and each of the selected variables has been calculated.[13] While this approach leaves much to be desired in terms of methodological niceties, it is sufficient to provide hypotheses for further research.

The variables selected include: (1) the median age of the population of each county, (2) the size of the population for each county, (3) the rate of growth of population between 1970 and 1980 for each county, (4) net migration into each county between 1970 and 1980, (5) the percent of the population identifying themselves as of Hispanic origin in the 1980 census, (6) the level of per capita income in 1979, (7) the rate of growth in mean family income from 1969 to 1979, and (8) the rank order of the counties moving from west to east along the border. The simple correlation between the 1979 Gini coefficients and each of these variables was calculated.

Of the six demographic variables examined, only two were found to have a statistically significant relationship (.05 level) with the distribution of income. These variables were the percent of the population identifying themselves as of Hispanic origin in 1980 (simple correlation coefficient = 0.554) and a migration variable defined to be the percent of the population in each county living in a different state in 1975 (simple correlation = 0.624) than in 1980. Of the remaining three variables, both per capita income (simple correlation = −0.404) and the geographic rank order of the counties (simple correlation = 0.618) exhibited a statistically significant relationship at the 0.05 level with income distribution as measured by the Gini coefficients.

There are a number of consequences of the pattern of income distribution found along the border in both the public and private sectors of the border economy.

Among the most important implications of the level of distribution of income are those related to the need to provide higher levels of public services along the border and the ability of the state and local governments along the border to raise the revenue required to provide those services.[14] A few examples include the fact that citizens of two countries often use the streets, roads, and highways and parks of border cities (on both sides of the border). Texas newspapers in particular are inclined to point to the use by citizens of Mexico of educational and health facilities available in Texas cities. Both the low level of income in the border counties and the more unequal distribution of income found especially in the Texas border counties reduce the ability of state and local government to raise the tax revenue needed to provide such services. Further, the low level of per capita income in parts of the border region may itself be a factor requiring additional public expenditures.

In the private sector, the level and distribution of income along the border have important implications in the areas of retail and wholesale trade—especially inventory requirements and advertising strategies. For example, retail stores along the border have an apparent tendency to concentrate on merchandise in the lower price ranges.

The distribution of income along the border is also related to the rate of economic growth of the region. The need for large amounts of both public and private investment in the border region is well known. The prospects for significant federal programs aimed at the economic development of the border region are limited, at best. Therefore, the ability of the local economy to generate investment funds and to create a favorable climate to attract private external investment is critical. The distribution of income described above suggests that the ability of the local economy in this regard is also limited. Further, this pattern of income distribution is not likely to make the border region attractive to outside investors.

The recent peso devaluation(s) and the subsequent economic disruptions on the U.S. side of the border have without much doubt altered the patterns of income distribution along the border described in this paper. In particular, the peso devaluations appear to be associated with the increase in unemployment and a rising rate of business failure in many of the border counties. Thus, it is likely that the degree of inequality in the distribution of income along the border has increased.

Notes

1. While both the size distribution and the functional distribution of income are important variables, the size distribution of income was selected as the central focus of this paper because this variable relates more directly to issues of poverty and inequality.

2. Hansen, for example, used the Bureau of Economic Analysis Functional Economic Areas (FEAs) along the border which include such cities as San Antonio, Texas, and Palm Springs, California. See Niles M. Hansen, *The Border Economy Regional Development in the Southwest*, University of Texas Press, Austin. 1981.

3. In 1980 three of the border counties (San Diego, California, Pima, Arizona, and El Paso, Texas) accounted for 58.9 percent of the total population and 72.3 percent of the total families in the 25 border counties. Given the obvious importance of these three counties in the region, the analysis in this paper will be based primarily on measures of income distribution calculated for each of the border counties individually. Thus, the distortion due to the three large counties which might be present in a single aggregate measure of income distribution may be avoided.

4. U.S. Bureau of the Census, *Summary Characteristics for Governmental Units and Standard Metropolitan Statistical Areas* (PHC80-3-33), Washington, D.C. 1983, Appendix B.

5. U.S. Bureau of the Census, *1970 Census of Population and Housing: Characteristics of the Population*, Volume I, Washington, D.C. 1973.

6. See, for example, Jan Pen, *Income Distribution: Facts, Theories, Policies*, Praeger Publishers, New York, 1971; and A. B. Atkinson, *The Personal Distribution of Income*, Westview Press, Boulder, Colorado. 1976.

7. Fossett, Mark, and Scott J. South, "The Measurement of Intergroup Income Inequality: A Conceptual Review," *Social Forces*, Vol. 61, No. 3, March 1983, pp. 855–871.

8. See the discussion of measures of grouped data in N. C. Kakwani, *Income Inequality and Poverty: Methods of Estimation and Policy Applications*, Oxford, New York. 1980.

9. Hansen, p. 142.

10. Yotopoulos, Pan A., and Jeffrey B. Nugent, *Economics of Development: Empirical Investigations*, Harper and Row, New York. 1976. Pp. 237–257.

11. Many of the demographic issues related to the distribution of income are discussed in *Income Distribution and the Family*, a supplement to Volume 8 of *Population and Development Review*. 1982.

12. The discussion in Pen, *Income Distribution*, is excellent on this point.

13. It should be noted that the choice of a particular measure of income distribution such as the Gini coefficient over some other measure of income distribution may influence the correlation coefficients described here.

14. Brook, Kathleen, James Peach, and Orman Paananen, "Local Government Revenues and Expenditures in the Border Counties," paper presented at the Western Social Sciences Association, Albuquerque, New Mexico, April 1983.

6
The Northern Border of Mexico and the Crisis of 1982: A Few Preliminary Observations

Jesús Tamayo

I

The border crisis cannot be fully understood without first examining, albeit in the most general manner, the national economic crisis. What follows is a reflection, frequently amplified, of the exhaustion of an expansionist-type economic development model which created grave problems for the external sector of our economy. In the last few years, the ready availability of crude oil made possible huge imports of resources for economic expansion (both public and private), subsidy of imports, enrichment of certain sectors of the political bureaucracy, and financial speculation. The accumulated deficit in the balance of payments led to an unaccustomed level of foreign debt. Suddenly, the paralysis of the only level available to conserve and reproduce our foreign credit led us into financial bankruptcy, known euphemistically as a liquidity or cash crisis. This has made it necessary to reexamine the national economic projections in other terms, and has forced renegotiation—between the "political class" and the rest of the social sectors—in order to determine the weight of the crisis which each of them will have to bear in the years to come.

Background

The stage for the national financial crisis, which became so openly manifest in February 1982 and appeared to reach its climax in August and September of that year, was set in 1976, when the political decision was made, at the beginning of José López Portillo's administration, to expand the oil-producing sector and, on this basis, to develop the national industrial capacity. For this purpose an overvalued peso was used as an important instrument in the expansion process. In fact, shortly thereafter, the Bank of Mexico was to prevent the rate of

81

exchange, supposedly "floating," from growing beyond certain limitations;[1] the availability of oil revenues would permit the maximum limit, unofficially established for the rate of exchange, to be maintained indefinitely.

After several months, however, factors both external and internal made it evident not only that a fixed and progressively overvalued rate of exchange was inefficient, but that the overall economic policy was likewise inefficient. The high interest rates prevailing in the international financial market (to which, for internal interest rates, a differential was added as "devaluation risk"), caused our internal interest rates to soar to very high levels. The "high cost of money" brought about a progressive decline in industrial activity, drove up the prices of manufactured goods, eroded their competitiveness and, consequently, put the brakes on non-crude oil exports. The increasing inflation rate inside the country operated in the same way; being significantly higher than the inflation rate in the United States, it subsidized all manner of imports and, even more, discouraged Mexican exports.[2] Given this scenario, non-oil export income plummeted, while at the same time expenditures increased significantly for imports and for the purchase, outside Mexico, of services by wealthy Mexican sectors.[3]

Within the group of Mexican importers subsidized during the period in question (in other words, within the group of those who received income transfers via the rate of exchange), the border population of northern Mexico figures prominently, being a traditional importer of a substantial part of their consumer goods.[4] For nearly five years, the increasing overvaluation of our money vis-à-vis the dollar subsidized the purchase, in itself heavy, of goods and services paid with American currency. Sales of neighboring border business enterprises in the United States increased to the point that, in some cases, they became dependent on Mexican consumption.[5] Trade in imports on the Mexican side of the border also flourished splendidly.[6] In more recent times, a substantial part of the national demand for imports was added to the strictly border demand, and the Mexicans' purchasing power was felt far into American territory.[7]

During the period in question, the prevalent rate of exchange made the scarce Mexican goods reaching the far north of the country seem relatively expensive. Not too long ago—during the first half of the sixties—"CEDIs" (Tax Return Certificates) had fostered the shipment of Mexican goods to "the border," but the overvaluation of the peso had progressively undone the effects of that program.[8] In summary, the overall economic policy from 1976 to 1981 in the extreme north of Mexico tended to foster the consumption of imported goods— already high in itself. The direct beneficiary of this was that business sector dealing in durable American goods, principally electric household appliances. This sector flourished on both sides of the border with the increasing regional propensity to import.[9] The border's "maquila" (assembly-line) sector, and the weak non-"maquila" manufacturing sector, for its part, showed no signs of having suffered any significant ill effects from that economic policy.

The Crude-Oil Crisis

Until 1981, Mexico had reported an unprecedented economic growth (more than 8 percent in the last few years). Internationally, this was considered a special case among developing nations. This crystallized, it was said within the country, in the confidence of international bankers in Mexico, and consequently, in the credits that Mexico had received. Halfway through 1981, however, the decrease in the price of crude oil on the international market (a reduction carefully sought by the purchasing countries), put the Mexican economy on the alert. With oil-export income reduced, the balance-of-payments deficit soared and had to be financed with foreign credit. The situation had suddenly changed. While the bankers continued to offer credits, they lowered the amount of credit they offered and set shorter terms— an average of two years instead of seven—for payment; in addition, the interest rates on the credits increased.[10]

Faced with imminent crisis, the Mexican government let the peso "slide" vis-à-vis the dollar. The rate of exchange was allowed to reach 1 to 26 by the middle of February. It was nevertheless obvious that the sliding rate was slow in relation to the political and economic impact provoked by the overvaluation of the peso.[11] Presidential appeals for solidarity did not prevent speculators, in the first weeks of February, in the words of José López Portillo, from "holding up the Bank of Mexico."[12] The flight of capital thus would precipitate the first devaluation of 1982.[13]

In May, with the country now experiencing the first austerity measures, newly-appointed Treasury Secretary Jesús Silva Herzog announced that Mexico would face, during the following twelve months, a period of zero economic growth and an annual rate of inflation of not less than 50 percent.[14] He did not, however, announce that the international bankers had not only suspended new credits to Mexico but also the delivery of currency for credits previously approved.[15] The exhaustion of reserves was foreseeable.

The crisis does not spread its effects homogeneously throughout the entire nation. Neither do the economic policy responses of the Mexican Government, the devaluation of the peso or monetary exchange. Likewise, the scarcity of foreign currency is felt at different levels and with different degrees of effect in divers places and national economic sectors.

While urban border cities are relatively insulated from the Mexican national system (and so their economies are relatively more integrated into the economic system of the United States), their population feels more strongly the effects of rate-of-exchange modifications, variations in monetary exchange regulations, or generalized shortage of foreign currency.[16] Put another way, the border population is more seriously affected by these occurrences, because if it is true that they "earn in pesos," it is no less true that they "buy in dollars" a substantial part of their consumer goods.

The February devaluation, as would also be the case with the August and December devaluations, drove violently upward the cost of basic subsistence goods along our northern border areas. Consequently, the brakes were put on the traditional tendency to buy products from the United States, reorienting the local demand toward nationally produced products. Prior to February, almost any imported product purchased at the 26 to 1 exchange rate proved more economical than its national equivalent; after February, and principally after August, the majority of nationally produced goods proved more attractive than their imported counterparts purchased at the rate of 70 to 1, to say nothing of those purchased after December at the rate of 150 to 1. It must, however, be pointed out that the soaring Mexican inflation has tended to wipe out the concomitant competitiveness of Mexican goods.[17]

The cost-of-living increase (or the decrease in real income) at the border affects principally those employees with fixed income. This group includes federal, state and city government employees, laborers and employees in "maquila" (assembly-line) operations, the few laborers in the weak local manufacturing industry, and employees of local business. Other groups of border employees are in a better position to resist the effects of the crisis or to transfer them to others. First among these are those who sell goods and services to the border visitors; second is that group in private practice of the professions. There is, of course, a group of workers who are even benefited by this situation. This is the group of emigrés known as "commuters" or "green carders," who are Mexicans with legal residence in the United States who take advantage of this status to work in the United States and live across the border on Mexican soil.[18]

Mexican business has been affected by the economic crisis. To the extent that this causes a lowering of real income for the majority, business activity feels the decrease. The first groups to be affected have been those who deal in goods highly elastic vis-à-vis income, among which are our luxury or superfluous imports. In addition, every devaluation alters the system of relative prices, which is important to any importer and especially for the Mexican consumer living at the border. Thus it is not strange that, regionally, among the first to be affected by the crises are the American merchants along the border. Likewise, regional Mexican commerce in imported goods has seen its level of activity plunge. On the other hand, Mexican commerce in basic, non-durable goods of national origin has received that demand which has been progressively lost by its American counterpart.[19]

The border "maquila" (assembly-line) sector has also benefited from the crisis. The wages paid to employees and laborers was reduced for those companies in proportion to the devaluation of the peso. Alongside the across-the-border sector is the value-adding sector (small and medium-sized industries) which tends to decrease slowly but surely. It is not yet clear whether the crisis will benefit these or, on the contrary, hasten their extinction.

Finally, that sector selling services to American visitors, the so-called tourist "industry" at the border, has, as a result of the devaluation, found itself in a position to increase its gross sales volume, which had been in the doldrums for years as the result of peso overvaluation. The increase in the sale of tourist services, however, has not been immediate.[20]

The Financial Slump

The flight of capital from the Mexican system, which according to unofficial reports reached $15 billion in the space of eighteen months, opened out into a new peso flotation/devaluation at the beginning of August. In an effort to protect non-speculative activities, it was accompanied by a dual-dollar-parity system—a *free* rate of exchange and a *controlled* rate. A week later, the Mexican Government announced the prohibition of transfers of funds outside the country and mandated the payment in pesos of dollar accounts in Mexican banks.[21] (These obligations reached a total of twelve billion pesos according to figures reported by the private banking industry.)[22] August was characterized not only by the exhaustion of dollars in the national money market, but also by the breakdown of controls over the administrative banking apparatus, the high degree of "dollarization" of savings and the unstoppable flight of capital.[23]

The August crisis practically paralyzed international transactions along the northern border. This forced the federal government to announce an urgent salvation plan for the border areas. On Wednesday the 18th, the Secretary of the Treasury reported that this plan would consist mainly in the authorization of preferential (low-cost) dollars to local merchants for the purchase of basic and semi-basic goods in order to offset their temporary scarcity in those areas.[24] The Mexican crisis also had repercussions in the southwestern United States, which led the Council of American Chambers of Commerce and California Governor Edmund Brown, Jr., to ask President Reagan to declare the border a disaster area. (United States economic aid would not be forthcoming, however, until the first days of September.[25])

The exchange controls mandated on September 1, signaling the final exhaustion of the state's reserves, suspended—*de facto*—the actual validity of the special custom regulations which gave a free import status to the border area. Not until September 18 would it be clarified that imports by border residents, under the customs law, would be exempted from the prior permit requirement.[26]

The brief duration of monetary exchange controls was characterized, in the Mexican border cities, by the non-supply of basic products, by the strategy of accepting pesos on the part of American business,[27] by the pertinacious scarcity of dollars, and by peso-dollar speculation aided and abetted by money-exchange facilities across the border.[28]

The federal government soon had to take backward steps, allowing the establishment of money-exchange facilities on the Mexican side of the border; that is, regionally suppressing exchange controls, later permitting border companies to open dollar accounts in the nationalized banking industry and, finally, granting an extension of the free zone status in the Mexican northwest. This time, however, those who imported American goods could not easily buy dollars in the Mexican banks.

The negotiating strategy of the Mexican government in the face of the crisis was orthodox. It consisted of seeking help from the international financial system itself (this time supported by some authorities in the United States), and in rejecting a number of Arabian offers to provide financial aid.[29]

On November 10, the Secretary of the Treasury and the director of the Banco de Mexico (Central Bank) made public the text of the letter of intent sent to the IMF by the Mexican Government. This supposed the surmounting, at last, of initial Mexican resistance to the adoption of the economic austerity measures insisted upon by that financial institution. The preliminary agreement—definitive IMF approval would be forthcoming in December—would open the door to renegotiation and restructuring of the foreign debt and would make it possible to receive, over the next three years, a total of $4.6 billion and to negotiate additional credits for $6 billion in 1983. Mexico, for its part, agreed to abandon its policy of financing its economic development with indebtedness, to reduce the public sector debt (measured in relation to GNP) from 16.5 percent to 8.5 percent, to cut back governmental subsidies, to reduce the rate of foreign indebtedness, to increase internal interest rates, to dismantle "tariff barriers" to foreign goods, and to soften exchange controls in order to return to "normalcy" in foreign transactions.[30]

On November 17, the Treasury secretary, Silva Herzog, said that the agreement included no wage ceiling and that IMF had accepted, unconditionally, the economic readjustment program proposed by Mexico.[31]

New Policy

On December 1, Miguel de la Madrid assumed the presidency of Mexico. In his inaugural address, he announced an economic reordering plan which raised to the rank of a principal economic-program measure one of the economic policy conditions demanded by the IMF, that of reducing public expenditures. In order to ensure the reduction of the public debt, he announced budgetary and tax reforms (to increase public revenues), and the restructuring of the administration of the federal government. The bureaucracy cutback and the reduction of public investment thus appear as the principal instruments to be used in fighting inflation and "in recovering the dynamism of economic development." Other important facets of the reordering plan were an employment protection program and another program for stimulating and protecting programs for producing, importing, and distributing basic foodstuffs. The plan promised honesty and efficiency in government and the reaffirmed commitment to qualitative relevance of the public sector within the mixed-economy regime.

It is worth pointing out that while de la Madrid affirmed that the nationalization of the banking industry was irreversible, he did suggest a turn toward a mixed banking system. He also announced, on that occasion, forthcoming adjustments in exchange controls, a "realistic" rate of exchange, import controls and the rationalization of government protectionism.

On December 10, the new administration authorized the partial opening of the exchange market.[32] The adjustment of exchange controls would surely tend to soften the Draconian nature of the measures taken during the first days of September, reducing the pressure on hypersensitive "middle-class" sectors of the population and giving them a certain amount of dollars for their immediate needs. The adjustment would also serve to devalue the currency once again by modifying the rate of exchange in the "controlled" parities,[33] taking care that those debtors with debts in dollars suffered a blow less than proportional with regard to the overall impact. It would also strive to ensure, via the control route, the income derived from exports in foreign currency. Finally, the adjustment would provide an opportunity to lay the blame, politically, for the twin springs of the crisis (financial bankruptcy and administrative chaos) on the populist strategies of the late administration. Explicitly, the new Exchange Control Decree reaffirmed the government's intention "not to interfere with the natural economic and social relationships of the border population with neighboring, alien zones." It also stated that it is "highly undesirable to have on the books regulations which tend to be massively violated, as well as to encourage the fostering of exchange markets outside of the banking institutions." Finally, it added that "experience has shown the impossibility in practice and the high administrative cost implicit in the effort to control foreign exchange inflows . . . especially that derived from tourism and border transactions."[34]

II

New Problems

The overall implications of the tactics followed by Mexico in the face of the economic crisis are well known. Our economic recovery program is, then, of a restrictionist nature, with clear limitations on salary increases (while not explicit, then at least implicit and evident), with a marked tendency to eliminate employment subsidies and transfer capital resources to manufacturing capital with debts in dollars. It is lost on no one that, during the first one hundred days of the new government, a clear sign has been shown of the political willingness to reduce the volume, if not the quality, of state intervention in the economy, to reopen the nationalized banking industry to private capital, to liberalize foreign commerce as far as the shortage of foreign currency permits, to eliminate price controls and to leave peasant (non-market) economies throughout the countryside to die a slow and natural death in this new social framework. All of this within a rhetorical anti-inflationary framework.

Toward the end of February, new problems cast doubt on the viability of the Mexican recovery program. Internal squabbles in OPEC led to the slashing of the price of crude oil on the international market.[35] Thus it is that Mexico heads a long list of debt-strapped countries with the risk of having their income reduced even further. Under these conditions, nobody can predict the future development of internal events.[36]

In sum, the expectations of economic recovery in Mexico seem to depend more on external factors (economic recovery in the United States, a drop in interest rates, recovery of the crude oil market, etc.) than on internal decisions and willingness; thus it is predicted that achieving this recuperation in the short term is improbable.[37] Be that as it may, it will require intense diplomatic support (above all if the required mulitlateral decisions are made), and a heretofore unprecedented national effort to overcome the traditional levels of productive inefficiency and administrative corruption to hold in check the inevitable tendencies toward national disintegration.

At short term, a generalized decline in Mexican foreign commerce is probable. This has, and will have, a significant influence in the reduction of business activity between Mexico and the United States, especially in the importation by Mexico of American goods.[38] In sum, in order to amortize our debt we have to export more, much more than we import. Thus, what emerges explicitly is an obligatory, but no less well-defined, strategy of substitution of imports which will neither be permanently propped up by an undervalued peso, nor accept new overvaluation of our currency.[39] Thus, the imminent development of new Mexican exports, natural gas for example, is foreseeable. So is the more or less unrestricted opening up of the economy to direct foreign investment.

In the political watershed, this scenario cannot fail to accompany the crisis in the traditional apparatus of control of the work force. Increasing unemployment, lowering of real income and the disappearance of economic transfers to labor make predictable: (1) the renegotiation of the virtual social contract between the institutional government and the masses of workers, both rural and urban; (2) the reconstitution of present labor and peasant unions; and (3) the violent repression of extreme political demonstrations—in a nutshell, the reorientation of the social life of the nation.

We have stated above that the effects of the economic crisis are amplified in the urban areas in the northern part of Mexico. It must be added that, in addition to the direct impact on the price of imported goods caused by the devaluation, the process of substitution of imports in the overall system drives up the cost of living and (at least at the beginning) drives down the quality of life of the nation's people. This especially buffets the four million Mexicans who now live in the extreme north of the country.

Furthermore, with a new rate of exchange, a number of Mexican products, especially those which are labor-intensive, become attractive for the American consumer. That is, they are aimed at the non-local purchaser, and the internal inflationary effect of this process is significant. Moreover, the local demand for certain goods grows with the extra (non-Mexican) demand; and the shortness of supply of these products becomes characteristic in these areas, themselves only irregularly supplied with national goods.

In the near future, the conditions prevailing outside this region will make it plain that the Mexican border will no longer have the cheap dollars of yesteryear and that—on the contrary—it must reorient its demand somewhat permanently to the national production system. While some regional groups may manage to reestablish indefinitely the free zone or other economic-commercial exception schemes permitting tax-free importation of raw materials, machinery and electrical domestic appliances, "there is nothing that the government can do to give them cheap dollars."[40]

In other words, the border population must, along with the rest of the country, bear the implications of the new economic policy adopted by the federal government. Much as that government might wish, it cannot make many real concessions to regional interests. Everything seems to indicate that the majority of the border population understands the responsibilities arising out of the circumstances; one must, however, ask whether the bourgeoisie of the region will accept their part of the burden in the crisis, or with what weapons it will negotiate with the federal government the shifting of its responsibilities to other social sectors of the population. It would also be wise to ask whether or not this process will strengthen its tendencies toward regional political autonomy, whether it will manage, once again, to pass off its own interests as the general interests of the region,[41] and if so, to what degree it will achieve this; and, finally, what are the Mexican nation's possibilities and limitations in these negotiations. And what are the regional and federal interests of the United States in developing the center-to-periphery contradiction along the Mexican border?

It is obvious that we cannot answer these questions here. In conclusion, however, we could add some final considerations which, in any case, would help to clarify the formulation of these questions and draft new ones.

While the Mexican social structure, seen as a whole, is characterized by the weakness of the aggregate of organizations referred to by specialists as civil society and, consequently, by the relative strength of the governmental machinery and its tendency to occupy every nook and cranny of social life at the border regions, these characteristics appear to be less clearly defined.[42] Federal authority frequently materializes there in watered-down ministerial representations, governmental employees and officials of unreliable memory, and the relatively weak local presence of the state.[43] These factors provide a greater range of action for strictly non-governmental local organizations which, in addition, are aware of the democracy of the neighboring United States.

In some regions in the extreme northern part of Mexico, relationships with the central authorities are even more complicated, although a certain symbiosis has evolved there between the "political class" and the local business sector.[44] While in recent years this sector has been involved in the process of an increasing economic association with its American counterpart (and in this process has learned to align itself culturally with the neighboring sociocultural models), to the extent that it penetrates into the local political apparatus, there appear, within the aggregate of "regional interests," the defense and promotion of United States interests in the region.[45]

The present crisis precipitates the emergence of an aggressive public/private partnership. In the northern part of Mexico, the aggressiveness against the system is aggravated, perhaps because the center has frequently allowed itself to be represented by inefficient, if not corrupt, officials, and because the local authorities have not infrequently spearheaded the defense of outside interests. If this situation continues, what will it cost in the future?[46]

We have indicated on a number of previous occasions that the Mexican state must take full charge of the border question and elevate it to the national level. It would be necessary to add today that "the nationalization of the 'political class' at the border" stands out as a *sine qua non* when our country needs to summon its moral resources to confront internal crisis and outside pressures, and when it can be foreseen that the border societies, more than anyone else, must resist the reduction of their traditional standards of living and, at the same time, reaffirm their common interests and destiny with the rest of the Mexican nation.

SUMMARY

The devaluations of February, August, and December of 1983, the monetary controls and generalized shortage of foreign currency in national financial circles have had a regional, border-long impact of unaccustomed magnitude, whose medium- and long-range effects are, for the most part, still unpredictable.

In principle, the requirements of the State have taken precedence over any regional considerations; more recently, the former appeared to be yielding in favor of private local interests which, in addition, enjoyed full press coverage. Independently of the results of this initial skirmish, a long financial crisis is foreseen, and the negotiations concerning the weight which each of the national social classes will have to tolerate in the years to come, is barely under way. Likewise, the national polemic over the role of the nation's periphery, in the national economic plans, is far from over.

The main purpose of Section I is to reproduce—based on the chronological sequence of the events of the second half of 1982— the counterpoint comprising the following factors: foreign conditions on the Mexican system, some of the Mexican government responses to those conditions, and finally, the effects or repercussions involving exclusively the border area, as well as certain regional responses and initiatives.

Section II identifies certain overall economic tendencies permitting prediction of a likely regional scenario at short term. Finally, this paper asks about the possibility of whether the private sectors and certain groups of the "political class" support and favor the present economic policy, with its orientation toward the substitution of imports.

Notes

1. In recent years, international financial centers have promoted the existence of floating rates of exchange in order to eliminate distortions and stimulate international trade. However, the vulnerability of the Mexican government to speculative "runs" or "stampedes," causing abrupt changes in value, makes a number of analysts long for the time-tested, rigid systems, and reach the conclusion that a "restricted flotation" system is necessary.

2. See a detailed analysis of the economic crisis in the final months of 1981, in the article written collectively by the analysts of the Mexican Economics Department of the CIDE: "A hard government's night," in *Nexus* (50), February 1982. The "Communiqué of the Banco de Mexico announcing that its institution would withdraw temporarily from the exchange market" (published in *Comercio Exterior*, Volume 32, No. 3, Mexico City, March 1982), provides the official interpretation of events.

3. The import-company sector, public and private, has not been the only sector to benefit greatly from the economic policies of the last few years. There is also the urban petty bourgeoisie, who import all manner of consumer goods from the United States. This sector, "carried along" as a beneficiary of the overvaluation of the peso, soon discovered how relatively inexpensive it proved, for example, to travel abroad or buy real property or medical services outside Mexico.

H. Rudnitsky, in *Forbes* magazine, pointed out beginning at the turn of the year that the flight of Mexican capital prior to the first devaluation, in February, reached $100 million daily. (*Forbes*, March 15, 1982). Prior to this devaluation, *Fortune* magazine and *Texas Business* stated that Mexicans had $16.4 billion deposited in Texas banks, and that Mexican real-estate investment in principal Texas cities has risen from $2 billion to $6 billion. On September 1, 1982, José López Portillo would state that recent bank accounts opened by Mexicans abroad totaled at least $14 billion, and that the value of urban and rural real estate in the United States, property of Mexicans, was estimated at $25 billion.

4. The high percentage of imports among consumer products in those areas is their most prominent economic characteristic; this materialized, until August 1982, both in the large number of American products with dollar price-tags and sold in dollars in urban markets in the extreme northern part of the country, and in the also numerous purchases by Mexicans in border stores on the U.S. side. One must bear in mind that, unlike the situation for Mexican tourists, for border residents the use of imported goods is, in fact, largely inevitable. Reasons geographical, historical and economic explain that our border markets today may not be predominantly under the jurisdiction of the nation's capital. See Jesús Tamayo, "The integration of the border population to the production and consumption of American goods: interdependence or a dependent articulation?" in *El Día*, June 5 and 6, 1981.

5. In 1979, within the context of an exhaustive investigation carried out in the CIDE, we attempted a preliminary approximation of the volume of Mexican purchases in United States border cities. Our results showed that in 1972, McAllen, National City, Harlingen, and Laredo, Texas, were the cities most sensitive to the fluctuations of Mexican expenditures which, in extreme cases, contributed more than one-third of all local commerce. See "Labor-intensive export operations in northern Mexico border areas," final research report, Economic, Research and Teaching Center (CIDE), Mexico, 1979 (mimeographed copy).

6. It is well known that the economic activity of most of our border cities was born specialized, aimed basically at tertiary activities. As late as 1970, five years after the birth of the Border Industrialization Program (BIP), those cities showed still a higher degree of business and service specialization than the aggregate of political-administrative organizations ("municipios," or districts) which are most densely populated in the country. (See "Labor intensive export-operations.")

7. According to a study undertaken by the San Antonio, Texas, Chamber of Commerce, in 1980 3.2 million tourists visited the United States and spent a total of $2.6 billion which, in accordance with the distribution provided by the Department of Commerce, should have been distributed as follows: Los Angeles: 960,000 Mexican tourists, who spent $780 million; San Antonio: 512,000, $416 million; Houston: 480,000, $390 million; San Francisco: 320,000, $260 million; others: 928,000, $754 million. Source: *Uno más Uno*, December 8, 1981.

8. Ever since they were established, the "CEDIs" have had a dynamic development, even greater than that of the importation of *artículos* "gancho." Despite their success, they were suspended following the 1976 devaluation. Buttressed by this experience, the Treasury Department established similar incentives, the so-called "CEPROFIS."

9. Official Mexican statistics for 1977 showed that imports by the border population, i.e., by 5 percent of the nation, totaled 18% of all imports. The following year, 1978, total Mexican imports which, due to the organization of the Mexican accounting system, do not include "border transactions," reached 183 billion pesos at the present rate of exchange; within these, imports to "free zones" totaled 12 billion, and importation of "bargain" or "display window" merchandise totaled 2 billion. In addition, expenditures by Mexicans that year in "border transactions" reached 36 billion. Thus, actual border participation in national imports appeared to exceed 20 percent. See *Mexican Foreign Commerce Statistical Yearbook*, SPP, Mexico, 1978; Banco de Mexico, *Annual Report*, 1978.

10. See "U.S. banks reassess Mexico credit. Lenders say it's good risk, but are more cautious," *Los Angeles Times*, April 27, 1982.

11. Two days before the devaluation, the president of the CANACINTRA affirmed that maintaining a fixed or semi-fixed peso parity "protects Japanese, European or United States industrialists from the competition of Mexican industry" ("Portafolios," in *Excelsior*, February 16, 1982.)

12. First public statement by José López Portillo with regard to the devaluation. Speech shown on Mexican television the morning of February 20, 1982.

13. It is also possible that the decision by the United States to raise the prime interest rate—a decision announced during those same days, which seems to have caused extreme annoyance in European capitals and even to have influenced the devaluation of several European currencies—could have precipitated the Mexican decision to devalue. See "Shots heard across the Atlantic," *Time*, March 1, 1982; also "Europe vs. Reaganomics," *Newsweek*, March 1, 1982.

14. See "Mexico forecasts 50% inflation, zero growth," *Los Angeles Times*, May 19, 1982; and "Drastic growth slump predicted for Mexico," *The San Diego Union*, May 20, 1982.

15. The polemics over the national economic situation were conditioned by the Mexican political calendar. The forthcoming presidential elections would clearly detract from the visibility of the rising internal inflation which would lead almost inexorably to a second devaluation. Thus it was that from February to July, together with massive speculation in capital that was betting on the second devaluation of the peso, the purchase of dollars by the Mexican middle class became a practical necessity in order to protect family savings.

16. The relative remoteness of the border areas vis-à-vis the country's principal production centers, their size and spatial distribution—all added

to the incipient development of the nation's productive capacity and the strength of the corresponding United States apparatus—explain the almost ancestral incompetence of national products in those markets, where they have frequently been introduced under conditions disadvantageous in terms of price, time, variety and quality. See Jesús Tamayo, "Two problems of the economic development of the border," in *Mexico–United States Relations I*, UNAM/Nueva Imagen. Mexico, 1980.

17. See "The devaluation and the northern border area," in *Mexican Foreign Trade Charter*, Year 2, Number 3, Mexico CIDE, May 15, 1982.

18. In some areas, the number of "emigrados," (the "resident immigrants") is highly relevant. This is the case in San Luis Rio Colorado, Sonora, where there are an estimated five thousand workers in this category. While the Immigration and Naturalization Service periodically enumerates them, it does not publish the magnitude of their numbers.

19. Regional trade, both Mexican and American, has for years served not only the border residents but also Mexican visitors to the border, who traditionally take advantage of their stay there in order to *introduce* (more often than not, illegally) articles originating in the United States. Thus, the border trade obtained an advantage from the economic-commercial exception policies which the residents of the extreme north of the country have traditionally enjoyed. This policy materialized only as of September 1, 1983 in the *free* "domestic" importations legalized by the Customs Regulations, in *free* imports into the "free zone" as well as the importation, also *free*, of "bargain" merchandise. The overall volume of border importations is unknown; what is known is that their approximation by the Bank of Mexico under the heading of "border transactions" is an undervalued estimation of actual volume. See Jesús Tamayo and José Luis Fernández, CIDE *Collection of Essays on Political Studies*, Mexico, 1983.

20. The prospective visitor to the border envinced hypersensitivity to local reports which at that time presented an image of Mexico emphasizing social conflicts and governmental inefficiency and corruption as well as a supposed tendency toward socialism.

21. See "Regulations for payment of bank deposits made in foreign currency," *Diario Oficial* (Official Gazette), August 13, 1982.

22. See: "Dollar freeze called act of desperation" in *The San Diego Union*, August 14, 1982; also see "With no more reserves, the government is closing in on dollars in bank accounts," in *Proceso*, August 16, 1982, pp. 23–26.

23. "Acute shortage of dollars in Nogales (Sonora): government lacked foreign currency to pay," in *Excelsior*, August 19, 1982; "Uncertainty and chaos as market reopens," in *Uno más Uno*, August 20, 1982; "In Nogales, in less than 48 hours, the money (sic) dropped 35 pesos," in *Excelsior*, August 21; "The city of Tijuana faced with the worst crisis in its history," in *Excelsior*, August 22, 1982. The flight of capital increased during August. See: "Peso devaluation fails to halt run of dollar" in *The Tribune* (San Diego), August 10, 1982; "Peso hits 150 to dollar on black market," in *The San Diego Union*, August 16, 1982; "Trade on decline in San Ysidro; banks swelling with dollars of Mexican depositors," in *Excelsior*, August 22, 1982.

24. Beginning with the February devaluation, but even more following the August devaluation, the border residents decried on several occasions the scarcity of basic goods in these areas. This scarcity, to a large measure provoked by the Americans living in border cities on the other side of the border, was

exacerbated by the increasing local demand for Mexican products, which demand grew out of the devaluation. See: "U.S. bargain hunters 'sacking' Tijuana Shelves," in *The San Diego Tribune*, August 12, 1982; "Now they come from the U.S. to buy basic commodities on this side," in *Uno más Uno*, August 10, 1982; and "Scarcity of basics in border area," in *Uno más Uno*, August 17, 1982.

25. "Southern U.S. businesses nearly bankrupt," in *Excelsior* on August 21, 1982; "Economic disaster in U.S. border area," in *Uno más Uno*, August 21, 1982; "Sales plunge in McAllen despite attractive specials," in *Excelsior* on September 7, 1982, and finally, "U.S. economic aid to cities on its Mexican border," in *Excelsior*, September 8, 1982.

26. See "Generalized exchange-control decree" in the *Diario Oficial*, September 1, 1982; and "Prior permit requirement decree by the Commerce and Industry Secretariat for all imports covered under the General Importation Tax Schedule, including the importation of said merchandise to the country's free zones, with the exceptions as indicated, until December 31, 1983." *Diario Oficial*, September 17, 1982.

27. By accepting pesos, the Americans had found the way to attract Mexicans who no longer turned out as they had before to patronize American businesses; at the same time, it prevented dollars from entering Mexico. The pesos captured on the other side of the border went to the labor-intensive factories to meet their payrolls; they were also used to pay balances due to Mexican exporters.

28. This was promptly reported in the Mexican press. See: "Mexican politicos linked with U.S. exchange houses," in *Excelsior*, October 31, 1982. On November 8, José Luis Mejías wrote in his column, "The Untouchables," in *Excelsior*, that Roberto de la Madrid was the owner of a chain of exchange-houses on both sides of the border.

29. See: "*Financial Times* publishes that Mexico rejected credit from Saudi Arabia," in *Excelsior*, October 5, 1982.

30. See Letter of Intent sent by the Mexican Government to the International Monetary Fund (Text in full, published in the City of Mexico, November 11, 1982.)

31. See *Excelsior*, November 18. 1982.

32. Hereafter, foreign currency in actual cash may be purchased on the "free" market in border cities, and in international airports. In cities beyond the border, foreign currency may be acquired only as documents. See *Diario Oficial*, December 13, 1982.

33. On November 20, when the decree took effect, the dollar on the *free* market was also devalued, being quoted at 150 pesos.

34. "Exchange Control Decree," *Diario Oficial*, December 13, 1982.

35. See "the unrigging oil prices," in *Newsweek*, March 7, 1983.

36. While some analysts foresee a strategy of *consolidation* of the international debt, there are those who believe that the collapse of the international system is dangerously imminent, as a result of the impossibility, from the accounting standpoint, of coping with that debt. This, they maintain, would crystallize in a domino-theory series of *defaults* (more or less involuntary) by debtor countries. The disjunctive between "eating and paying the debt," in which the debtor nations in question find themselves, is obvious; a number of local voices suggest putting national requirements ahead of international obligations. It is obvious that this could be done, either unilaterally or by

mutual agreement with other debtor nations. Joint action presupposes the existence of international covenants between countries with highly differing levels of development and divers political planning, whereas unilateral action, aimed at reducing or suspending payment, would have disastrous economic and political consequences, and significantly damage the nation's productive capacity by wiping out foreign trade almost completely. See Remarks by Mexican Treasury Secretary Jesús Silva Herzog in *Excelsior*, March 8, 1983.

37. See: "World Bank Report on Mexico—until 1989, the debt will be overwhelming."

38. In addition, this scenario tends to be aggravated if, on the other hand, American protectionist trends prosper against precarious Mexican non-oil exports; it is therefore natural to expect that the Mexican exporters affected insist in their demand that Mexico join the General Agreement on Trade and Tariffs (GATT).

39. One must, however, recognize the favorable impact that this will have in the long run on the nation's productive capacity through the substitution of imports in both local and border markets.

40. Miguel Mancera Aguayo, Director of the Banco de México in *Excelsior*, January 16, 1983.

41. Recent events show how the regional private-sector interests, affected by the decline in commercial intercourse, were presented as the overall interests of the region, affected by the lack of understanding of the "central" government. The interests of workers in that region, for example, did not receive the same preferential press coverage.

42. The communities which we have grouped under the heading of border cities are notoriously heterogeneous and it would, therefore, be wrong to generalize facts which, while strictly local or regional, might be applied improperly to other cities or groups thereof. Accordingly, it is interesting to clarify that herein below we refer to clearly observable circumstances in the extreme northwest of Mexico. Concerning these mistaken generalizations, see: Jesús Tamayo and Berta Helena de Buen, "Some mistaken concepts about Mexico's northern border"; Working Papers Series, Overseas Development Council, Washington, D.C. 1982.

43. The governmental presence has not been measured exactly in terms of the number of government officials or public employees in a given region, but principally by their political density and the legitimacy of their social function.

44. It is no coincidence that in recent lists of aspirants to the candidacy of the ruling party for the Baja California Norte governorship, the overwhelming majority comprise distinguished regional businessmen.

45. This explains that it may be the state government from which labor legislation advocating exception of labor-intensive factories is protected; and, lately that the Treasury Secretariat is asked to reduce federal taxes for the Americans established in that area, and to eliminate retentions at border customs inspection facilities so as not to alter the outgoing flow of basic goods.

46. To date, the civil organization has sprung from the middle-class strata, suggesting defiance of public authority. Together with this may be observed the opposition on the right in certain sectors favorable to autonomist ideas. The National Action Party (PAN) has in recent weeks spearheaded the civil disobedience movement in refusing to pay automobile registration fees and increases in electrical energy usage rates.

7

Industrial Integration of the Northern Border Regions of Mexico into the National Economy

Alfonso Corona Rentería

Introduction

In May 1982 the Mexican and U.S. steering committees of the First Conference on Regional Impacts of U.S.-Mexico Economic Relations met at Grand Canyon in Arizona to discuss the organization of this second conference. It was agreed then to assign to this meeting the name "Challenges and Opportunities."

More than a year has elapsed since we held that preliminary seminar. The economy of Mexico was showing signs of deterioration; the February 1982 devaluation had already occurred—the first of three that would take place in that unfortunate year. The economy of the United States was sinking into recession and unemployment. Yet nobody then imagined the changes in border relations that in the course of one year would give a new and acute meaning to that conference title. Cross-border regional economies have reached an historical crossroads. Picking up the challenge and taking advantage of opportunities to reorder their growth and development are now even more important if we are to reduce inequities and create economic links and development patterns in the rapidly changing border regions of Mexico and the United States.

Overall Economic Relations in Recent Years

It seems necessary to underscore at the outset that the study of regional impacts in economic relations between the United States and Mexico is, in the first place, set in the overall context of the unequal and hierarchically classifiable interactions between two countries—one of them highly developed, the other developing and exhibiting a high degree of dependence on the first.

The asymmetry in degree of development regions situated on one side of the border and the other is directly attributable to the effects of the economic system of the world's most powerful capitalist nation on its neighbor to the south. Evidence of Mexico's dependence on the American market is recognition that 69 percent of Mexico's exports are destined for the United States, while 63 percent of her imports come from that country. Mexico's relations with the American market are reinforced by direct investments aimed increasingly at the manufacturing and food sectors. A small number of American firms are the owners of the vast majority of direct foreign investments in Mexico. Mexico's foreign debt was concentrated in American banks during the last ten years, for a number of reasons: the lack of equilibrium in that country's cash account; the limitations on the capital market inside Mexico; the low level of savings and, in consequence, of available credit; the increase in the rate of bank interest in the United States; the need for outside financing due to the Mexican federal government's budgetary deficit and the expectations of economic growth aroused by the take-off of the oil industry.

In recent years, the U.S. economy has recorded the highest unemployment levels since the 1930s, and while presently the economic weathervane points to recovery, unemployment will not wane substantially for another two or three years. Adding this to the serious disturbances in the Mexican economy results in a set of increasingly complex economic relationships with implications, both political and social, for both countries, internally as well as on the international plane.

During the period from 1979 to 1981, when the worldwide recession became acute, the Mexican economy soared, overstimulated by an enormous and unbalanced public expenditure. A drop in the price of Mexican crude oil halfway through 1981, together with the stagnation of the price and volume of Mexican exports, changed the course of the Mexican economy. In order to compensate for these losses, international credit was contracted at a high level and a short term.

The years of prosperity in Mexico had given rise to an extremely high volume of imports, encouraged by the substantial reduction in customs tariffs; internal inflation hastened it along and the imbalance in trade reached unprecedented levels. The resulting instability in the money market was aggravated by monetary speculation. The international polarization process was intensified with the massive flight of capital.

The enormous investment of Mexican capital in fixed-income securities and real-estate in American cities and recreation centers contributed mightly to the destabilization of Mexico. Meanwhile, the February and August 1982 devaluations took place. That year also saw a decrease in the influx of foreign capital and tourists to Mexico. The American market contracted and continued to shrink as far as

Mexican exports were concerned. A very recent example is the exclusion of 57 Mexican products from the United States Generalized Preference System.

The contraction in the money market, the recession in the Mexican economy and the peso devaluations affected imports from the United States, which were down 60 percent during the period including the final quarter of 1981 and ending with the final quarter of 1982, while estimates for 1983 indicated a reduction of American exports to Mexico by about $10 billion. This phenomenon was to cause the unemployment of some 231,000 persons, of whom approximately 48,000 live on the border with Mexico.

The second devaluation of the Mexican peso, which signalled the exhaustion of the country's foreign-currency reserves, left national-ization of the bank as the only alternative, along with exchange controls and the instant appearance of a black market in dollars in the large cities and along the northern border. The unprecedented immigration of Mexican workers to the United States is a measure of the social effects of the Mexican crisis. The third devaluation, mandated in December 1982, consolidated a new reality for border transactions.

The economic and social environment of the border has always been a reflection of the intense and complex overall relationship between Mexico and the United States. Comprising different geo-economic regions, permeable with regard to the flow of people and contact between them, as well as the flow of capital goods, ideas and political pressures, the border area, with its differential costs, permits American investors to take advantage of the relatively low cost of Mexican labor to turn out finished goods for transnational companies.

In the recent past, the lack of a national supply of intermediate and finished goods, and the non-existent interindustrial integration of the border states, have combined with the overvaluation of the Mexican peso, fostered by the "free zone" system, to hugely stimulate importation of consumer goods while undermining the possibilities of a regional industrialization integrated into the Mexican national economy.

The current Mexican economic crisis sets forth in the most spec-tacular form a previously underestimated aspect of the asymmetrical interdependency across the border of the twin cities. This is the dependence of American retail stores and other business enterprises on Mexican trade. The suspension of exchange operations arising out of the astronomic new rates of exchange meant that Mexicans could no longer buy the dollars necessary to make their daily purchases of durable and semi-durable goods in the stores on the American side of the border. For example, exports originating in San Diego, California were down 16 percent from the first quarter of 1981 to the final quarter of 1982. Declines were similar in the majority of American cities along the Mexican border. The effect has been devastating on the economy of American cities along the entire three-thousand kilometers—one thousand and eight hundred miles—of American border with Mexico.

On the Mexican side of the border, 15 percent of the businesses closed their doors for want of imports. The country's industry works with less intensity due to the lack of imported raw materials. The supply of merchandise is insufficient to satisfy a demand which has increased by 300 percent.

We now find a situation with two neighboring economies in unequal development, which have suffered greatly as the consequence of the respective crises in both countries. One must ask if such disorder could occur in two cross-border economies less dependent on retail merchandise, more closely linked one to the other by flows of inter-industrial raw materials and products, and more closely integrated into the overall economies of their respective countries.

Beginning with the bank nationalization and the establishment of exchange controls, the northern border has begun a process of economic reordering; the dollar is no longer the prevailing currency in any transaction, and the peso has now taken its rightful place.

The national market has a captive potential of 10,000,000 inhabitants along the border, who formerly bought their food on the American side. A similar number of Mexicans, residents of the southern part of the United States, likewise constitute a potential market for Mexican exports. Both markets will be a reality only if the national supply can supply the necessary quantities and qualities in timely fashion. Regional industrialization and commercialization policies must be formulated, based on the complement of intersector links of inter-mediate goods (raw materials) and finished products between the border states, and with regard to the rest of the economy. The intersector and interregional raw material/finished goods links must be reinforced with interurban liaisons east to west and north to south.

If action is not taken promptly, the high domestic inflation rate could return—in the space of a year or two—the traditional price advantage of American-manufactured goods, without our being able to capture on behalf of Mexico the market of our own border. The recent increases in the price of Mexican gasoline which now, although inferior in quality, is nevertheless more expensive than American gasoline, has brought about a resurgence of the proclivity to import consumer goods from north of the border.

If action is taken, imaginative action based on fairness and reason, Mexico can derive great benefit from industrial-regional integration via the creation of employment and the uplifting of the standard of living in the border states. An interchange network for intermediate goods (raw materials) and finished products can be constructed, complementing interregional production processes aimed at both the domestic and the international markets. Greater regional integration of the economies in the southern United States may also be required. Border trade then would occupy an important place in the economies of those regions, but it would cease to be the dominant economic activity and, therefore, would become much less vulnerable to the cyclical or structural changes typical of the capitalist system.

Economic Relations Between the North of Mexico and the Center

From the regional standpoint, interindustrial integration of the border states is justified because those entities have a relatively small impact on the economy of the nation, considering the size of their territory, their development potential and sparse population. In fact, the northern states, with more than 44 percent of the nation's territory, in 1980 had only 16.1 percent of the national population and barely reached, in that same year, 20.2 percent of the overall gross national product. Except for Chihuahua, the border states achieved an internal gross product per capita higher than the national average, however. The region's 1980 share in the gross national product included 22.9 percent in the agricultural and cattle industry, 21.2 percent in the distribution sector, 21.2 percent in the electrical sector, 20.1 percent in manufacturing, 18.3 percent in mining and 17.8 percent in construction. The population density in terms of residents per square kilometer in the border states is below the national average, with the exception of Nuevo León, where it is slightly higher; of the 50 largest cities in Mexico, 16 are in northern border states.

The problems facing the economies of the northern border states are, among others, a marked imbalance between the supply and demand for goods and services generated in the region; a deficient economic integration in the area; the geographical dispersion of the largest cities and the lack of communication between states and the rest of the country. This situation has limited the possibilities for development of a goodly number of activities requiring a substantial market as well as those activities with export possibilities. To all of the foregoing may be added the problem of the influx of people arriving at the border with the objective of working in the United States.

The expanse of this area, and its human and natural resources potential, as well as its potential for generating more trade in nationally-originating goods, justifies a development study specific to the northern states. While the in-bond plant industries have achieved their objective of generating employment, their legal basis limits the possibility of taking them seriously as a stable source of employment, and their production of goods does not presently influence the development and industrial integration of the country. Economic relations between the northern states and the rest of the country comprise principally the export to the central states of steel products, machinery and equipment as well as cattle, agricultural products and fish. The central states, in turn, export a large number of goods to the northern states, but these prove insufficient for consumption by the border regions. It is consequently seen as urgent that a policy be put into effect to achieve an intersector and interregion industrial integration contributing to the resolution of the problems set forth above. Such a policy should take into account the American markets for the supply of raw materials and the export of finished goods of national manufacture.

Objectives and Goals

A general national priority should be reduction of the border states economies' dependence on the United States, while increasing the contribution of the border regions' economies to the national economy and development. A second general objective should be encouragement of the industrial and population decentralization of the adjoining zone of the central states, fostering the development of medium-sized cities as well as the abatement of underemployment and the creation of employment and regional income distribution. Specific goals should include formulation of a model for international, intersectoral, and interregional integration of the border-state industries with those of the central and southern states of Mexico.

One quantitative result to be expected from this research would be the identification of productive activities made possible and supported by local resources and by raw materials of interregional and/ or American origin and, along with this, identification of the limits of the market—whether national or international. A qualitative result would be a set of policy regulations for north-south regional industrial integration as well as recommendations of policies for investment incentives in the proposed activities in the areas selected. The integration policy model would have to have congruence with the divers industrial development plans. A number of cities in border states should be selected in accordance with a strategy involving geographical location; size; population; endowment with natural, economic and human resources; and infrastructure and urban layout for the location of industrial and agricultural investments articulated both intersectorally and interregionally. Specific complementary policies should be designed relative to different economic and social spheres, fiscal and monetary tools, rates of exchange, foreign trade, commercial supply networks, family expenditure distribution, employment training, etc. These would reinforce the interindustrial policies and be congruent with the objectives of integration of the nation's economy.

The foregoing objectives cover an enormous amount of territory. Going beyond the exclusively economic aspects, they include social, political, environmental and other dimensions. The primary objective, however, is to increase regional production in northern Mexico. The attainment of this economic objective would necessarily contribute to the realization of sets of objectives such as the reduction of regional pockets of underemployment, better allocation and exploitation of resources in the region, improved distribution of income between regions, etc. To the instruments of economic policy such as direct public investment in the regions, subsidies, controls, etc., may be added the set of non-economic instruments adapted to regional requirements and levels of development such as energy policies, infrastructure, housing, educational and environmental-protection policies. The relative effectiveness of the instruments is a function of their pertinence in mobilizing production and location factors specifically required by certain production sectors.[1]

Strategies for the Implementation of Regional Industrial Integration Policies

Policies for regional industrial development must rest on a two-dimensioned strategy—one dimension being spatial, the other sectoral. The former is related to the location, size and number of cities selected for the allocation of investments and the latter to the selection of the sectors and the industrial branches proposed for development in priority cities. The instruments of location factors analysis are used for both.

Selecting the number of cities to be developed forms part of the industrialization strategy, whether the decision is for concentrated decentralization in a number of industrial centers or for dispersal of decentralization in many cities. Here we are dealing with a problem of strategic choice. Some authors consider that the ideal urban size for industrial growth in Mexico is a population of 500,000. Only Tijuana and Mexicali, in Baja California, and Ciudad Juárez, in Chihuahua, meet this criterion. These cities present a very high rate of growth, with many problems of overcrowding; they are highly polarized by the American side, and it is preferable to regulate their growth and keep it stable, thus fostering growth of other medium-sized cities in the interior of these states.

It is very important to remember that the integration of the northern states into the rest of the country depends on the possibilities of creating new technical sectoral linkages as well as the existence of a highly active network of cities and highways to reduce travel time to the center of the country. We must seek and find the best combination of size and geographical location to permit a city to meet both requirements: that of external economies and that of an urbanization capable of attracting industrial investments. The other criterion is a local resources potential that permits an urban industrial takeoff capable of integrating intersectorally and interregionally with the rest of the country.

The selection of industries based on the analysis of interindustrial ties is especially appropriate because once a small number of key industries are established in the regions in question, rapid, innovative growth must follow. The industries chosen must stimulate technological progress and be exporting industries in the region. Such industries require intense capital investment, improved interregional ties and lower occupational levels.

The other point of focus, mentioned previously, emphasizes a policy of industrial diversification, making the region in the throes of development less vulnerable to cyclical fluctuations and thereby fostering greater employment stability and regional income. These industries may be more labor-intensive than those mentioned above, may maintain greater intraregional ties and weaker interregional ties.

The degree of isolation of a region is a decisive factor. The greater the degree of isolation, and the greater the distance to be covered to reach an important regional center, the greater the tendencies toward intensive use of the labor force and toward inward integration, that is, intraregional integration. On the other hand, the sparsely developed but open regions, with solid ties with the central regions of the country, have the capacity to absorb a labor force, maintain strong intraregional links and encourage an industrial process with greater equilibrium between capital intensiveness and labor intensiveness.

The foregoing observations are useful in the adoption of strategy decisions regarding the concentration or dispersion of industrial capacity, as well as the relative capital- or labor-intensiveness of the regional investment projects. Notwithstanding, the use of raw materials-finished goods analysis appears to favor from the outset those projects which are well integrated interregionally and require high capital- and low-labor intensiveness, relatively speaking.

It is desirable that the intersectoral, interregional and international industrial integrational model proposed should be constructed on the basis of concepts of threshold of growth and regional profiles which allow—within the framework of locational theory—discovery of the determining factors for specific industrial activities and the quantification of the influence which these factors have on sectoral growth within the regions in question, in order to situate these regions with regard to a critical threshold of growth.

This threshold of growth may be in reference either to regions in expansion or stagnation. A variable may be chosen as representative of the growth of these regions, for example the employment increase rate or production increase rate, to serve as a synthetic indicator of regional characteristics. This variable is assigned a value serving as a scale of measure. For example, if a region achieves a coefficient of production or employment increase rate below that scale, it may be considered as belonging to the group of regions in stagnation. If, on the other hand, it obtains a score higher than this critical value, it will belong to the group of regions in the growth stage. The threshold concept will also serve as a diagnosis of the status of regions lagging behind. This diagnosis will, on one hand, identify the specific elements requiring action and, on the other, identify the type of development policy required to permit regions to cross the threshold and get their growth process underway.

The second element is the notion of a regional attraction index. This index comprises a subgroup of location factors which are pertinent to the sector in question. The group of all the potential locational factors constitutes the "regional profile" represented by a coefficient which may be interpreted as "propensity to attract sectoral activities." The value of these propensities indicates the importance of the corresponding locality factor, determining the region's attractiveness for the sector. Its content may be organized in a certain number of profiles, such as that of attractiveness *per se*, comprising essentially supply-and-demand elements for raw materials and finished goods, which is the classic profile of production-factor availability. Simply put, this means the natural, economic and human resources within a region or specific population nucleus. It is the sociocultural or political profile, which involves the regional institutions and policies, the environment, etc. All of these elements may be present in the regions to varied degrees, and their pertinence for the location of specific sectoral activities will vary from one sector to another. Regional development policies propose modifying the profile (diagnosis) at the regional level in order to create conditions favoring growth where conditions favoring growth do not yet exist.

The model considers regional interdependence explicitly. The regions in our system are not closed systems; on the contrary, both the raw materials market and that for finished goods in the majority of modern industrial sectors extend far beyond the borders of the region selected. Technological interdependencies likewise have an interregional space dimension, based on the location of industrial activities within a given region. This is the case not because of the attraction of the region itself, but (1) because it is contiguous to an important market (for example, that of the United States) for the products of the sector, (2) because of spatial relationships between different regions which offer markets for products or access to raw materials, and (3) because of a group of the services required for the sector to function.

Programs

Analysis of interregional, intersectoral, and international fluxes would indicate the following:

1. Which raw materials are produced in the border states, and are susceptible of being incorporated into the productive processes

of other Mexican regions. The market areas for the finished goods will be determined.

2. Which raw materials originating in one or another Mexican region can be incorporated into the production processes of the northern Mexican regions. This market may be either national or international.

3. Which American raw materials are required for integration into the border state regions, both horizontally and vertically, with strong links to the rest of the country.

4. The final demand of the border areas with regard to both the national economy and that of the United States.

The matrix of flows, covering the origin and interregional destination of raw materials, will make possible the identification of lines of production with comparative advantages for the national market and for exportation. It will underscore supply-and-demand patterns, both nationally and externally, as well as the regional location. The contribution of these activities will be evaluated as regards the achievement of such objectives as decentralization of economic activity, generation of employment, interregional economic integration, a decrease in the balance of trade deficit with the United States, the development of medium-sized cities, and others.

If the information concerning these flows permits, interchange matrices will be prepared for each northern state, setting forth in relief the regional supply coefficients for different sectors (the local sectors are comprised of local production.) A paradigmatic model may propose that 60 or 70 percent of the regional demand for certain products be covered by local production. The remaining demand may be covered by other regions, whether Mexican or American. In order to put together the conditions for the regional integration paradigm, a three-sector matrix is required: that of border regions; that of the other Mexican regions, especially Monterrey, Guadalajara and the Metropolitan Federal District area, including Toluca and Puebla, and, finally, the American sector.[2]

The purpose of the foregoing analysis is discovery of the raw material–finished goods coefficient and final demand in the border regions with respect to the Mexican national economy and that of the United States. It is also possible to model the interregional economic effects and ties which may be achieved by new investments in a sector which may be either national or international.

1. Location Factors. The interregional integration model rests on a strategy of decentralization of the industrial establishments distributed throughout a number of border state areas which, given their geographical location and their resources, present a viable situation for sustained development of underpopulated regional areas separating the north of Mexico from the country's center. It is with this purpose in mind that the analysis is made of regional economic activity location factors.

2. Inventory of Resources. Evaluation of the geographical character-istics; the natural, economic and human resources of the urban areas selected in order to determine their potential for the provision of resources required for development.

3. Urban Development.

- An urban framework and structure of functions and services for the cities in question,
- The polarized region of each city,
- Urban infrastructure and development,
- Interurban networks, and
- Systems and hierarchies of inter-border cities within the national framework.

4. Investment Profiles. A portfolio of preinvestment projects. This information will contain a manageable number of viable projects which may be located in the northern border states.

- Market study: demand, supply, prices, commercialization, the product.
- Technical study: size, production process and location, physical works, organization.
- Financial study: financial resources for investment, financial anal-ysis and projections, financing.
- Economic evaluation: the relationship between the project and the economy as a whole, the anticipated impact of the project.

5. Policy Model. A synthesis and harmonizing of projects, which is the equivalent of an industrialization policy model, with the char-acteristics described on the preceding pages.

SUMMARY

The Mexican crisis which began in 1982, and the recession in the American economy which has lasted nearly three years, have dem-onstrated the fragility of border economic relations based mainly on retail trade transactions, which collapsed as the result of the Mexican currency-exchange controls.

These facts indicate the need to reorder the economies of the northern border states of Mexico through the planning of intersectoral and interregional integration of the industrial plants of the northern states—both with each other and with the main industrial regions of Mexico. For this purpose, a research program has been proposed, consisting of the following: (1) intersectoral and interstate input-output flow analysis to discover investment opportunities at the input-output intersections of the states' matrices, this analysis to include transborder flows pointing out the origin and destination of inputs and outputs; (2) location and quantification of local, natural, economic and human resources in selected urban regions in order to discover their economic capability for sustaining industrial growth; (3) evaluation of infrastructures, urban resources and interurban networks in those urban regions which should, when possible, be located away from the international boundary; (4) preparation of a portfolio of preinvestment profiles as the result of the above analysis.

It is advisable that the American border states build a similar regional and intersectoral industrial linking-model showing the transborder input-output flows, on the one hand, and, on the other, evaluating the regional impacts on both sides of the border so as to refine the appropriate instruments of policy, avoiding possible negative feedback effects.

Notes

1. The research project leading to the implementation of the above-described economic integration policy is underway, and will probably be finished by June, 1984.

2. An important reason for the separation of the regional components in a flow matrix for national intersectoral relations is that in each country the distribution of economic activities by region is very unequal. For this reason a change of activity will have unequal impacts on the employment and income levels. Additionally, a regional model puts into relief the general effects caused by different production techniques, consumer habits and business customs between regions.

References

Ancot, J. P., "Politique Régional, Facteurs de Localisation et Seuils de Croissance." Annual Meeting of the French-Language Regional Science Association, Namur, Belgium, September 1982.

Beckman, Martin J., "Borders as Locations of Economic Activities." Department of Economics, Brown University. Revised from the paper delivered at the First Conference on Regional Impacts of U.S.-Mexico Economic Relations, Guanajuato, Gto., 1981.

Beutel, J., "The Location of Public Facilities in a System of Central Places: An Activity Analysis Approach," Papers of the Regional Science Association, Volume 47, 1981.

Bustamante, Jorge A., "Conceptualización y Programación del Desarrollo de la Región Fronteriza de México," *Estudios Fronterizos*, ANUIES, México.

Ceceña, José Luis, "Reflexiones sobre el Marco General de las Relaciones México-Estados Unidos." First Conference on Regional Impacts of U.S.-Mexico Relations, Guanajuato, Gto., 1981.

Censos Nacionales de Población, Secretaría de Programación y Presupuesto. México. 1970–1980.

Corona Rentería; Alfonso: "Polarización Internacional y Desarrollo de las Regiones Fronterizas de México." First Conference on Regional Impacts of U.S.-Mexico Relations, Guanajuato, Gto., 1981.

Luna Trail, Jaime, y Ricardo Guerra Quiroga, "Plan Regional de Desarrollo Urbano de la Franja Fronteriza Norte del País." First Conference on Regional Impacts of U.S.-Mexico Relations, Guanajuato, Gto., 1981.

Matrices de Insumo Producto. Secretaría de Programación y Presupuesto. Secretaría del Trabajo y Previsión Social—CENIET. Banco de México. 1960, 1970, 1980.

Mendoza Berrueto, Eliseo, "Historia de los Programas Federales para el Desarrollo Económico de la Frontera Norte." Simposio sobre el Desarrollo Económico y Administrativo de la Zona Fronteriza Norte de México, Ciudad Juárez, Chih., 1979.

Suárez-Villa, Luis, "Center-Down Development in Perspective: Labor Absorption and Interdependence in Brazilian Regional Industries," 29th North American Meetings, Regional Science Association, Pittsburgh, 1982.

Victoria Mascorro, Edmundo: "Patrones de Distribución Espacial de los Asentamientos Humanos en la Franja Fronteriza Norte de México." First Conference on Regional Impacts of U.S.-Mexico Relations, Guanajuato, Gto., 1981.

8

Internationalization of Industry: U.S.-Mexican Linkages

Joseph Grunwald

Introduction

Offshore assembly production is a sharp manifestation of the North-South dichotomy: capital-intensive, high technology production in industrial countries; low-skilled, labor-intensive production in developing countries. It has been a relatively successful way for threatened industrial-country firms to retain competitiveness and for developing countries to exploit their own comparative advantage. Nevertheless, the benefits of such activities have been questioned. In the North, the movement offshore creates adjustment problems for large pockets of the unskilled still remaining in manufacturing industry; in the South, the growth of assembly activities for exports raises the spectre of a trap which will perpetuate a low-grade labor force and rudimentary production activities.

It should not be surprising that Mexico has become the United States' most important partner in offshore assembly activities. As a developing country it shares a nearly 2,000-mile border with one of the world's highest-wage countries and by far the world's largest producer. The border is fairly accessible and transportation from almost any point in the United States to the border is cheap when compared to overseas trade. Not only geographically but also culturally, the distances between the two countries are not very great. Many U.S. entrepreneurs and business executives have been to Mexico, and

This article is a greatly reduced version of the original paper presented at the May 24–28, 1983, Second Conference on Regional Impacts on the U.S.A. and Mexican Economic Relations, Tucson, Arizona. This study is based on a chapter in a forthcoming book, *The Internationalization of Industry*, prepared by the author and Kenneth Flamm, to be published by the Brookings Institution. That chapter benefited from a collaboration with El Colegio de México. The views expressed here are those of the author and should not be ascribed to the staff members or officers of El Colegio de México or the Brookings Institution, where the author is a senior fellow.

for historical reasons as well as because of migration, its culture is diffused throughout many parts of the United States.

In the mid-1960s when 806.30/807.00 trade data first became available, Hong Kong was more than five times as important and Taiwan nearly as important as Mexico in processing and assembling U.S. components for reexport to the United States. By the end of that decade, Mexican operations were nearly double those of Hong Kong and about four times as much as those of Taiwan (Table 1). This shift took place despite Mexico's higher wages. Mexican assembly operations now produce a significantly different product mix than Asian assemblers, with relatively less of the low transport-cost electronics and apparel items and more goods with relatively higher transport costs. For this reason, Mexican output seems less sensitive to wage changes than Asian operations.

Proximity as a principal factor in that country's attractiveness was reinforced by Mexico's Border Industrialization Program, put into effect in the mid 1960s. Aiming to absorb the border unemployment left by the termination of the "Bracero Program" between the United States and Mexico in 1964, it allowed the duty-free imports of machinery, equipment, and components for processing or assembly, provided that all of the imported products will be reexported. Thus none of the output of the assembly operations, called "maquila" by Mexicans, could be sold within the country. (The assembly plants are called "maquiladoras.")

Subsequent Mexican legislation, decrees, and administrative regulations expanded the scope of the maquila by exempting the maquiladoras from the "Mexicanization" requirement of Mexican majority ownership,[1] by permitting the establishment of maquiladoras anywhere in the country, and by facilitating customs and other government procedures.

Despite the original conception of the "twin plant" idea, whereby U.S. firms would establish two plants under a single management, one on each side of the border, the great majority of U.S.-owned maquiladoras are supplied from plants quite distant from the border. Although quite a few twin plants have been established along the border, particularly in the El Paso–Juarez region, there are not enough of these to make that concept representative of the existing co-production activities between the United States and Mexico.

Importance of Offshore Assembly for Mexico

Since 1965, when the Border Industrialization Program got under way, a significant number of assembly plants have been established almost every year (Table 2). In mid-1983 about 600 maquiladoras were in operation, employing over 140,000 persons.

Although employment in offshore assembly production is significant within the context of Mexico's overall employment problem, the

TABLE 1

U.S. 806/807 Imports by Important Countries

1969 and 1980

(millions of dollars)

Country	1969		1980	
	Total 806/807 Impt.	U.S. Value (duty free)	Total 806/807 Impt.	U.S. Value (duty free)
Industrial Countries				
West Germany	627.4	11.6	2,203.6	63.3
Japan	137.9	25.4	3,284.1	46.2
Canada	340.1	118.7	1,231.9	389.5
Developing Countries				
Mexico	150.0	97.9	2,341.4	1,186.3
Malaysia	.4	.1	820.0	480.5
Singapore	11.6	3.8	773.3	409.4
Philippines	5.2	3.5	412.9	253.4
Taiwan	68.7	23.8	473.9	107.2
Korea	23.8	15.9	312.6	167.3
Hong Kong	91.4	51.3	468.1	114.1
Haiti	4.0	2.4	153.8	105.3
Brazil	4.1	2.5	111.5	15.9
Dominican Republic	.1	.1	97.5	66.1

(continued)

TABLE 1 (continued)

Country	1969		1980	
	Total 806/807 Impt.	U.S. Value (duty free)	Total 806/807 Impt.	U.S. Value (duty free)
El Salvador	.2	.1	88.9	51.4
Colombia	.4	.2	19.9	12.1
Total 15 Countries	1,465.3	357.3	12,792.4	3,468.0
Total All Countries	1,838.8	442.1	13,999.2	3,741.7

SOURCE: U. S. Tariff Commission, Economic Factors Affecting the Use of Items 807.00 and 806.30 of the Tariff Schedules of the United States, TC Publication 339 (Washington, D.C., September 1970); and the U.S. International Trade Commission, Tariff Items 807.00 and 806.30 U.S. Imports for Consumption, Specified Years 1966-80 (June 1981).

maquila labor force is quite small, less than 1 percent of the total. In the border region, however, maquiladoras are among the most important employers.

Underemployment estimates range from 27.4 percent to 52 percent of the labor force in 1978.[2] The unemployment rate at the border seems to be higher than in the rest of the country and, according to fragmentary information, appears to be rising.[3]

The value added generated by the maquiladoras in Mexico has been increasing sharply since the beginning of the border industrialization program. At the end of 1981 it was running at an annual figure of over $1 billion according to peso figures from the Mexican Secretariat of Programming and Budget converted at the current rate of exchange.

Therefore, the maquila operations make a substantial contribution to Mexico's foreign exchange earnings. The precise magnitude is difficult to determine, primarily because of the leakage of Mexican maquila wages across the border to the United States. Some estimates indicate that more than half of maquila wages are spent in the United States.[4] The net leakage will depend on the degree of over- or under-

TABLE 2

Mexico: Employment in Assembly Plants, Number of Plants and Hours Worked

1969-1981

Year	Number of Plants		Interior Plants as Percentage of Total Plants	Total Employment (All Workers)		Interior Employment (All Workers)		Production Worker Employment		Average Monthly Hours Worked by Production Workers
	Total	Interior		Number	Change from Previous Year Percent	Number	Change from Previous Year Percent	Number	Change from Previous Year Percent	Millions of Dollars
1969[a]	108			15,858						
1970	120			20,327	28.2					
1971[b]	251			29,214	43.7					
1972[b]	339			48,060	64.5					
1973	257	10[d]	3.9	64,330	33.9	4,200[c]				
1974	455	26	5.7	75,977	18.1	4,852	15.5			
1975	454	36	7.9	67,213	-11.5	5,069	4.5	57,830		10.8
1976	448	42	9.4	74,496	10.8	6,964	37.4	64,670	11.8	12.3
1977	443	45	10.1	78,433	5.3	7,752	11.3	68,187	5.4	13.1
1978	457	37	8.1	90,704	15.6	8,317	7.3	78,570	15.2	15.1
1979	540	60	11.1	111,365	22.8	10,828	30.2	95,818	22.0	18.4
1980	620	69	11.3	119,546	7.3	12,970	19.8	102,020	6.5	19.2
1981	605	72	11.9	130,973	9.6	14,523	12.0	110,684	8.5	21.1

(continued)

TABLE 2 (continued)

SOURCES: Secretaría de Programación y Presupuesto (SPP), Departamento de Estadística Industrial Secretaría de Patrimonio y Fomento Industrial (SEPAFIN).

[a]From El Paso Chamber of Commerce as reported in U.S. Congress, House Committee on Ways and Means, June 4, 1970, Exhibit G, p. 3,284. Figures, which may not be comparable, as of July 31, 1969.

[b]As of July 1971 and August 1972 from Leopoldo Solís, "Industrial Priorities in Mexico," in UNIDO, Industrial Priorities in Developing Countries (New York: United Nations, 1979), Table 15, p. 109. Figures may not be comparable.

[c]Estimate, Banco de Mexico SA, Encuestas, Cuaderno Semestral #1 (December 1978), Table 1, p. 15.

[d]Computed by subtraction.

Note: Data prior to 1974 may not be comparable, except for 1970.

valuation of the Mexican peso vis-à-vis the U.S. dollar.[5] The facts are, according to Banco de Mexico data, that both the border transactions and tourism have been consistent and substantial net foreign exchange earners for Mexico, exceeding $1 billion since the mid 1970s.[6] Whether, and by how much, the surpluses on these accounts would have been larger in the absence of offshore assembly operations is still an open question.

In any case, as a net foreign exchange earner, maquila exports are important, since all of the value added is exported.[7] Thus since 1973 the exports of maquila services have earned for Mexico about as much as total Mexican nontraditional manufactured exports.[8]

Characteristics of the Assembly Industry

Products, Location and Size

The variety of Mexico's assembly activities is wide and has been increasing. It ranges from toys and dolls and the sorting of U.S. retail store coupons to sophisticated electronic equipment. The ten most important product groups averaged about 80 percent of total value of assembly output imported by the United States from Mexico during 1969–1971 but only about 70 percent during 1979–1981. If television receivers and parts are excluded, the percentages drop from 60 percent to 45 percent, indicating a diversification over the decade (Table 3).

While the variety has risen, the composition of the product mix has changed. Textile products (including apparel), toys and dolls and similar simple light industry constituted one-quarter of all maquila output in 1969, but in 1981 they accounted for only one-twelfth. Television receivers and parts now make up about one-quarter of the total, thus being by far the most important single product group in Mexico's assembly operations. Semiconductors and parts which, with over 16 percent of the total, were almost as important as the television group in 1969, accounted for less than 6 percent in 1981. Motor vehicle parts were not a significant assembly product in 1969, but in recent years they have occupied between third and seventh place in order of importance in Mexico's maquila operations.

The maquiladoras operating in 1981 assembled at least $2.7 billion worth of total output. That is the amount that was imported by the United States under tariff items 807 and 806 that year (Table 4). If Mexican assembly products for other countries (mainly Japan) are added, the maquila output may well have reached $3 billion in 1981. About half of the output consisted of U.S. components.

Most of the plants are located along the border, concentrating in six towns from Tijuana, just south of San Diego, California, on the Pacific Ocean, to Matamoros opposite Brownsville, Texas, near the Gulf of Mexico. About 12 percent of the total (72 plants) were in

TABLE 3

The Most Important 807.00/806.30 U.S. Imports from Mexico

(U.S. ITC Categories), 1969-1981

Most Important U.S. ITC Products	1969 % of Total 806/807 Value	Rank	1973 % of Total 806/807 Value	Rank	1978 % of Total 806/807 Value	Rank	1981* % of Total 806/807 Value	Rank
T.V. Receivers & Parts	17.1	1	22.3	1	25.0	1	23.2	1
Semiconductors & Parts	16.3	2	12.0	3	5.0	5	5.6	6
Toys, Dolls & Models	12.0	3	2.8	9				
Textile Products	11.5	4	12.2	2	10.2	2	7.5	3
Office Machines	9.0	5	7.5	4	2.8	10	3.5	8
Electronic Memories	3.9	6						
Scientific Instruments	3.8	7					3.3	9
Piston-Type Engines & Parts, etc.	2.9	8	2.6	10				

(continued)

TABLE 3 (continued)

Most Important U.S. ITC Products	1969 % of Total 806/807 Value	Rank	1973 % of Total 806/807 Value	Rank	1978 % of Total 806/807 Value	Rank	1981* % of Total 806/807 Value	Rank
Hand Tools, Cutlery, etc.	2.4	9						
Resistors & Parts	2.2	10						
Electric Motors, Generators, etc.			2.8	8	3.8	6	5.8	5
Equipment -- Electric Circuits, etc.			4.2	5	5.7	4	6.8	4
Motor Vehicle Parts, etc.			2.9	6	6.2	3	$3.8^{\dagger}$	7
Capacitors			2.9	7	3.7	7		
Electrical Conductors					3.4	8	8.6	2
Other Misc. Elec. Products & Parts					3.4	9	3.0	10

(continued)

TABLE 3   (continued)

	1969		1973		1978		1981*	
Most Important U.S. ITC Products	% of Total 806/807 Value	Rank	% of Total 806/807 Value	Rank	% of Total 806/807 Value	Rank	% of Total 806/807 Value	Rank
% of 10 Most Important Products	81.1		72.2		69.2		71.1	
TOTAL 806/807 Value (Millions of Dollars)	145.2		651.2		1,539.8		2,655.6	

* Includes only 807.00 imports.

† Including 806.30 imports, this percentage would be 4.3 in 1981.

SOURCE: For 1969–1978, special magnetic tapes prepared by the U.S. ITC;

for 1969–1980, "Tariff Items 807.00 and 806.30 U.S. Imports for

Consumption, Specified Years 1966–80," U.S. ITC (June 1981); and

for 1981, U.S. ITC, special tabulations.

the interior of the country in 1981 (Table 2). The proportion, while still small, has been increasing steadily. (In 1973 there were only 10 plants—or less than 4 percent of the total at that time—located away from the border). The interior plants are situated now in nearly every part of the country, including the three largest cities, Mexico City, Guadalajara, and Monterrey.

Not only the number but also the size of plants in Mexico's maquila industry increased. Estimates indicate an average of about 120 workers per plant during the early 1970s. This rose to about 160 during the mid 1970s, an average of about 200 workers per plant at the end of the decade and about 220 by mid-1982.[9]

Ownership

The majority of the maquila output in Mexico is produced by foreign subsidiaries operating in that country. And since 90 percent

TABLE 4

U.S. Imports Under Tariff Items 807.00 and 806.30 from Mexico,

Total, Duty-Free and Dutiable Value in Millions of U.S. Dollars

and Percent Dutiable Value of Total Value

1969-1982

Year	Total 807/806 Imports (1)	Duty-Free 807/806 Imports (Millions of Dollars) (2)	Dutiable Value of 807/806 Imports (3)	Dutiable Value as Percent of Total Value (3÷1)
1969	150.0	97.9	52.1	34.7
1970	218.8	138.3	80.5	36.8
1971	270.4	166.0	104.4	38.6
1972	426.4	256.3	170.1	39.9
1973	651.2	364.8	286.4	44.0
1974	1,032.6	568.7	463.9	44.9
1975	1,019.8	552.4	467.4	45.8
1976	1,135.4	599.9	535.5	47.2
1977	1,155.5	631.1	524.4	45.4
1978	1,539.8	826.0	713.8	46.4
1979	2,065.1	1,049.4	1,015.7	49.2
1980	2,341.4	1,186.3	1,155.1	49.3
1981	2,709.3	1,437.5	1,271.8	46.9
1982	2,804.8	1,429.8	1,375.0	49.0

SOURCE: U.S. ITC, Tariff Items 807.00 and 806.30, U.S. Imports for Consumption,

various issues; and special computer printouts for 1981.

or more of the assembly is for the U.S. market, most of these subsidiaries are U.S.-owned or -controlled.

Mexican capital, however, has also played a role in the maquila operations. While U.S. companies control 90 percent of all maquila operations in Mexico, there is significant Mexican capital participation in almost half of the plants, particularly in the interior and in the small plants on the western section of the border region.[10] The industrial parks designed for maquiladoras are generally Mexican-owned and -operated.

In the past, most of the U.S.-controlled maquiladoras were subsidiaries of medium-sized multinational enterprises. More recently, however, some of the giants in U.S. industry have established offshore assembly operations in Mexico. At least 48 of the Fortune 500 had maquiladoras in 1978. In addition, three of the largest Japanese and four of the top European industrial concerns operated assembly plants in Mexico that year.[11] The interest of Japanese and European companies in Mexican offshore production appears to be increasing. While it is understandable that foreign participation would be higher in the maquila industry than in other economic activities, it should be noted that the share of all Mexican manufactured output produced by foreign transnational companies has increased in the postwar period.

Foreign companies, instead of establishing their own subsidiaries, also subcontract Mexican firms to undertake the assembly operation for them. Many of these are "captive" plants, i.e., they produce only for one foreign company; the majority, however, provide assembly services for two or more foreign enterprises. They can be found all along the border but a large number concentrate in the area bordering California near to their U.S. contracting companies. Most of the captive plants, principally in the apparel industry, and some of the others receive a major portion of the machinery and equipment on loan or on a rental basis from the subcontracting company in the United States. These are usually second-hand items and seldom represent up-to-date hardware. The fact that the equipment belongs to the foreign (usually U.S.) contractor means that it can be withdrawn after completion of an assembly job. The usual agreement, however, calls for a continuing contractual relationship.

A variant of subcontracting used in Mexico is a temporary arrangement, generally called a "shelter plan," under which local and special firms in Mexico, who "know the ropes," provide assembly services for a foreign concern until the foreign company is ready to establish its own subsidiary or enters into a long-term relationship with a Mexican firm or decides not to assemble in the country. The firms offering shelter plans range from consulting businesses—providing only advisory services to foreign companies wishing to set up shop in Mexico—to well-equipped plants that can engage in a variety of assembly operations with machinery and equipment provided by the client.

Thus the shelter plan permits a foreign company to try out offshore assembly operations without immediately having to make long-term commitments. The local firm "shelters" the foreigner from the red tape involved in starting up foreign production. This covers legalities in dealing with government offices, hiring and administration of workers and technicians and compliance with rules, regulations and customs. Since the foreign company's management will be on site, local procedures can be learned "on the job."

Capital Requirements

Almost by definition, assembly operations, even in foreign plants which generally make up the largest maquiladoras, tend to have very low capital-labor ratios compared with other manufacturing activities. According to one Mexican economist, capital investment per worker was less than 10,000 pesos in Mexico's maquila industries in 1974. This compares with 62,000 pesos in 1970 for all Mexican manufacturing industry.[12] This difference may be exaggerated because, on the one side, capital in the maquila industry may be underestimated[13] and, on the other, Mexico has a very high capital-labor ratio in manufacturing compared to other developing countries.[14] Nevertheless the gap between the capital requirements of maquila operations and the average for all manufacturing as reported in the Mexican industrial census is striking. Most likely the difference has narrowed since the 1974 estimate as larger and more capital-intensive plants have opened operations in the country during the last decade.

Value Added

The difference in capital per worker between assembly and the rest of manufacturing also means that value added by the worker in the maquiladoras is lower than in other manufacturing plants. In 1975, the only year for which Mexican industrial census data and maquila information from the Secretariat of Programming and Budget coincide, the statistics indicate that the maquila value added per worker is somewhat less than two-thirds of the total manufacturing value added per worker, approximately $4800 as compared to $7500 (converted to U.S. dollars at official exchange rates). If it is considered that average fixed capital per worker in all of manufacturing may be at least three times greater than in the assembly industries, then the output that can be obtained from a unit of capital in the latter is obviously much greater than in manufacturing as a whole.[15]

In recent years, wages have accounted for more than 60 percent of total Mexican value added at the border, but averaged about 40 percent in the interior plants. Materials have made up about 2 percent of value added at the border and five times as much in the interior. Rents and utilities also have been a higher proportion of value added in the interior (averaging well over one-quarter) than at the border (less than 20 percent). Since 1978, the same is true of profits and taxes (more than 20 percent in the interior, less so at the border).[16]

Wages

Maquila wages appear to have risen steeply during the mid 1970s, outpacing the consumer price index. The payroll per employee (blue and white collar workers) increased by about 16 percent in real terms in 1974 over the previous year and about 7 percent from 1975 to 1976. Since 1978, remunerations per worker in maquiladoras have declined in constant prices so that by 1981 they were—in real purchasing power in Mexico—just 5 percent above the 1973 level. This does not mean that real maquila wages have fared much worse than wages in other manufacturing sectors. The average national index of official minimum wages, put into constant prices, showed similar changes and so do the fragmentary average wage data as published in the IMF's *International Financial Statistics*.

For some purposes, however, it is advisable to put assembly wages into dollar terms. Converted into dollars, maquiladora wages increased enormously until 1981, interrupted only by a temporary decline as a result of the 1976 peso devaluation. Thus dollar wages increased by more than 50 percent between 1973 and 1975 (compared to only a 13 percent increase in Mexican purchasing power) and by about 80 percent between 1977 and 1981. The dramatic devaluations of 1982 have again diminished Mexican incomes in dollar terms despite significant peso wage increases.

Wage changes in dollar terms have two implications. One relates to the production costs of U.S. firms that do their assembly operations through U.S. subsidiaries in Mexico. Although they pay their Mexican workers in pesos, it is the dollar costs of the wages that is the relevant figure for U.S. firms. It is obvious that during the 1970s their Mexican wage costs have increased much more rapidly than U.S. wages.

The other effect is on the behavior of assembly workers as consumers. Given the fact that the Mexican peso was freely convertible throughout the period under discussion, the sharp increases in border wages in dollar terms compared to their stagnant or declining peso purchasing power in Mexico, was a strong inducement for maquiladora employees to spend as much as possible of their wages across the border in the United States. Until 1982, assembly workers on the Mexican side of the border found that the easily obtainable dollar equivalent of their peso wages rose much faster than prices in the United States.[17]

Minimum wages for the border areas tended to be considerably higher than the national average, exceeding the latter by more than half at the beginning of Mexico's border industrialization program.[18] The influence of the high wages and prices on the U.S. side helped create this differential. Since then the border average has fallen behind so that by 1980 the difference between it and the rest of the nation was reduced to under 30 percent.

Despite some problems with comparability, the data show that average remunerations in the assembly industries have been significantly higher than official minimum wages. In the border plants they have been running almost 10 percent above the border minimum level and, in the interior, assembly wages averaged about 14 percent above the national average minimum wages during 1975–1980 (Table 5).[19]

Assembly wages paid in plants in the border region have been consistently higher than in maquiladoras in the interior of Mexico. While the gap appears to have declined in recent years, it still averaged well over 25 percent during 1980–1981.

To summarize: Mexican wages in the border regions adjoining the United States are on average considerably higher than in the interior of the country. The difference has been declining, apparently as a result of deliberate government policy and weak labor unions at the border. Wages in the assembly industries have followed this pattern. Nevertheless, both at the border and in the interior the wages paid in assembly industries have been higher than respective minimum wages.

Insofar as wage differentials are important for offshore assembly operations, the lower wages in the interior of Mexico provide a powerful attraction relative to the border areas. The operations of the maquiladoras in the interior appear to have been successful. Value added by worker there averaged well over one-third above the value added by worker in the border maquiladoras during 1974–1980. After 1977, profit shares of the maquiladoras in the interior have been above those at the border.

Use of Mexican Materials

The share of materials and supplies provided by the domestic economy is an important indicator of the linkages that offshore assembly activities have for the Mexican economy. That percentage has been exceedingly small. With the exception of 1976 when it rose to 3 percent, it hovered around 1.5 percent of the total use of components and supplies (imported and domestic) during 1975–1981. In the plants in the interior, however, the usage of domestic materials has been considerably higher, the domestic content ranging from 6 percent to 15 percent of total materials used.

The Main Issues of Offshore Assembly Operations in Mexico

Because of the magnitude of Mexico's involvement in offshore assembly activities, its merits for the country have been debated extensively. Benefits have been questioned and serious negative effects for the Mexican economy and society as a whole have been attributed to the assembly arrangements. The critique centers on three principal issues: (1) the absence of significant linkages of assembly activities to the Mexican economy; (2) the effects on the labor force and on society in the areas where maquiladoras concentrate; and (3) the vulnerability of maquiladoras to swings in the U.S. business cycle and their general dependency on decisions made in the United States and elsewhere outside of Mexico. These three issue areas are discussed below.

TABLE 5

Mexico: Production Worker Payroll per Hour in Assembly Industries Compared with Mexican Official Minimum Wages per Hour, by Region

1975-1981

| | Assembly Production Worker Wages Paid per Hour* (Pesos) | | Relationship of Border to Interior Assembly Wages (Percent) | Minimum Wages per Hour (Pesos)† | | Relationship of Assembly Wages to Minimum Wages (Percent) | |
| | Border Plants | Interior Plants | | Border Region | National Average | Border | Interior |
	A	B	A + B	C	D	A + C	B + D
1975	11.1	8.0	138.8	10.1	7.0	109.9	114.3
1976	13.8	9.3	148.4	12.7	9.0	108.7	103.3
1977	17.3	13.2	131.0	16.2	11.6	106.8	113.8
1978	19.8	15.9	124.5	18.1	13.2	109.4	120.5
1979	22.3	18.3	121.9	20.5	15.4	108.8	118.8
1980	26.3	20.4	128.9	23.2	18.2	113.4	112.1
1981	32.9	26.7	123.3				

NOTES:

*Assembly Production Worker Payroll does not include fringe benefits.

†The Official Minimum Wages are given as a per day wage, including non-working Sunday pay. In order to calculate the hourly wage, the daily minimum wage is multiplied by 7/6 and then divided by 8 (following method by Van Waas—see sources below). Since the minimum wage was changed in October of 1976, a month-weighted average was calculated for that year.

(continued)

TABLE 5 (continued)

SOURCES: Columns A and B -- calculated from published and unpublished tables of SPP, Mexico;

Columns C and D -- calculated from Van Waas, The Multinationals' Strategy for Labor, Table 10, pp. 276-77; method of

multiplying daily minimum wages by 7/6 and then dividing by 8 was stated in note to Table 1, p. 83. See also SPP,

Boletín Mensual de Información Económica, 6, 3 (Mexico, June 1982), Tables 3.6.1 and 3.7.

Linkages

The institutional framework for maquila operations reinforces their economic isolation. In general, maquiladoras have not been permitted to sell on the national market but have had to export their total production. This is understandable since these are "in-bond" industries, their imports of components being exempted from Mexican import duties provided that they be reexported after assembly.[20]

Thus most of the commercial relations of the maquiladoras are with foreign companies, especially with U.S. multinationals, rather than with Mexican producers and consumers. Add to that the fact that even when maquiladoras are not U.S. subsidiaries, many plants, particularly in the apparel industry, operate with machinery and equipment provided and owned by the U.S. contractors, and one gets a picture of an enclave of Mexican assembly activities that is tied much more strongly to the United States than to the rest of Mexico.

Interviews with U.S. as well as Mexican managers of maquiladoras indicate that attempts were made to increase the usage of Mexican components and materials in assembly operations. According to the managers, most of the attempts failed because of one or another deficiency of potential Mexican suppliers: rigorous specifications could not be met due to deficiencies in quality control (important particularly in the electric and electronic industries); delivery schedules could not be met; production capacity was insufficient; and, mentioned most often, prices were too high. All of these are typical symptoms of the import-substituting type of industrialization in which protected firms have not attained international competitiveness.

The other side of the coin is that there are no strong incentives for Mexican manufacturers to do business with maquiladoras or for Mexican capital to establish assembly operations. Given the protection of Mexican industry and the uncertainties of foreign markets, producing for secure domestic markets may not only yield higher returns but may also be easier than meeting the demanding requirements of foreign firms and consumers. Moreover, the image of the maquiladora as the foreigner with weak roots in the domestic economy does not encourage Mexican firms to engage in long-term commitments in the assembly business.

The low participation of Mexican capital and entrepreneurship in maquiladora activities will limit the transfer of technology from offshore production to the Mexican economy. This limitation is itself a barrier to greater Mexican involvement in coproduction with foreign companies. Unless the circle is broken linkages will remain weak; Mexican enterprises will continue to furnish primarily packing materials and janitorial supplies for the maquiladoras rather than the manufactured components for assembly in substitution of foreign materials.

The enclave image is fostered also by the near absence of any "forward" linkages, because the sale of maquiladora output on the domestic market is all but forbidden. Among other things, maquiladoras could provide Mexican producers with sophisticated subassemblies at cheaper prices than available now. This might enable Mexican firms to use high technology inputs which they now cannot afford. If so, the maquila could contribute to the technical upgrading of Mexican industrialization.

Employment and Migration

The striking aspect of the labor force in Mexican assembly industries is the high proportion—more than three-quarters of the total—of women. Some observers attribute this to the hiring practices of maquiladora managers who want to obtain a docile crew of production workers. Most of these women are very young and were previously not in the labor force.[21]

What seems to be clear is that maquila workers in Mexico are not drawn from the traditionally unemployed or underemployed but from a sector of the population which never worked or looked for work. Therefore, one of the original principal objectives of the Mexican border industrialization program, which aimed to absorb the rural male migrant workers left stranded by the termination of the bracero arrangement with the United States, has not been met by the establishment of offshore assembly operations in the country.

On the other hand, women who enter the labor force through maquila employment do not tend to leave the labor force when they become separated from their jobs. Once they have gained a certain measure of independence through working, they will probably look for work after they have lost their first job, particularly if they are under pressure to continue making the financial contributions which have helped them and their families to achieve higher living standards. It is argued therefore that the maquiladoras create their own labor pool.

Questioning of maquiladora executives about the high female worker proportion in their plants almost invariably brings the same responses: women are more dexterous for assembly tasks than men (also their hands are smaller, which is an asset, particularly in the assembly of electronic microcomponents). They are more used to and, therefore, more patient with routine assignments, and in any case, according to the managers, comparatively few men apply for such jobs.

There is little support for the assertion that women workers have greater manual dexterity than men, even for delicate, small-size assembly operations. Further questioning of plant managers in Mexico and Haiti reveals that men on the assembly lines, whether in sewing or electronics, are at least as efficient as women.[22]

The fact is that the preponderance of female workers in assembly production seems to be universal and not confined only to developing countries. The proportion in the United States appears to be higher than in Mexico, ranging from 80 percent to over 90 percent in most assembly activities.[23]

The employment of women in occupations such as sewing appears to be culturally determined in most parts of the industrial and industrializing world. It seems to be a small step from experience with the needle to the learning of electronics assembly, which requires detailed attention to small components. It may also be culturally determined that men are more impatient with delicate repetitive routines. It is not clear, therefore, whether one can single out Mexico in the employment of women as a design for exploitation in order to maintain lower wage scales through easier control and manipulation of a more docile work force. What seems to be clear is that Mexican assembly plants are not unique in employing a high proportion of women.

It seems safe to say that the employment of a greater proportion of women previously out of the labor force is a phenomenon of the path of economic development in modern times. There will be disintegrative effects on the traditional family. Social adjustments of this type are painful and sometimes costly, but they are a part of the contemporary process of economic development. Perhaps the introduction of offshore assembly activities into particular regions of Mexico has accelerated the coming of the adjustment problems there.

In surveying the negative aspects of offshore assembly production regarding labor, it is important to put them within the context of the whole Mexican economy lest one lose perspective. It was found that maquiladora wages have averaged above minimum wages everywhere and minimum wages at the border are still well above those in the rest of the country. Therefore, it is quite certain that maquila wage averages are higher than wages elsewhere in the Mexican economy for equivalent work.[24]

It would be useful to compare labor conditions, upward occupational mobility and other employment characteristics in maquiladoras with those existing in non-assembly plants. At present, reliable data resulting from such comparisons are not available, but impressionistic information indicates a not unfavorable position of maquiladoras vis-à-vis other factories in Mexico.

One important point regarding the supply of labor in Mexico remains to be made. The usual discussion centers on the large pool of persons available to do low-skill jobs. The scarcity of skilled and highly trained persons urgently required by the growing Mexican economy has not often been an important concern. Yet this scarcity has become a significant obstacle to efficient economic development. The assembly plants also are in constant need of trained manpower (engineers, technicians, managers, plant supervisors, accountants, and so forth). Technical and administrative personnel has been increasing, both in absolute terms and as a proportion of the total maquiladora work force, rising from about 13 percent in the mid-1970s to 70 percent in 1982.

To some extent maquiladoras import their skilled labor, in some cases they train high-level manpower, and they also hire trained Mexicans. In the last case, the assembly plants compete with other Mexican enterprises. This competition will be to the detriment of the country's economic development if the maquiladoras have "unfair" market power because of their foreign connections and resources.

The Dependency Issue

The U.S. recession of 1974–1975 was a traumatic experience for the promoters of Mexican assembly industries. Some maquiladoras closed down; many workers were laid off. The Federal Reserve Bank of Dallas reported the closing of 30 maquiladoras by April 1975 and the loss of about 35,000 jobs, or over 40 percent of the 1974 labor force.[25] Nevertheless, the decline was relatively short-lived. By 1977 employment was above the 1974 level and there was a net addition of about 100 plants in the following two years.

Only border-plant production volume declined; in the interior, real value added as well as employment increased between 1974 and 1975. The shock wave of the U.S. recession concentrated on the electrical and electronic assemblies. Apparel and textiles were not touched (their employment increased slightly between 1974 and 1975). Ciudad Juarez—in the center of the border region, and the major maquiladora city in terms of value added—suffered no net declines in employment and production. Although many plants closed there, new maquiladoras opened and employment increased by 45 percent between 1974 and 1977.

The most striking relative drop in both employment and output had nothing to do with the U.S. recession. It took place in Nuevo Laredo, on the far eastern Texas border, where employment fell by almost 70 percent and real value added by more than that between 1974 and 1976. What happened there was primarily the consequence of inter–labor union conflicts.[26] Nuevo Laredo accounts for more than one-third of Mexico's temporary net loss in assembly employment and output attributed to the 1974–1975 U.S. economic downturn.

The bulk of the remainder of Mexico's temporary job and production losses of 1975 in the maquiladoras can be accounted for by Tijuana and Nogales. Most of the affected maquiladoras in the two towns were plants of "fly-by-night" firms with small, easily portable investments. Such firms are particularly sensitive to the business cycle as well as to increases in wage rates.

A sharp rise in Mexican wages aggravated any effects of the U.S. recession. Since all of the output was exported and the peso rate of exchange remained fixed, wage costs for assembly firms rose with the nominal peso wage increases. Minimum wages in U.S. dollars doubled between the early and middle 1970s. (Wage increases also outpaced Mexican inflation after 1973.)

The jump in minimum wages was reflected in the payroll cost per employee which rose in dollar terms by more than 60 percent between 1973 and 1975. This, added to the sharp price rises of the other components of Mexican value added, such as rent and utilities, led to a cost squeeze that the weaker assembly companies could not withstand. Despite the devaluation of 1976, many of the small firms that closed their Mexican plants during the mid-1970s did not return.

The deep U.S. recession of 1980–1982 had similar effects. Some of the weaker maquiladoras disappeared. After an initial drop in the second half of 1982, employment and output in the Mexican plants rose to unprecedented levels in 1983. While the number of plants by mid-1983 was still lower than in 1981, plant size was almost double what it was at the beginning of the previous decade.

Thus, given a mix of more responsible companies and a higher investment in assembly operations, one can assume that maquiladoras will be less prone to "pack up and go" whenever negative, but temporary, forces are encountered. Of course, a severe and prolonged economic recession in the United States, combined with a deterioration in the political situation in Mexico, may well lead to drastic cuts in maquiladora income and employment.

Maquiladora and Migration

Three assertions have been made about the role of maquiladoras in respect to migration. The first is that the establishment of assembly plants at the border has stimulated massive internal migration of persons from the interior of Mexico to the border; the second is that the maquiladora serves as a jumping-off place for migration to the United States for the persons it has brought to the border from the interior. The third, inconsistent with the former assertion, is that the creation of assembly jobs in Mexico will diminish migration to the United States.

Regarding the first point, most of the rapid growth of the border population took place before the start of the maquiladora program. The average yearly growth rate between 1950 and 1960 was 6.3 percent compared with 4.1 percent between 1960 and 1970, the period during which the maquiladora program started. Some attribute the slowdown to the ending of the bracero program in 1964.[27]

Studies of maquiladora workers found that a minority of the migrants came to the towns in order to work in maquiladoras.[28] The more comprehensive study by Seligson and Williams found that "at maximum 5% of the entire 1978 work force of the BIP [Border Industrialization Program = maquiladoras] may be defined as contributing to interstate migration to the North."[29] Plant managers tend to prefer to hire persons who have had a few years of residence in order to get more

stable employees.[30] About 80 percent of the interstate-migrant maquiladora workers had lived in the city where they were interviewed
more than three years and only 8 percent less than one year.[31] In
conclusion, at least until the late 1970s assembly plants appear not
to have been important in provoking internal migration to the northern
border.

Regarding the second assertion, none of the above-mentioned studies
has found any evidence that maquiladoras at the border have served
as a significant jumping-off point for migration to the United States.
These results are not surprising, given the nature of the maquiladora
work force. Most of it consists of women, primarily of urban background, a quite different population group from the male rural workers
and peasants who in the past have constituted the aliens who have
entered the United States illegally.[32]

This same reasoning invalidates the third assertion often made that
"for each job that is created by the maquiladora industry there is
possibly one less alien that would go to the United States."[33] The
people who cross the border into the United States without documents
are generally not potential maquiladora workers. Just as the establishment of the border industrialization program through the creation
of the maquiladora system could not absorb, as intended, the unemployed and underemployed men who were left stranded when the
bracero program ended, this system also cannot stem the migration
to the United States.

The establishment of maquiladoras in the interior of Mexico may
be much more effective. It may help keep potential interstate and
intercountry migrants in place. Seligson and Williams found that
almost half of the migrants working in assembly plants at the border
said that they would go back home (to the interior of Mexico) if
similar employment were available there.[34]

Policy Implications and Conclusions

Despite their positive and important contributions, assembly activities have been viewed with some ambivalence by Mexican policymakers. Few are proud of assembly operations. They are considered
by some as a demeaning activity, a service performed for foreigners
comparable to taking in their dirty laundry.[35]

In part, the lack of enthusiasm is due to the isolated nature of
assembly activities. In Mexico these activities are geographically concentrated. Add to that the perception that offshore assembly constitutes
a stage of international capitalism serving the interests of foreign
owners, that it does little to train and upgrade the labor force, that
domestic inputs are small, that there is hardly any transfer of technology,
that it creates an industrial structure dependent on the whims of
foreigners who, searching the world for opportunities for easy profit,

are quick to transfer their business to the lowest-wage country; and the image emerges of an enclave activity that indeed makes a small contribution to economic development.

This picture, although a caricature, prompts the question in Mexico as to whether domestic resources put into assembly operations might not be better used in other sectors that would produce immediate and strong linkages for national industrialization. While one critique of offshore assembly focuses on the lack of integration of offshore activities into the national economy and polity, another criticizes assembly production as "dead-end" industrialization. Policies emerging from the first kind of critique will seek to increase the linkages of assembly activities to the rest of the economy. Policies based on the second view will do just the opposite: they will aim to divert national capital to areas deemed more socially productive. Therefore the enclave nature of this production may be a deliberately created outcome.

Thus, either one judges these activities to be ill-suited for national capital and seeks to create a controlled foreign enclave, or one considers them potentially productive areas for national entrepreneurship and strives to break down the enclave-like aspects of assembly operations. But it makes no sense to hold both views and pursue contradictory policies.

If it is held that offshore assembly is of more than trivial significance for Mexico and has been an important generator of income, foreign exchange, and employment, policies to link these activities more directly to the Mexican economy would make sense. As long as trade restrictions insulate the national producer from foreign competition, special incentives might be needed for national capital to venture into assembly activities as suppliers or operators. A strong inducement in the case of Mexico would be to eliminate the restrictions on firms simultaneously to produce for the domestic market and assemble for exports. This would permit the fuller utilization of capacity in existing plants and reduce the risk for national capital of investing in assembly plants. Both domestic and foreign business fluctuations can be smoothed by being able to shift production between the domestic market and exports. In order to avoid charges of unfair competition from powerful foreign subsidiaries, it might be considered that, at least initially, the opportunity to sell on the domestic market be limited to companies that have at least Mexican majority ownership as would, under current Mexican law, apply in any case to non-assembly investment.

The attractiveness of assembly for local enterprise could be enhanced by lifting the restrictions on the sale of in-bond assembly products on the domestic market. Although these sales would not be exempted from customs duties on imported materials,[36] they would make available to the domestic economy assembled items at lower cost than if they had to be reimported after their return to the United States. The August 1983 decree is a step in the right direction.[37] Lower prices would benefit not only consumers but also Mexican producers, who might use sophisticated subassemblies—previously too expensive—as inputs in their industries.

It is clear that subcontracting with local firms in Mexico is more conducive to the transfer of technology than operating offshore assembly plants through U.S. subsidiaries. The subcontractor would not only benefit directly from working with the U.S. principal, but could also transfer the acquired knowledge to production for the domestic market, thus spreading the effects. The shift from subsidiary assembly production to subcontracting would thus not only eliminate the intermediary in technology transfer, but also the delinking of assembly plants from the United States would remove the pejorative enclave image of offshore assembly.

The big question is whether growth in offshore assembly operations will not be interrupted by a movement toward automation. Until now automation has not been cost-effective except when production runs are sufficiently long and quality requirements are high. So far, manual assembly has been more flexible. As automated methods become more sophisticated, robots will be able to make the changeover from handling one product line to another in much less time. This will reduce costs of operation and also make automation worthwhile in short production runs for articles with rapid technological and/or style changes.

Will automation, then, bring offshore assembly production back home to industrial countries? If automation becomes economically viable, it might still be rational to transfer automated assembly abroad as long as cost differentials persist and are not outweighed by the perception of greater risk.

While the automated operation itself is not labor-intensive, the ancillary operations can be quite labor-using. Materials handling, preparation work, cleaning and inspection can be done by relatively low-skilled workers. Only the design, programming and maintenance of the equipment requires skilled technical personnel. Thus as long as wage cost differentials greatly outweigh transportation costs, even automated assembly for the U.S. market might be cost-effective in developing countries. Furthermore, as an example, it might make sense for Japanese and other foreign firms to automate assembly for the U.S. market in labor-abundant Mexico as long as there are significant savings in transporting components rather than finished products across the ocean.

The transfer of automated assembly abroad involves substantial capital investment. Risks in foreign lands will have to be weighed much more carefully, and sensitivity to political and social factors needs to be much higher than with manual assembly technology. It is likely, therefore, that when automation becomes profitable, the motive for offshore assembly will diminish and a major portion of assembly operations will return to the United States. This will be particularly true if the cost advantage of offshore assembly in developing countries is eroded by increasing political instability, rising labor militancy, growing bureaucratic obstacles and other heightened risks. Such conditions would accelerate the movement toward automation and bring offshore production back to the United States.

Nevertheless, it would take an enormous improvement in the economic efficiency of automation to offset the economies derived from the vast, inexpensive and easily trainable labor pool of the developing world. As long as Mexico enjoys relative political stability and the enormous wage differentials persist, its large, easily trainable labor pool will continue to participate in the production of industrial country output.

Notes

1. The exception is the textile industry, whose exports are subject to the imposition of quotas by the United States. In that industry, assembly plants must have at least 51 percent Mexican ownership, the usual minimum ownership requirement for economic activities in Mexico.

2. Michael Van Waas, "The Multinationals' Strategy for Labor: Foreign Assembly Plants in Mexico's Border Industrialization Program" (Ph.D. dissertation, Stanford University, March 1981), note 253, pp. 195–96.

3. According to official Mexican census data, open unemployment in 1970 was 4.2 percent at the border as against 3.8 percent for the country. See Joaquín Xirau Icaza and Miguel Díaz, *Nuestra dependencia fronteriza*, Archivo del Fondo 48 (Fondo de Cultura Economica Mexico, 1976), Table 11. Since these figures do not include those seeking work for the first time, they are underestimates.

4. Jorge A. Bustamante, "El Programa Fronterizo," pp. 186–87. See also Van Waas, *The Multinationals' Strategy*, p. 195; *Comercio Exterior de Mexico* 24, 6 (May 1978), p. 208; Donald Baerresen, *The Border Industrialization Program of Mexico* (Lexington Books, 1971), p. 35; U.S. Congress, House Committee on Ways and Means, Hearings, June 4, 1970, "Exhibit H," p. 3286; and *Actualidad*, a Mexican monthly review, 2, 7 (May 1, 1981), p. 14.

5. Surely a higher proportion of Mexican wages near the border was spent in the United States during the 1970s when the value of the peso was relatively high than after the 1982 devaluation when the U.S. dollar became expensive for Mexicans.

6. Banco de Mexico, *Indicadores Económicos*, various issues.

7. Maquila exports are included in the "service" rather than the merchandise export category in Mexico's balance of payments statistics. They therefore do not correspond to U.S. import statistics under tariff items 807 and 806. The latter include U.S. and other non-Mexican components as well as the Mexican value added. The dutiable value of 807/806 imports should reflect Mexican value added plus non-Mexican and non-U.S. components. Mexican maquila exports data include Mexican assembly exports to all destinations, not only to the United States.

For these reasons, statistical discrepancies will emerge between U.S. and Mexican data. In addition there are the usual discrepancies between f.o.b. and c.i.f. values, and because of lags in the recording of transactions, as well as because some U.S. 807/806 imports come from Mexican assembly plants not under the maquila regime (plants that are in a free zone and prefer to export under the free zone regime) and therefore are not listed in Mexican maquila statistics. On the other hand, there are maquila exports which contain no U.S. components or otherwise do not qualify for 807 or 806 U.S. tariff exemptions, and therefore are not listed in U.S. data.

8. For the definition of nontraditional exports see UN ECLA, *Economic Survey of Latin America*, various issues.

9. Airgrams from the U.S. Embassy of Mexico: A-265 dated June 4, 1971; A-388 dated June 30, 1972; and A-61 of February 14, 1973; as well as SPP unpublished tables.

The largest-size plants tend to be located in modern industrial parks; in Ciudad Juarez, where the country's largest industrial park for maquiladoras is located, the average was 350 workers per establishment in December 1980. Small plants prevail in the Far West: Tijuana averaged only 100 workers and Mexicali less than 90. Maquiladoras in the interior on average are slightly smaller than at the border. Plant size also varies with type of products. Furniture assembly is generally done in small plants, assembly of electrical machinery and equipment in large plants.

10. Ernesto Calderon, "Las Maquiladoras de los paises centrales que operan en el Tercer Mundo," in *Maquiladoras,* Lecturas de CEESTEM (Mexico: CEESTEM [Centro de Estudios Económicos Sociales del Tercer Mundo], 1981), p. 92.

11. Van Waas, *The Multinationals' Strategy,* p. 34.

12. Leopoldo Solis, "Industrial Priorities in Mexico" in United Nations Industrial Development Organization, *Industrial Priorities in Developing Countries* (New York: United Nations, 1979), p. 108 and Table 15, p. 109.

13. Machinery and equipment on loan (by the principal) to independent subcontractors, particularly in textile assembly, may not be reported to census takers.

14. See World Bank, *Mexico, Manufacturing Sector: Situation, Prospects and Policies* (Washington, D.C., March 1979); and Xirau and Díaz, *Nuestra dependencia fronteriza,* Table 34.

15. Using the relationships of $3:1$ for the capital-labor and $1.5:1$ for value added-labor ratios, the value added/capital ratio in the assembly industry is twice as high as in the total manufacturing sector in Mexico.

16. The numbers in this and the following two sections were calculated on the basis of data in unpublished SPP tables.

17. With the 1982 devaluations, not only did the dollar become much more expensive but convertibility became more difficult at the border (in the interior of Mexico free convertibility became practically nonexistent). It can be assumed that since 1982 a much smaller proportion of Mexican border wages has been spent in the United States. This will remain so, unless major disparities in the movement of purchasing power between peso wages and their dollar equivalent again emerge.

18. The border average was calculated by Van Waas, *The Multinationals' Strategy,* Table 10, pp. 276–77.

19. It should be noted that hourly minimum wages were calculated on the assumption that Mexican workers receive non-working Sunday pay. To the extent that the law is not followed, minimum wages would be about 15 percent lower than indicated in the tables, thus enlarging the gap with maquila wages.

In a sample of 224 maquiladora workers in Tijuana, Monica-Claire Gambrill found in 1977–1978 that 18 percent of all the workers received a wage less than the minimum. Among the unskilled it was 21 percent (the percentages for women were higher, for men lower). About 36 percent of all workers and 20 percent of the unskilled received more than the minimum. See "La fuerza de trabajo en las maquiladoras," *Maquiladoras,* Lecturas de CEESTEM (Mexico: CEESTEM, 1981), Table 2, p. 15 and Table 3, p. 16.

20. A recent decree issued in August 1983 allows maquiladoras to sell up to 20 percent of their output on the domestic market. It is not yet clear whether approval must be granted on a case-by-case basis. If so, this provision may not be effective as long as maquila products are seen as competing with domestic production.

21. About two-thirds of the women workers are less than 25 years of age. In electronics the proportion is 85 percent, with a median age of less than 20 years. The average age is considerably higher in the apparel industry, about 26 years (Fernández, "Chavalas de Maquiladora," Table 1, p. 163).

22. See also Fernández, "Chavalas de Maquiladora," pp. 109–10; and Van Waas, *The Multinationals' Strategy,* pp. 200–01.

23. In the U.S. semiconductor industry, for example, 92.4 percent of the assembly operators were women in September 1977. (Bureau of Labor Statistics, *Industry Wage Survey: Semiconductors, September 1977,* Bulletin 2021, U.S. Department of Labor, 1979.) In the U.S. apparel and accessories industry, 81.4 percent of the total was female employment. (Bureau of Labor Statistics, *Employment and Unemployment During 1979: An Analysis,* Special Labor Force Report 234, U.S. Department of Labor, 1980.)

24. Nearly all assembly plants along the eastern part of the border with the United States are unionized. Going west, the rate of unionization diminishes and in Ciudad Juarez, the largest assembly concentration, it is only about 50 percent. Further west, as in Tijuana, there is relatively little union activity.

25. "Border Industries," *Business Review,* July 1975, p. 1. See also Solis, who gave the same job loss figure in "Industrial Priorities in Mexico," p. 108.

26. For an interesting description and analysis of this "worker rebellion," see Van Waas, *The Multinationals' Strategy,* especially pp. 296–310. By 1980 Nuevo Laredo's maquila employment and value-added in real terms were still well below half of 1973–1974 levels (Mexican SPP data).

27. See Bustamante, "El Programa Fronterizo," p. 191.

28. Gambrill, "La fuerza de trabajo," p. 29 and Table 10, p. 28; and Fernández, "Chavalas de Maquiladora," Tables 7 and 8, p. 180.

29. Seligson and Williams, *Maquiladoras and Migration,* p. 5.

30. Van Waas, *The Multinationals' Strategy,* p. 207.

31. Seligson and Williams, *Maquiladoras and Migration,* Table III.2, p. 67. The migrant maquiladora workers had lived an average of 10.3 years at the border in mid 1978.

32. Ibid., pp. 83–90, 112–22; and Wayne A. Cornelius, *Mexican Migration to the United States* (Cambridge, Mass.: MIT, 1978), discussed in Seligson and Williams.

33. Ramiro Zuñiga of the Maquiladora Trade Association, speaking on National Public Television on "Border Business," *The MacNeil/Lehrer Report,* March 12, 1979.

34. Seligson and Williams, *Maquiladoras and Migration,* Summary, p. 9.

35. The government of Mexico did not go out of its way to promote investments in offshore assembly operations. In a 16-page special advertising supplement sponsored by Mexico, maquiladoras or assembly activities were not mentioned once, although investment in manufacturing was featured conspicuously. See "Mexico's Sunny Economic Climate," special advertising section, *Newsweek* (June 1, 1981). The U.S. businessman would not know by reading the supplement that offshore assembly opportunities existed in Mexico, much less that such activities generated over $2.3 billion of U.S. imports (including U.S. components) from Mexico in 1980.

36. Normal import duties should be paid in order to avoid unfair competition of in-bond assembled items with entirely locally produced goods.

37. See note 20 above.

9
Evaluating the Benefits and Costs of Mexico's Border Industrialization Program

Haynes C. Goddard

Introduction

Recently, Mexican researchers and policy makers frequently have raised questions about whether Mexico's border industrialization program (BIP) has yielded positive net benefits to the country. These doubts have arisen because (1) the composition of the labor demands generated by the program has been different from that expected by the government, leading to an increase in labor force participation among border residents rather than a decrease in the unemployment rate along the border; (2) the program may have stimulated migration to the border area, swelling the labor pool and further exacerbating the unemployment problem there; (3) substantial leakages to foreign exchange have generated back into the United States, thereby diminishing the net additions to the foreign exchange generated by the program; and (4) the reported profits, and therefore the profit taxes, have been less than expected.[1]

Of these concerns, only induced migration seems to be less of an issue today than it once was, since apparently there is no strong evidence that the program has been a strong inducement to migrate to the border. Rather, it seems that the lack of employment in rural areas and the allure of employment in the United States are more important determinants of increased migration rates to the border areas.

Today, the discussion of the issues emanating from the BIP is no longer put in terms of whether or not Mexico benefits in net terms from the program. Although we still do not have good estimates on the overall net economic impact of the program (aside from the payroll and value added), most observers seem to believe that the country does benefit from the program. Rather, appropriate attention has been turned to estimating the magnitude of the net benefits. Knowing the sources and the magnitudes of the benefits and costs that arise from the operation of the assembly industry can help Mexican policy makers devise policies that maximize the net benefits of the program. For example, this knowledge can serve as a basis for computing how many resources should be dedicated to resolving some of the aspects of the operation of the industry that numerous observers have indicated need improvement. Principal among these are an improved workplace environment and worker training and education.

This investigation addresses two economic factors that figure centrally in the calculation of the actual and potential net benefits of the BIP in Mexico: (1) the impact of an overvalued exchange rate on the use of the foreign exchange generated by the program for consumption, and (2) the impact on the benefits of the program occasioned by the fact that the opportunity cost of labor is less than the nominal wage. We present some partial and tentative information on the magnitude of the reduction in consumption at the border that would accrue under an (estimated) equilibrium exchange rate and also on the additional benefits that result from using a shadow wage rate rather than a market wage rate to compute labor costs. These two issues are essentially unrelated except in the sense that they both constitute elements of the measurement of the real (versus pecuniary) gains to the country of the operation of the assembly industry. Our choice of these two aspects of the problem area has been influenced by the nature of the discussion in Mexico (in the case of exchange leakages) and by the availability of previous research on which to build (opportunity cost of labor).

While leakages at the border are not attributable to the operation of the assembly industry *per se*, critics have perceived these leakages as attenuating the value of the industry and the BIP to the country. Our purpose is to measure how the contribution to the economic development of the country could be increased were the government to follow a different exchange rate policy.

As a final note of introduction, it should be pointed out that economic analysis of the BIP is difficult because of the severe limitations that characterized both the quantity and the quality of data on industry operation and the associated behavior of its workers, both as suppliers of labor and as consumers. It is in studies of this sort that the art as opposed to the science of benefit-cost analysis becomes very apparent. Nonetheless, we think that the figures presented below give a reasonably valid picture of the magnitude of the additional value to the economy of the two factors that we examine here. No attempt has been made at this stage to extend the formal modeling of the questions treated here beyond what the available data permit us to quantify. Finally, the present study addresses only part of what is required to do a complete cost-benefit analysis of the industry. In particular, nothing has been said of the externalities nor of social cost-benefit analysis (e.g., distribution of income), nor are present-value calculations developed here. These tasks remain for future work. We begin by reviewing some of the background of the BIP.

Background and Issues

During World War II Mexico and the United States signed an agreement that allowed Mexican laborers, principally agricultural workers, to cross into the United States to work. This program was conceived as a temporary measure to ease the manpower shortage created in the United States by the need to expand the number of men under arms during the war. After the war, Mexico came to depend on the program as a source of foreign exchange earnings and as an outlet for its "excess" supply of labor. The program continued until 1964 when it was unilaterally terminated by the United States, largely in response to pressure exerted by organized labor in the United States. The abrogation of the program led to a substantial increase in unemployment in the border regions of Mexico, and partly as a measure to alleviate this problem, the new Mexican president, Díaz Ordaz, announced in 1965 a new program that would permit United States firms to import into Mexico capital equipment and materials for the purpose of further processing of duty free finished products for re-export.[2] The Johnson Administration agreed to this program, whereby use would be made of items 806.30 and 807.00 of the United States tariff schedules which permit reimport of finished or partially finished goods (goods sent abroad for further processing, usually assembly) with duty to be paid only on that value added to the product while outside of the United States.[3] In Mexico, the plants set up under this program are called "maquiladoras"; the industry is called the "maquila" industry.[4]

Since the United States has a relatively high real-wage economy in comparison to that of Mexico, United States firms have ample incentive to move segments of production processes that are labor intensive to lower real-labor-cost areas. Real labor cost as a whole is lower in Mexico because labor productivity in general is lower, and because Mexico has abundant supplies of unskilled labor. The country has been one of the most frequently chosen locations for labor intensive production processes, mainly assembly. The industries represented in the maquila sector include those of television receivers and parts, semiconductors, toys, textiles, office machines, scientific instruments, electric motors, lumber and paper products, electrical equipment, motor vehicle parts, ceramic parts and luggage, among others. These operations are concentrated along the border, but have been expanding into the interior of the country as well.

U.S. investment in the maquiladoras has grown substantially over the years; by 1969 there were 108 different plants employing about 16,000 individuals. By the end of 1980 this had expanded to 620 plants (69 of them in the interior) employing 120,000 people (13,000 in the interior). See Table 1.[5] The value added in this program was US $770 million in 1980 ($440 million in payroll), constituting a significant source of foreign exchange earnings. On a gross basis, these $770 million in 1980 represented 5 percent of all of Mexico's non-petroleum exports on current account, and 3 percent of all current account exports (US $15.390 billion and $24.820 billion, respectively). The importance of this industry continues to grow apace with the weakening of international oil prices and of Mexico's oil export earnings.

A salient issue is the fact that a large percentage of the value added leaks back across the border in the form of consumer goods purchased by maquiladora employees. The net impact on foreign exchange earnings therefore is much less, and the net benefit to the country is held to be much less. Since the three devaluations of 1982, these leakages have probably diminished markedly. It should be pointed out that the use of the terms "benefits" and "costs" in describing the national value of the industry has frequently been less than precise and raises the question of what definitions various critics use. If it is held that the lost foreign exchange through these consumption leakages results in a loss for the country, then this implies that the shadow value of the exchange in other uses (presumably industrial development) is greater than in consumption. To the extent that the exchange rate is overvalued and leads to incremental consumption imports over what would otherwise occur, this would be an appropriate conclusion, and is an issue we seek to illuminate here. The analysis of shadow pricing, of course, can be extended much further.[6]

These comments suggest that the benefits of the maquila program have not developed quite as a number of Mexican policy makers and observers of this subject had anticipated, or would have liked. The principal economic criticisms have been as follows:

1. The segment of the labor force that has been employed in the maquiladoras is not the same as that which was displaced by the termination of the bracero program. Rather, maquila firms overwhelmingly employ young women, many with no previous work experience and who apparently would not otherwise have sought employment. As a consequence, the maquiladoras seem to have increased the labor force participation rate in the areas in which they are located and thus the BIP has not led to a reduction in the unemployment rate as had been hoped.

2. The potentially favorable impact on foreign exchange earnings is greatly attenuated by the leakages at the border in the form of

TABLE 1

Value Added and Total Payroll in Maquiladora Plants, by Location,

in Millions of Current U.S. Dollars

1973-1980

	1973	1974	1975	1976	1977	1978	1979	1980
Value Added								
All Plants	197.0	315.6	321.2	352.2	314.9	438.6	637.9	770.8
Border Plants	177.5	289.2	290.0	314.4	276.3	386.5	539.7	661.2
Interior Plants	19.5	26.5	31.1	37.7	38.6	52.0	98.2	109.6
Total Payroll								
All Plants	115.5	194.7	194.4	215.6	200.3	262.5	371.4	456.4
Border Plants	107.7	181.4	180.1	199.9	183.8	241.8	339.6	413.7
Interior Plants	7.8	13.3	14.2	15.7	16.5	20.7	31.8	42.7

SOURCE: Joseph Grunwald and Kenneth Flamm, The Internationalization of Industry, The Brookings
Institution, forthcoming

NOTE: The definition of value added in this table includes the payments of factors of production
in the standard definition as well as payments for Mexican materials and utilities. The
payroll figures are for the maquiladoras only.

purchases of U.S. consumer goods. It is estimated that the marginal propensity to import for Mexican residents at the border lies between 0.5 and 0.8,[7] whereas for the rest of the country, the MPM is estimated at only 0.071.[8] The concern expressed has been twofold: first, leakages across the border mean that potential backward linkages are lost to the rest of the Mexican economy, leading to opportunity losses (foregone benefits) that can be substantial, since the opportunity cost of labor that could be indirectly employed through domestic purchases is often substantially less than the nominal wage rate. We investigate this proposition for the maquila industry below. Second, since the foreign exchange gap is often the most serious resource shortage confronting developing countries (and is a problem for Mexico), the shadow value of exchange exceeds its nominal value, in large part because of a consistent and deliberate overvaluation of the peso.[9] This means that opportunity losses to Mexico are, in fact, greater than those measured by the nominal value of imports of consumer goods financed by maquiladora salaries.

3. Linkages and interactions with the rest of the national economy have been less than hoped for and desired. Mentioned already are the attenuated backward linkages to the industrial structure of the economy. In addition, there has been less training and imparting of skills with transferability to the rest of the economy than had been anticipated. We repeat that this is a criticism, not yet a fact, for little is really known about this dimension. Furthermore, there has been little transfer of technology (most of the capital-labor ratios for the industry tend to be lower than for the rest of similar Mexican industry[10]), largely because, seen from the viewpoint of the U.S. firms, the whole point of their investments is to use less expensive labor for those operations for which labor saving technologies either do not exist or are relatively expensive.

4. Lastly, there is the economic issue concerning the adequacy of the rate of return to Mexico's investment in industrial parks and other infrastructure designed to encourage maquiladora investments. There are also a number of noneconomic issues, principal among which is concern over the impact of the industrialization program on Mexican family structure, since most of the maquiladora employees are women.

The issue about which there seems to be the least information is that regarding the assessment of the benefits and costs of the program to Mexico. The salient elements were mentioned in point number two above. The economic issues are, of course, the central issues in the sense that a calculated level of positive economic net benefits would give Mexican policy makers a level of benefits to trade-off against non-economic costs in the process of deciding whether or not the program is worthwhile on balance or, more importantly, to what extent growth in the industry should be encouraged.

In this report, we focus on two aspects of the problem of benefit estimation: (1) the impact of an overvalued exchange rate on the foreign exchange available for investment that Mexico perceives from the maquiladora program, and (2) the opportunity cost of labor employed in the program. The first question relates mainly, though not completely, to those plants at border locations, while the second deals with the overall program. It is not novel to suggest that overvaluation of the peso relative to the dollar has affected the net benefits of this or any other industrialization program in Mexico; what has been lacking in this case, however, is measurement of that adverse effect.

This research pulls together findings from several studies in an attempt to shed more light on the topic, as well as providing new information on the dimensions of the problem. Critical to the analysis is the use of exchange rates to estimate equilibrium levels of imports at the border. A serious problem confronting this analysis is a lack of firm information on the critical functional relationships that describe border behavior, such as the relative price elasticity of demand for imports at the border. We begin with a discussion of the exchange rate question.

Mexican Exchange Rate Policy[11]

In the period from the late 1930s to the late 1950s, Mexico followed a development policy of import substitution, especially in the consumer goods sector. Over this period, it used relatively frequent devaluations in attempts to close a persistent balance of payments deficit, without any real success. The structuralist view of the matter holds that the ineffectiveness of devaluations to eliminate imbalances in international payments resulted from price-inelastic and income-elastic demands for imports in the early stages of development and that persistent disequilibria should instead be financed by public and private capital flows. As indicated, Mexico followed an import substitution program and much of the potential for import substitution in the consumer goods sector had been achieved by the mid-fifties. At the same time, Mexico's policy makers had become convinced that devaluations did not solve balance-of-payments deficits; and, until the mid-seventies, Mexico had fairly successfully (at least viewed from the short-run perspective of being able to finance the payments deficits) followed a policy of "stabilizing development" ("desarrollo establizador"), characterized by fixed exchange rates and finance of deficits by external debt, principally public.[12] In the period 1955–1975 the exchange rate was fixed at M $12.50 to the dollar and various quantitative restrictions (mainly import licences) were used to help control the payments deficits. They still grew from US $117 million in 1956 to US $3.7

billion in 1975, the year before a major devaluation. (Petroleum became a significant source of foreign exchange earnings only in the second half of the decade.) Central to our purposes, however, is the evidence produced by Villarreal that it was precisely at this time of switching the previous development policy to that of "stabilizing development" (1957–1959) that import substitution in Mexico had proceeded to a point where the inflexibilities imposed by structural factors in the economy had come to be greatly diminished, so that devaluations now had more potential for contributing to the attainment of balance of payments equilibria and, therefore, for reducing reliance on external debt to finance the deficits. We will rely on that flexibility, as measured by Villarreal, to calculate changes in border consumption.

Techniques for Estimating Shadow Exchange Rates

During this period of fixed exchange rates (1955 to the end of 1982), the general price level in Mexico increased relative to the U.S. price level. A standard method for estimating long run equilibrium exchange rates between countries is to employ the monetarily based theory of relative purchasing power parity (RPPP) for computing the necessary adjustment factors. We have computed the degree of peso overvaluation based on relative wholesale price movements in the United States and Mexico (65 percent of Mexico's trade is with the United States); the official and adjusted exchange rates, along with the percentage overvaluation, appear for the period 1970–1980 in Table 2.[13] The purchasing-power parity theory of exchange-rate determination has its limitations, but the evidence on the general correspondence between relative price levels and exchange rates over long periods is persuasive.[14] We will discuss shortly a possible limitation to its use during the decade of the 1970s.

As can be seen from Table 2, the movements in the price levels of the two countries suggest that the peso was consistently overvalued on the order of 20 percent and more in the 1970s (and around 13–15 percent in the 1960s). In this investigation we will use these shadow exchange rates for the analysis of impacts of a different exchange rate on border consumption of imports.

An alternative approach to the problem of estimating shadow exchange rates is to employ a real model (as opposed to monetary models, as in the RPPP), seeking to answer the question of what magnitude of exchange-rate adjustment should occur in order to achieve any desired level of adjustment in the balance of payments.[15] A simplified version of Floyd's model is described as follows. Define the deficit as $D = M - X$. The condition for eliminating the payments imbalance is that $\Delta(X - M) = D$, or $M - X = \Delta X - \Delta M$. Employing the definitions for the long run elasticities of a country's demand for imports and supply of exports, we have

TABLE 2

Rates of Exchange for Mexico, 1970–1980

(1958 Base)

Year	Official Exchange Rate	Theoretical Exchange Rate	Percentage Overvaluation
1970	12.50	14.37	15.0
1971	12.50	14.44	15.5
1972	12.50	14.20	13.6
1973	12.50	14.55	16.4
1974	12.50	15.00	20.0
1975	12.50	15.16	21.3
1976	15.44	17.73	14.8
1977	22.58	23.58	4.4
1978	22.77	25.31	11.2
1979	22.81	26.61	16.7
1980	22.95	29.10	26.8

NOTE: The exchange rates are yearly averages.

SOURCE: 1970–75 from Villarreal Arrambide; 1976–80 by author from official

publications.

$$e_{dm} = \frac{d \ln M}{d \ln r} \simeq \frac{\triangle M}{M} \bigg/ \left[\frac{r_2 - r_1}{r_1} \right]$$

where r_2 is the new exchange rate, and r_1 the old. We have a similar expression for e_{sx}. Solving e_{dm} and e_{sx}, respectively, for M and X, and substituting into the condition for balance, we have

$$M - X = e_{sx} \frac{r_2 - r_1}{r_1} \cdot X - e_{dm} \frac{r_2 - r_1}{r_1} \cdot M$$

Solving for r_2 we obtain

$$r_2 - r_1 \left[\frac{M - X}{e_{sx} \, X - e_{dm} \, M} + 1 \right]$$

The basic advantage of this approach is that it makes the real side of the economy explicit. A shortcoming is that it requires estimates of the long-run elasticities, more difficult to obtain than information on relative price levels, especially where several important trading partners are involved.

It should also be indicated that the estimates of the absolute exchange rate yielded by either approach would be influenced by the many trade restrictions that Mexico has applied to its external trade. Removal of these would undoubtedly have an important effect on the initial level of the exchange rate, since the use of quantitative restrictions or rationing can be viewed as a partial substitute for price rationing. However, removal of the restrictions would lead to a one-time adjustment, and once the change had sufficient time to work itself out, we would expect the yearly changes in the relative exchange rates again to reflect the differential movements in the price levels, as suggested by the RPPP theory.

Last, we should mention the implications for our estimations of the extraordinary economic and financial events of the decade of the 1970s. The recent literature on the performance of the RPPP as a predictor of exchange rates in the 1970s has produced evidence that this performance was not good.[16] The main explanations for this poor performance (not yet adequately tested for Mexico) seem to lie in important relative price changes that occurred in those economies that have floated their currencies, and perhaps also in the impact of changing inflationary expectations, such as those predicted by the asset market pricing model, for example. In the case of Mexico, the peso has never really been allowed to float during the period of examination, so using the RPPP to estimate the degree of overvaluation is still valid. The fact that capital flight grew rapidly, even after the discovery and exploitation of the nation's large oil reserves, lends support to this position.

Impacts of Exchange Rate Policy on the Maquila Sector

Viewing this sector as a whole (imports, exports and employment), we can indicate a number of important impacts that the exchange-rate policy pursued by Mexico has had on the economic benefits flowing from the maquila sector. These impacts are those on (1) leakages of the income generated in this sector to the United States, (2) demand for employment and the rate of expansion of the industry, and (3) backward linkages. What we can say about each of these topics varies considerably at this stage of our investigation; there are substantial data gaps and uncertainties that plague any research in this area.

Expenditure Leakages at the Border

As mentioned earlier, it has been estimated that 50–80 percent of income generated by border maquiladoras eventually is spent in the United States. We can calculate the reduction in such imports that would be occasioned by an appropriately valued peso if we have the import demand function for the border (or the export demand function from the United States side of the border; this in fact may be easier to obtain). What is available at the moment, however, is the countrywide (as opposed to the border) import demand function for the period 1958–1970, as estimated by Villarreal (p. 146). This equation is:

$$\ln M_t = -0.605 + 0.810 \ln Y_t - 1.536 \ln (P_m/P_d)_t$$
$$\quad\;\; (1.026) \;\; (13.046) \qquad\quad (4.298)$$

$$R^2 = 0.0614 \quad n = 12 \quad \text{D.W.} = 2.1397$$
$$(\;) = t \text{ values}$$

where

$$M = \text{imports}$$
$$Y = \text{gross domestic product}$$
$$P_m/P_d = \text{ratio of wholesale price indices for Mexico and United}$$
$$\text{States, respectively.}$$

Before using this equation, we should assess the potential biases its use may introduce into our analysis. First, the coefficients are estimated with national data, not border data. On this account, we might expect that, from the standpoint of predicting the response of border transactions, both coefficients are biased downward (a measurement bias, not an estimator bias) and that the border response to exchange rate adjustments would be greater than that predicted by this equation. This is because the domestic content of border consumption has been significantly lower than in the country as a whole, so that significant substitution of domestically produced consumer goods is technically feasible. Also, the data used in the regression were not on a *per capita* basis, and as such the estimated coefficients are subject to specification error bias; we expect, however, that it is the GDP and the excluded population variable that are collinear rather than the relative price variable and the excluded population variable. We do not use the income term from this regression in our analysis, thus the possibility of specification error, at least as discussed above, does not present a problem.

Another potential problem is that today's relative price elasticity is quite likely to be greater than −1.536, a figure that was estimated over an earlier period, due to additional import substitution that has occurred, further altering the structure of the Mexican economy. Indeed, one of Villarreal's theses was that the progress of import substitution caused this elasticity to increase in absolute value (it was not significantly different from zero for the 1945–1958 period).

Finally, the elasticity reported here was estimated with data measuring total imports, not just imports of consumer goods. Since we expect consumers to have more national substitutes available than do producers, and also that the opportunity cost of going without a consumer good is less than for an input in general, we expect the reported elasticity to underestimate the consumer response to a change in the exchange rate. In the light of these several considerations, then, we conclude that we may be significantly *underestimating* the reduction in imports occasioned by a properly valued exchange rate, and thus we can be relatively confident that the magnitude of the incremental benefits (reduced exchange leakages) would in fact be greater than what we are able to estimate.

Using the expression $\Delta M = -e_m \, (\Delta r/r) \, M$,[17] we compute the savings in foreign exchange (reduction in imports at the border) for the various degrees of overvaluation shown earlier in Table 2. These savings are valued at the original overvalued exchange rate. Our calculations suggest that Mexico could have saved 110.7 million dollars in lost foreign exchange had it used a more appropriate exchange rate in 1980, a rate based on RPPP adjustments (see Table 3). Since December, 1982, the government has adopted a policy of setting an undervalued "free" market rate for the peso, and letting the "controlled" rate slide, reflecting internal inflation. Once these two rates coincide, if the government maintains a policy of not permitting the exchange rate to become overvalued again, then we should expect the kinds of gains calculated here to be realized in practice.

Backward Linkage Effects

We can indicate only in general terms a number of backward linkages relating to both the border and national economies that would be stimulated if Mexico were to maintain a closer parity to the dollar for the peso.

In general, we should expect the usual economic forces in an economy characterized by moderate supply elasticities (relatively few structural bottlenecks) to come into play in the long run. These would lead to greater import substitution and greater internal multiplier effects on national income. There are a number of caveats, however, that need to be taken into account when discussing the border economy in these terms. First, it is misleading to focus only on the first round or iteration effects of the border leakages of maquiladora payrolls as

TABLE 3

Reductions in Foreign Exchange Leakages for Border Maquiladoras

(Millions of Current U.S. Dollars)

	1973	1974	1975	1976	1977	1978	1979	1980
Payroll[1]	107.7	181.4	180.1	199.9	183.8	241.8	329.6	413.7
Imports[2]	70.0	117.9	117.1	129.9	119.5	157.2	220.7	268.9
Percentage overvaluation[3]	16.5	20.0	21.3	14.8	4.4	11.2	16.7	26.8
Saved foreign exchange	17.7	36.2	38.3	29.5	8.1	27.0	56.6	110.7
Savings/imports	0.25	0.31	0.33	0.23	0.67	0.17	0.26	0.41

NOTES: 1. Border plants only; source: Grunwald and Flamm.

2. Computed at 65% of payroll; 0.65 is the mean of a uniform distribution with lower limit of 0.5 and upper limit of 0.8.

3. From Table 1.

is implied by the 50–80 percent leakage cited above. Taking into account the subsequent iterations may reveal a different picture of net border transactions. For example, increased income on the U.S. side occasioned by the leakages can be expected to lead to subsequent increases in the purchases by U.S. residents of Mexican goods and services ("tourism"). Secondly, many Mexicans (including the undocumented) cross the border each day to work on the U.S. side and bring back many of these dollars.

Because the border is fairly distant from the major industrial sections of Mexico (except for the Monterrey area), and because the transport links to the rest of Mexico still need development, we should expect that supply responses to a revalued peso will be somewhat more inelastic and slower in developing than would be observed in the rest of the country. Nonetheless, a close parity relation between the peso and the dollar would have the effect of making such import substitutions more economic, including any associated long run infrastructural improvements designed to integrate the border more fully into the economic fabric of the nation.

Aside from substitutions leading to greater supply of Mexican consumer goods to the border areas, we should also expect increased use of Mexican materials in the maquila operations, not a distinguishing characteristic of the current operations. The aforementioned study conducted by CIDE surveyed some 571 maquilas, asking the reasons why Mexican material inputs were not substituted for imported materials for the three most important inputs. The two most frequently mentioned reasons were inadequate quality (frequency of 27.6 percent), and higher prices in Mexico (18.8 percent; CIDE, p. 633). The high-price problem would be directly ameliorated by an adjusted exchange rate, and quality insufficiencies would be indirectly so. This is because quality is ultimately a matter of cost (for a given technology); it is a matter of better machinery and materials and more skilled manpower. If a foreign maquiladora operator has sufficient reason (potential cost savings) to believe that he can further lower costs by substituting Mexican materials, he can be expected to do so. The only limit to this process is that the total costs of developing an acceptable local supply of inputs not exceed that of importing them; the exchange rate of course directly affects these decisions.

Valuing Labor Cost in Maquiladoras

If a proper analysis of the economic net benefits of the maquiladoras is to be undertaken, care must be taken that the major inputs are valued in accordance with their scarcity values or opportunity costs. This section gives some preliminary evidence on the social cost of labor employed in the maquila industry.

As an input, labor is treated as a cost in cost-benefit analysis. However, its nominal or financial cost often differs from its economic cost, that is, its opportunity cost. This is true for Mexico in general and for the maquiladoras in particular. Total payrolls for the border maquiladoras for the year 1973–1980 are shown in the first row of Table 5, repeated from Table 1. The dip in 1977 is related to the U.S. recession but is mostly due to labor difficulties in Nuevo Laredo and the subsequent closing of virtually all of the maquiladoras there.

While Mexico is generally characterized as a labor surplus economy with substantial underemployment, indicating that shadow wage rates should be used to value labor's real cost, not all of the positions created in this sector should be treated in this manner. In a 1975 survey of 31 maquiladoras, König found that 82 percent of the workers were unskilled workers; of the remaining 18 percent, 10.5 percent were supervisors and 7.6 percent were technicians and managers, of which only 0.4 percent were foreign.[18] König estimates that 45 percent of the operators (37 percent of total employees) would not have looked for work in the absence of the maquiladoras, and that the 55 percent who would have looked for work (45 percent of total employees) would, conservatively, have received perhaps 70 percent of the minimum wage.[19] It is assumed that the wages of the trained employees reflect their opportunity costs, as this type of manpower is scarce in Mexico.

We employ the following model to make use of the data in König's study for the purpose of calculating the global economic cost of labor employed in the maquiladoras. This economic cost will be shown to be less than the financial cost, and the difference between these two figures should be treated as additional benefit to the operation of this industry. By definition, total payroll equals the average wage multiplied by the number of employees. Let $\bar{w}_n$ be the nominal mean wage, $\bar{w}_s$ the shadow mean wage, P_n the nominal payroll, P_s the shadow (opportunity cost) payroll and L the number of employees. Thus $P_n = \bar{w}_n \cdot L$; $P_s = \bar{w}_s \cdot L$ and $P_n/P_s = (\bar{w}_n L)/(\bar{w}_s L) = \bar{w}_n/\bar{w}_s$, so that $P_s = P_n/\bar{w}_n/\bar{w}_s)$, where $\bar{w}_n/\bar{w}_s$ is greater than one. It follows that we can estimate the total opportunity cost of labor in the industry if we can calculate the ratio of the mean wage rates. Using official data (Table 4), we are able to compute this ratio as follows.

We have three groups: (1) trained employees whose wages we assume to reflect their value in alternative employments; (2) the untrained who would not have been employed had it not been for the maquiladoras (that is, according to the interviews would not have sought work); and (3) those who would have been employed in the absence of the maquiladoras at a wage 70 percent of the minimum. These percentages are respectively 18 percent, 37 percent and 45 percent of the maquila labor force.

Since

$$\bar{w}_n/\bar{w}_s = \sum_i^k f_i w_{in} / \sum_i^k f_i w_{is}$$

TABLE 4

Average Salaries for Production Workers and Technicians

in Maquila Industry, 1974-1979

(current pesos)

Year	Production Workers	Technicians	Differential
1974	23,994	47,999	24.005
1975	24,287	48,785	24,498
1976	30,575	61,995	31,420
1977	39,097	57,105	18,007
1978	44,915	65,650	20,724
1979	50,487	84,230	33,743

SOURCE: Estadística de la industria maquiladora de exportación 1974-1980,

Secretaría de Programación y Presupuesto, Mexico, November, 1981.

155

TABLE 5

Nominal and Shadow Labor Costs and Employment Benefits of Border

Maquiladoras, 1974-1979

(Millions of current U.S. dollars)

	1974	1975	1976	1977	1978	1979
Nominal labor cost[a]	181.4	180.1	199.9	183.3	241.8	339.6
$\bar{w}_s / \bar{w}_n$ [b]	0.57	0.57	0.57	0.53	0.53	0.55
Shadow labor cost	103.8	103.1	114.7	98.1	127.8	186.5
Net employment benefits	77.6	77.0	85.2	85.7	114.0	153.1

NOTES: a. Grunwald and Flamm.

b. Percentage

where f_i is group frequency, $k = 3$ and w_{in} and w_{is} are the subgroup wages. Using the above data, we compute the ratio of (annual) wage rates, which appear in the second row of Table 5 (using an alternative procedure with hourly wage rates, but holding the proportions of the wage rates for the three groups constant across the years yielded virtually the same estimates). For the period studied, the average opportunity cost of labor in the maquiladoras was only 55 percent of its nominal cost, with very little variation across the years. The shadow labor costs are shown in the third row of Table 5, and are the values for labor cost that should be employed in any analysis of the net benefits of the maquila program in Mexico.

With this information, we can then compute the yearly increment to net benefits occasioned by the fact that the weighted average opportunity cost of labor is less than its financial cost as $NB_t = P_{n,t} - P_{s,t}$. These increments are shown in the fourth row of Table 5. Since these figures do not include estimates of rent (the compensating variation for labor supply), they are biased downward, although rents likely exist only for the group of technicians and managers, as the supply of unskilled labor is quite likely to be perfectly elastic at the wage rates offered by the maquiladoras. Conversely, using interview data as a guide to prospective future individual behavior is well known for imparting potential biases; in this case, it is quite possible that fewer than 45 percent of the operators would not have looked for and found work, so that our calculations have an upward bias. We cannot evaluate the degree to which these biases may be offsetting.

Examination of Table 4 reveals some trends that merit further explanation and investigation. Table 4 indicates that while workers' salaries continued to grow in current pesos during the period examined, in 1977 they declined absolutely for the technicians. The year 1976 was one in which a major devaluation occurred (see Table 2) after 18 years of a fixed exchange rate, and was a year in which economic activity in Mexico declined. We hypothesize that the worker's salaries continued to rise mainly because of the adjustments in the statutory minimum wage (which maquila firms are careful to follow), but that technicians' salaries declined due to the softening demand for their services in the rest of the economy, with a resultant increase in competition for these positions. Employment of both groups in the maquila sector continued to rise throughout the period, with no declines. This is explained by the continued growth of the industry, reflecting the devaluation itself and the expansion of the U.S. economy at that particular time.

SUMMARY

This report has concerned itself with the estimation of two aspects of the economic appraisal of the maquila or offshore assembly industry in Mexico: (1) the addition to foreign exchange reserves that could be attributable to the presence of the industry under a different exchange rate policy, and (2) the additional benefits that occur from the fact that the opportunity cost of labor (foregone production elsewhere in the economy) is less than the wages actually paid. The addition to foreign exchange reserves comes from a reduction in the consumption of imported goods on the part of the workers. For the year 1980, a year of substantial growth in the industry, in payroll and therefore in estimated imports of consumer items at the border, and a year of a substantially overvalued exchange rate, a properly valued exchange rate would have led to an estimated increase of $110 million available for investment or other more highly valued uses. In 1979, we estimate that due to an opportunity cost of labor that was only 55 percent of its nominal cost, additional benefits to the economy were $153 million.

While the estimates presented here are subject to as yet unquantified error, caution was exercised to make them conservative, that is, to underestimate the contribution (or potential contribution) to the economic welfare of the nation. The two aspects investigated here of course represent only two of the many elements that would constitute a complete benefit-cost appraisal of the industry, which must be made if a consistent policy to maximize this sector's contribution to Mexico's economic welfare is to be developed.

Acknowledgments

I would like to acknowledge the assistance of Elda Maldonado Triana and the helpful comments of Manuel Silos Martínez, both of the Facultad de Economía, UANL, and of Joan Anderson, University of San Diego.

Notes

1. Some of these issues and criticisms are reviewed by Manuel Martínez del Campo, "Ventajas e inconvenientes de la actividad maquiladora en México," *Comercio Exterior,* Vol. 33, No. 2, February, 1983.

2. A history of the border industrialization program can be found in Michael Van Waas, *The Multinationals' Strategy for Labor: Foreign Assembly Plants in Mexico's Border Industrialization Program,* Ph.D. thesis, Stanford University (University Microfilms International), pp. 143–191.

3. For a description of the provisions of the U.S. tariff law, see *Imports Under Items 806.30 and 807.00 of the Tariff Schedules of the United States, 1977–80,* publication 1170, U.S. International Tariff Commission, July, 1981.

4. "Maquila" means "measure" in Spanish in the sense that a miller of grain kept a measure or part of the grain in payment for his services. The parallel here is that the Mexican plants (mostly U.S.-owned) provide only labor services, never owning the product. The plants are also called "in-bond"

plants, since the products they assemble never legally leave the parent company, although they may be out of the home country.

5. A complete description of the maquila program can be found in *La industrialización maquiladora de exportación en las zonas fronterizas de México,* Centro de Investigación y Docencia Económica (CIDE), México, D.F., 1980. A more recent review can be found in Joseph Grunwald, "The Assembly Industry in Mexico," in Joseph Grunwald and Kenneth Flamm, *The Internationalization of Industry,* Brookings Institution, Washington, D.C., forthcoming.

6. See L. Squire and H. G. van der Tak, *Economic Analysis of Projects* (World Bank publication), Johns Hopkins University Press, 1975. See also John Weiss, "Cost-Benefit Analysis of Foreign Industrial Investments in Developing Countries," *Industry and Development,* UNIDO, No. 5, 1980, pp. 41, 58.

7. *Comercio Exterior,* Vol. 21, No. 4, April, 1971, p. 333.

8. CIDE, p. 721.

9. The historical rationale for this is explained in René Villarreal Arrambide, *El desequilibrio externo en el crecimiento via sustitución de importaciones: el caso de México, 1939-1975,* Fondo de Cultura Económica, México, 1976.

10. Luis Suárez-Villa, "La utilización de factores en la industria maquiladora de México," *Comercio Exterior,* Vol. 32, No. 10, 1982, pp. 1129-1132.

11. This section relies on Villarreal A., *El desequilibrio externo.*

12. A critical factor in the change in Mexico's attitude toward development policy was the publication of the volume by the Economic Commission for Latin America (ECLA), *El desequilibrio en el desarrollo económico latinoamericano: el case de México,* Bolivia, 1957.

13. Villarreal A. estimated the figures for the 1955-1975 period; we have updated them to 1980, keeping the 1958 base.

14. See Leland B. Yeager, *International Monetary Relations: Theory, History and Policy,* Second Edition, Harper and Row, 1976.

15. See J. E. Floyd, "The Overvaluation of the Dollar: A Note on the International Price Mechanism," *American Economic Review,* Vol. 55, No. 1 (March, 1965), pp. 95-106. Floyd's technique was applied to Mexico at a sectoral level for an earlier period by Gerado Bueno A., "La paridad del poder adquisitivo y las elasticidades de importación y exportación en México," *El Trimestre Económico,* Vol. 41 (2), No. 162, Abril-Junio, 1974.

16. Jacob A. Frenkel, "The Collapse of Purchasing Power Parities During the 1970s," *European Economic Review,* Vol. 16, 1981, pp. 145-165.

17. Derived from the expression for the relative price elasticity of demand, $e = (\Delta m/m)/(\Delta r/r)$.

18. It is not clear from the article how randomized, if at all, is König's sample, and as such it may contain elements of non-randomness. See Wolfgang König, "Efectos de la actividad maquiladora fronteriza en la sociedad mexicana" Roque González S., compilador, *La frontera del norte,* El Colegio de México, 1981, pp. 95-106.

19. König actually makes several disaggregated estimates; we have chosen one that is conservative, that is, one that probably overestimates the free market wage the workers would have received in the absence of the maquiladoras. See König, "Efectos de la actividad maquiladora fronteriza," p. 100.

10

New Policies and Strategies of Multinational Corporations During the Mexican National Crisis 1982–1983

Guillermina Valdes-Villalva

Mexico's economic crisis includes an unstable currency of its own plus a high commitment, because of international and foreign bank loans, to accept foreign currency. Thus the country's development policy will probably depend, perhaps increasingly, on corporations oriented to foreign capital, multinational labor, and exported products.

While national industry and non-maquiladora foreign corporations lost their 1982 profits, the export maquila industry in Mexico did not suffer severe consequences either from the world recession or from the crisis within Mexico. On the contrary, given that maquiladoras pay their labor in pesos, the downtrend and devaluation lowered production costs for this export industry.

In 1982 the Mexican labor rate was the equivalent of US$1.65 an hour; by May 1983 direct labor cost had dropped to US$0.43 an hour. This, states Richard L. Bolin, director of the Flagstaff Institute, "is less than what is paid in most Asian countries."

If added to this, one considers the nearness of Mexico to the United States, and the fact that transporting raw materials to Asian countries involves 30 days shipping time, our nearness results not only in cost and expenditure savings, but also saves time, which for all corporations is part of production costs.

Taxes paid by these corporations to their countries, upon the return there of the finished product, are taxes estimated exclusively on value added, whose principal factor is the cost of labor. Therefore the collapse of salaries and other production costs in Mexico constitute a tax saving for these corporations upon the return of their products to the country of origin and, consequently, a considerable decrease in tax revenue for the "producer" country.

Support Within Mexico for Maquila Industry

Federal government agencies have expressed support for recruiting these corporations, and for providing greater incentives for their operations in Mexico—such as lowering the proportional national integration requirement, and facilitating all importation and exportation procedures for raw materials and, later, for manufactured goods.

The state governors, jointly with the promoters of this type of industrialization, have become negotiators and defenders of the export maquila industries, especially those with a high unemployment rate. Thus, the governor of the State of Hidalgo, Guillermo Rosell de la Lama, offers employment to his constituency and requests maquila industry to move his state and Oscar Ornelas of the State of Chihuahua, proudly refers to his state as "maquila country."

Eighteen years after having established the Border Industrialization Program, Mexico seems still to believe that maquila industry means jobs and dollars for Mexico.

Promoters of this type of corporation contend that tax savings to the maquila corporation mean 124,000 jobs and approximately $1 billion in foreign currency. Several important factors decrease the effect of these benefits, however.

Unfulfillable Promises

Given the national crisis and the devaluation of the peso in relation to the dollar, actual employment figures are considerably lower than the 150,000 jobs which this same group promised during the "Alliance for Production" held when President José López Portillo took office. And how the promised billion in foreign currency will enter Mexico is also problematic. Contradictory criteria from the Banco de Mexico have caused the corporations which originally promised the money to keep their currency abroad. For multinational corporations to maintain a dollar account in Mexico, and these dollars to be exchanged by the Banco de Mexico at the official rate, would mean a differential of 34.50 pesos. (This requirement includes no guarantee that the Banco de Mexico or nationalized banking will retain the foreign currency.) Therefore most maquiladoras still operate outside the official guidelines; and all indications are that Mexico will receive only an amount in pesos equivalent to the corporations' operating costs, the highest of which is the direct weekly wage disbursement to their Mexican labor.

Unequal Competition

A greater danger to the national, especially the border, industry comes from the demand of maquila agents that their companies be allowed not only to produce in Mexico for export, but also to sell a percentage of their production within Mexico. This demand was nearly approved during the last days of the López Portillo administration. If it *should* be approved at a later date, it would obviously result in unfair competition for the national and border industry. Unlike maquiladoras, they have no importation franchise for machinery, commodities or raw materials; nor are they located within subsidized industrial parks. And, compared to the maquila industries, these firms have to pay large amounts in dollars for patents and technology.

Maquiladora and the Female Labor Force

Although there have been studies which define the type of labor employed by the maquila industry as young women between the ages of 16 and 25, who enter the labor market with temporary employment, to date Mexico has not made a clear analysis of what in real terms it means that the maquila provided Mexico, at least during this year, 124,000 jobs. Not only new-employment rates or new jobs per se must be considered, but also the maintenance of job openings. We cannot help suspecting that new labor enters the maquila export industry at the expense of the already employed—what on other occasions I have called disposable female labor.

The prejudice of economists, as well as of those who try to solve statistical problems concerning women and the economically active population (PEA) is seen when they systematically eliminate female unemployment from national statistics. They ignore female labor introduced to the economically active economy and later displaced due to the labor policies prevalent in the maquila type of corporation.

"The difficulty in measuring female unemployment," say scholars, "is that if women were included in the count, these data might not be valid. It would be difficult to know which women are unemployed and which are housewives." Thus, in all statistics having to do with the economically active population, we find that a male worker who is included in the PEA from the moment that he becomes employed is also part of the labor force when he loses his job and can therefore be considered unemployed or underemployed. A woman, presently employed, earning a salary, is included in the PEA, but a woman without a job has been redefined since 1950 as a housewife and is excluded from the PEA. Consequently, when the labor market contracts and female unemployment increases, women disappear from the unemployment figures, creating a whole class of statistically invisible women.

The maquila industry's strategy of using female labor that never grows old and is statistically invisible does not mean that this unemployment does not exist or that it is not measurable. A high rate of female unemployment does exist within this type of industry. The Centro de Orientación de la Mujer Obrera A.C. has undertaken ongoing research on this phenomenon during the past eight years, and the figures confirm the research done by other scholars in this field. The last research, done by C.O.M.O. in 1982–1983, showed the following figures: rotation, lay-offs and settlements reached 30 percent yearly; and only 12.9 percent of all the female population employed by the maquila industry in Ciudad Juárez, Chihuahua, are able to work in two maquilas during their productive or working life. The research also shows that the mean age of women in the export maquila in Ciudad Juárez is still 22 years, that 84 percent are single, 13.5 percent are married, and only 2.3 percent of the population employed in this industry cohabit with a male partner, are divorced or are widowed.

That females remain the priority labor force for the export maquila is seen in the 1982–1983 study, which shows figures of 93.8 percent women and 6.2 percent men.

The mean in formal schooling is 8.8 years, the majority having finished the second year of secondary school. Seventy-nine and six-tenths percent work in electronics, 9.2 percent in textiles, 7.7 percent in another type of assembly and 4.2 percent in other areas of production. Fifty-nine and seven-tenths percent work in companies of 500 to 1500 employees, the mean being 1,153; only 5.5 percent were employed after 23 and 94.5 percent were employed between the ages of 16 and 23. For the great majority, it is their first employment; 88.9 percent consider there is no possibility of promotion within the company. Only 23.7 percent have been able to change their activity within the export maquila. Only those below 20 years of age can obtain such changes; the rest have not been able to make satisfactory change of maquila, given the policies followed; and they also are prevented from going from the maquila to the national industry, to other service sectors, such as trade, etc., because national capital companies imitate the selection criteria set by the export maquila industries.

In May, 1983, when the export maquila corporations again began employing, there were approximately 50 applications for each job offered. A great percentage of the candidates did not meet the requirements because of their age, others were rejected because they were daughters of the first generation of maquila workers, because they belonged to the "cholo" movement or because they did not meet the educational requirements.

The selection criteria were radically changed. All who had not lived in Ciudad Juárez for at least six months were now excluded. Some union leaders stated that it would be necessary to bring young girls from nearby towns and areas near the Sierra of Chihuahua, since there were no young girls in Ciudad Juárez to qualify for export maquila labor. Other companies followed another tactic, that of going out to the peripheral "colonias" with loud speakers and others, a few, accepted older women.

Some companies drastically changed their employment policies because they found, especially among the border population, that the daughters of first-generation female workers or of migrants at the beginning of the Border Industrialization Program, were a new generation of young women who had changed radically. The traditional docility of women could not be relied upon and many young women were already organized, if not within a class organization identified with a labor struggle, at least within an organization of young rebels. In certain cases these were violent.

We can only conclude that, in spite of the contraction of industry in general, from which the maquila industry was not excluded, maquila production in general was subsidized collaterally by the national crisis, especially the sudden change in monetary differential. These corporations, by the fact of being in Mexico, "saved" from $15,000.00 to $18,000.00 a year per worker in 1982–1983. This is equivalent to an absolute subsidy by the Mexican workers in general, and in particular by the female workers in the export maquila industry, of approximately $560,640.00 Mexican pesos a year. Discarding from its arguments the acute inflation which has beset the country, and especially the border, *Forbes Magazine,* in its issue of May 23, 1983, still quotes a general manager of a plant saying, "I employ women because they are better at manual labor and are not interested in making better salaries."

Response from the Private Sector

With "savings" such as these, some companies now see their stay in Mexico as longer than the 10–15 years they originally had foreseen. These companies are now beginning to follow the suggestions of Joseph Grunwald, economist for the Brookings Institution, who says that American manufacturers must take the initiative of attracting Mexican partners by offering technical assistance to potential suppliers. "It is crucial," says Grunwald, "because in the long term, if this activity remains in an enclave, it will become less and less popular politically."

While governments consider what changes to make in this new phase of the relationship and how to negotiate new bilateral policies, the private sector has begun to move and some corporations are actively looking to Mexican companies for supplies, while providing molds, machinery and technical experience to the Mexican companies.

Originally, export maquila companies which located in Ciudad Juárez, and throughout the border, were doing primitive assembly work, under the hypothesis that plans for development of Mexico and salary increases would take Mexican labor out of world competition in the short term. This prediction failed to materialize as did the objectives of the Border Industrialization Program, which were:

1. The creation of jobs,
2. Transfer of technology, and
3. Training of Mexican personnel.

Originally, admits Edward M. Nicoletta of General Electric's plant in Ciudad Juárez: "The concept was only assembly . . . and no technology, but after seven years we decided that we could and were able to perform the same operations we have any place else . . . , now, 14 of the maquiladora plants of General Electric are being developed to become self-sufficient and innovative Mexican companies." "The third step," says Nicoletta: "is a company totally integrated into Mexico, buying and selling from and to Mexico, if tax laws are changed."

Implications for Mexico of the Private-Sector Position

In spite of a certain logic in the way the export maquila sees itself, there are inherent problems to this conception, which must be questioned and analyzed in the national interest.

1. The success of maquiladoras is based on the *sine qua non* condition that labor is cheaper and docile. Thus it competes effectively in cost with that in countries of lesser industrial development, perpetuating their dependency on external industrialization.

2. Maquiladoras fail to comply with the objectives of the Mexican law that established the program. The intent of the law is subverted by:

   a. Creating one-time employment of short duration using mainly the strategy of temporary labor contracts, as well as female labor.
   b. Denying north-south technology transfer, while taking advantage of innovation occurring in production lines and patenting the same without benefit to Mexico as the host country. It would be more just to register the innovation patents in our country to avoid Mexico's added cost of fees when such patents are reintroduced to the country as technological innovation.
   c. Failing to train a national production entity at the line workers' level. Formal training, according to statistics, in 92 percent of the cases has been limited to one full day, while 5.6 percent have received from one to three days training, and only 1.2 percent have received training from one week to continuously.

   By this, we do not mean to imply that learning does not take place on the production line or that this is not transferable to other areas of production. But what must be underlined is that, since the inception of the Border Industrialization Program, the maquila export industry has not intended either to create stable and permanent employment or to employ that population which appears as unemployed in the census or in PEA statistics.

We are not suggesting either that the export maquila does not give jobs to young women, a traditionally unemployed and easily replaced population, or that their production-line innovations are not taken advantage of. However, the export maquila to date has never had the intention of providing on-the-job training for management or middle management, much less for labor, which must be considered skilled labor in order to obtain the minimum wage for skilled labor, with accompanying better income and opportunities for promotions.

3. The export maquila demands social peace in return for staying in the country, defining "social peace" as the nonemergence of independent organizational forms. It is important to recognize that those companies which sign collective bargaining contracts do so with unions loyal to their interests and known systematically to repress autonomous movements, using an exclusion clause when such movements occur within a unionized plant. Luis Martínez, president of the Maquiladora Association in Ciudad Juárez, states: "The foreign investor can definitely count on the fact that the state of calm that Mexico enjoyed for 50 years will not be broken and that the country is a place which propitiates work and mutual advantages."

Advantages of Mexico for the Maquiladora

In spite of the premise that Mexico's ambition is to become a new Japan, the international media refer to Mexico as a "New Taiwan." In Ciudad Juárez, Lic. Aureliano González Paz states: "We have power and a huge, cheap, and hard working labor force, which has brought 600 maquiladoras to Mexico. These maquiladora plants have made cities such as Juarez, Nogales, Tijuana and Chihuahúa work-intensive centers, small Taiwans and Hong-Kongs."

The devaluation and the national crisis have made Mexican female workers, frequently said to be 40 percent more productive than any other nation's labor population, also the cheapest.

Miguel Van Wass, in a dissertation presented to the Political Science Department of Stanford University in California in 1981, estimated that at the rate of exchange of $12.50 Mexican per U.S. dollar, the net yearly profit of operating in Mexico for 1983 would be 1,700,000,000 pesos a year for 1983. If we estimate this figure at the rate of exchange of 150 pesos per dollar during 1983, the net profit would be 255,000,000,000 pesos—this without so far having obtained authorization to enter the Mexican market as national companies.

Under the banner of preserving the country's social serenity, export maquila corporations demand and obtain tax privileges that range from expediting import and export permits to privileged foreign investment, and to preferential treatment by the Secretaría de Hacienda y Crédito Público, Comercio y Fomento Industrial, as well as by state and city governments.

Following the lead of Peter Evans in his study of maquila industrialization in Brazil, Susan Kristopherson has investigated transactions in Ciudad Juárez involving public landholdings and industrial-park promotions. These appear to be related through the reciprocal activities of federal, state, and city governments, on the one hand, and private enterprise on the other.

The effect is striking. While federal, state, and municipal governments introduce legislative bills which allow the free transfer of land for the creation of industrial parks, private enterprise obtains federal credits at preferential interest rates to develop these parks and to bring industry. At the same time, urban development plans let the private sector know which areas are going to be designated to become industrial parks, so that the executives and members of private enterprise buy the land adjacent to the proposed parks, inevitably raising land prices. Speculating with land holdings in Juárez has reduced the city's public land reserve to less than 10 hectares. The municipality is therefore unable to solve severe housing problems because the only land available is in areas of difficult access, on hillsides where it is technically impossible to provide the most essential public services at a reasonable cost to the city and to the dwellers.

Maquiladora Versus National-Industry Incentives

In direct contrast to the privileges granted to transnational corporations, and to the benefits and huge profits which they obtain, as well as to the perhaps "legal" prosperity of officials and members of private enterprise and industrial promoters who are beneficiaries of the maquila export strategy, are the opportunities of the social sector and social capital companies such as cooperatives, even when these occasionally obtain export permits.

In October, 1982, a social capital cooperative in Ciudad Juárez, after months of petitioning, obtained several permits to export their materials. As with all permits for exportation, prices were based on kilogram weight, volume and total invoice price. In spite of the company's having been founded more than eight years before, their exports were suddenly halted because of changes in market prices and changes in the exchange rate from those they had estimated. The cooperative, SECOFIN in Ciudad Juárez, declaring that it could not reasonably make the necessary changes, went to Mexico City; to date, the permits have been neither renewed nor reestimated. No company of national or social capital has been authorized to have foreign currency in order to pay for export transactions; nor, if they had the currency, is there a mechanism whereby the banks would exchange it at the controlled rate of exchange.

In the same manner, the Ministry of Finance still maintains a tax structure which does not allow the few national or social capital companies that exist in the border to move their products into the interior of the country—although here they could take advantage of the great human resource of displaced female workers from the maquila industry to produce quality products at low cost for Mexico. Contending that all products from the border are "contaminated," since customs cannot determine, through purchase invoices of national raw materials, the origin of the components, the Customs Director has determined that all articles produced in the border area must pay duties as if they were imported products.

During the last few months, in comparison to the incentives offered to foreign investment in general and to the export maquila in particular, national industry has lost all incentives, franchises or subsidies. While the national industrial entity disappears, and unemployment increases, export maquilas offer fictitious employment which is starting to create a neo-migration towards the borders, based on rumors nationally that labor in the border areas is becoming scarce.

Population Growth, Neo-Migration, and the Plight of the Social Sector

Gerónimo Martinez has presented results of studies seeming to demonstrate that the growth of Ciudad Juárez has decreased from 5.7 percent to 4.4 percent annually. However, in hypothesizing that growth in the border cities is decreasing because they are no longer attractive to the population of the interior, Martinez omits several considerations.

One is the likely future population increase through reproduction. Sixty percent of the population of Ciudad Juárez is less than 24 years old, and 38 percent between the ages of 16 and 24 years old, ages when normally most of the Mexican population enters its reproductive stage. The studies made by the Centro de Orientación de la Mujer Obrera during the last four years show that persons who have chosen to bear children do not limit childbearing to one or two offspring; rather they follow the large-family model of their own parents. Only a small elite have limited themselves to the magic figure of 2.2 children. Psychosociological studies have established that family patterns tend to be repeated; only on rare occasions are these patterns rejected. Further, because of inflation, high male unemployment/underemployment, and the very brief working life of the female worker, the family requires for its support the incomes of two daughters employed at minimum wage plus those of several underemployed males and children. The pattern normally observed in the countryside, where children mean a source of income for the family, is thus repeated.

Martinez also omitted, in his projections, the neo-migration to the border since February 1983. On one hand, the differential between Mexican and U.S. wage scales has again become a powerful attraction; on the other, new U.S. undocumented-worker policies, such as Operation Work, have returned an average of 1,500 to 2,000 persons weekly through the El Paso–Ciudad Juárez border.

If in addition we consider the recruiting strategy of the maquila export companies, and of the unions which recruit labor without previous city residency requirements, the potential magnitude of neo-migration becomes incalculable. We can only underline its consequences:

- Uncontrollable human settlements,
- Frustration and desperation,
- Insufficient supplies and basic goods,
- Popular defense organizations,
- Public demonstrations, and
- Systematic repression and the creation of anti-riot corps to preserve social peace.

All of the above is intimately linked to the suffering of the social sector: workers, farmers, any who suddenly find themselves at the border with no alternatives. The salaries of the employed do not cover their basic needs. There are no supplies, and transportation expenses exceed 2,000 pesos a month. Promises to promote social organization for work and cooperatives have become vain: no authorization has been given for the establishment of a cooperative in over a year, with the excuse that the Ministry of Labor will not authorize more until the existing ones have been reviewed. This, together with the new policy that any cooperative project must reduce its social objective to the minimum, make for an anti-economic policy which destines the projects to bankruptcy.

Social Disruption and the "Cholo" Movement

For others, desperation cannot even be channeled creatively, as would be the case with work organizations. They turn instead to groups which very often become violent movements.

Youth—who have always gravitated toward movements which in one way or another reject structure—currently favor the "cholo" movement. This has characteristics of the "pachuco" movement of the fifties: "cholos" divide the city by territories which often are defended to the point of death; girls and boys obtain the respect of their peers through the number of times they have been put in jail or in youth detention centers. A longer or harder sentence only increases peer acceptance and respect. Pragmatism is also involved, and openly expressed. An example is one boy—a beneficiary of the National Education Project implemented by COMO—whose guardianship we accepted so that he could obtain his freedom. Afterward, he said, "Why did you get me out? I've got a bed here. I eat three meals a day—and the table is served by some real good-looking chicks."

A company which finally opted for not excluding women of the "cholo" movement found internal discipline to be totally disrupted. The "cholitas," their co-workers called them, stopped the production lines at will; not even the leader of the line, nor the supervisor nor the personnel department, dared to bother them. Once, when a production line of "cholas" was running toward the dining room ahead of their scheduled lunch break, an armed guard was sent to intervene. When the guard commanded, "Girls, don't run," he was surrounded by the entire line. One of them said: "Meddle with us and you'll be sorry." Knowing their reputation, the guard answered, "All right, just run more slowly."

At a COMO center located in a seminal "cholo" area of Ciudad Juárez, "cholas" and non-"cholas" discuss the benefits of the movement. Non-"cholas" included both those who were displaced from a company and those others whom the same company later hired. After a series of confrontations among the three groups, the displaced and the later-hired non-"cholas" admit that they do not know how to defend their rights. They feel at a loss and look upon the "cholas" with admiration.

COMO intends slowly to reorient the "cholo" organization toward more positive and solid manifestations with a broader community. The process is necessarily slow and must include changes in the "cholo" worker. The "cholo" code includes violence; reorientation requires the arduous task of becoming aware of what about the "cholo" movement was appealing enough to allow it into their lives. They must also reach individual and group awareness of themselves as women and as workers. Last, they must be integrated into a new type of movement with other ideals.

The Present and Future for Border-Area Maquila Workers

For displaced maquila workers in Ciudad Juárez, the job options are still few or none. A considerable group has opted for migrating without documentation and returning to domestic labor in the United States, in spite of their training and experience in production. Housewives offer them $60 a week live-in or $20 for a day's work plus lunch. Those 36,000 pesos a month are comparable to the salary estimated for technicians and skilled personnel.

These women have a greater possibility of going unnoticed in the United States, since they usually remain from one to six months within a household without going out. Often they are protected by the owner of the house, also a working woman.

If we were to construct a scenario in which the owner of the house, also a working woman in the United States, had to do without servants and had no access to day care centers, it would not be difficult to imagine an impact on the economy of American border cities which would reach manufacturing companies, almost all retailers, and all services. The non-working woman, too, would be incapable of devoting time to volunteer work in museums, symphonies, charities, or hospitals. All types of private social-action organizations which depend on volunteer work would be in danger of disappearing.

This strange problem, where interests of women meet in mutual service, transcends the need of documents and appears as a solidarity based on need. But it is still a cause for concern that the domestic worker is the invisible undocumented woman. Without a Social Security card or any other document, she will never be able to prove that she has been employed and so obtain the residency rights that, upon approval, any amnesty law would give her. She is a victim of the informal contract, where no rights are obtained.

For older women, between 30 and 45, a few opportunities of entering into the labor force in Ciudad Juárez are opening up. The export maquila companies are beginning to recruit a small percentage of women over 30 with either no schooling or a maximum of primary-level education, and no previous experience in the maquila industry. (To date only one company has specifically requested women over 30 with experience in export maquila. It is interesting to note that this company is a textile manufacturer; textile companies traditionally have employed an older labor force with less education.) Other companies are beginning to recruit men, those whose age and education are the same as those of their female counterparts—i.e., males aged 16 to 23 hired for production-line work. Employment among these two new types—older women and young men—will need to be studied and followed up carefully. Areas for attention include length of contract, turnover levels and reasons, and interaction within the plant among various groups—younger with older and experienced with inexperienced women and, especially, the relationship between these groups and the young men.

In 1981 Van Wass cited the response of the female manager of a Guadalajara-based company on finding that the company planned to stay longer in Mexico. As a means of combating labor turnover, she said that the possibility was being studied of employing older women with school-age children whom they needed to support. This manager blamed the instability of younger women for the high turnover. To us, instability seems rather to result from the strategy of the export maquila and the recommendation of Mexican advisors to implement temporary jobs; from settlements upon discharge after a number of years worked; and from the use in certain companies, with union complicity, of the exclusion clause. To the aforementioned may be added other internal maneuvers which increase pressure and stress and ultimately end in "voluntary" resignations.

Maquila Policies and the Future of Mexico

Mexico has had experiences along the northern border that must not occur in the rest of the country. The Border Industrialization Program has proven that the export maquila will never employ those who appear in the unemployment and underemployment statistics: men between 20 and 46 years old. Instead, maquila companies will continue using primarily younger women and incorporating older women forced by their personal and their family's economic needs to remain on the job for whatever period of time the company determines; later, both will be displaced. To date 30 percent of the productive force with two or more years of experience within the export maquila industry is still being displaced systematically, causing the turnover rate, far from decreasing, to increase 50 percent every three months.

Given the national crisis, and the use of export maquilas as a strategy for the creation of jobs and development, the export maquila can be expected to remain at least until the end of the century. Moreover, a "boom" period of two to five years may be anticipated which will change Mexican labor, both male and female, into the most vulnerable sector, while the nation becomes more dependent.

Findings and Recommendations

It is urgent to adopt strategies of job creation complementary to those of the export maquila, because in the final analysis this type of job has as its main characteristic instability and lack of permanence.

Even to begin protecting the interest of maquila workers, one of the most important and urgent criteria is that—for any company locating within the country—a bond be set to guarantee the rights that the Federal Labor Law grants to Mexican workers. Such a bond would be reviewed and raised in proportion to growth and personnel employment.

It is also urgent that measures be adopted in regard to the border, now existing in an emergency situation. We, as "fronterizos," require a series of agreements that would allow us to make optimum use of our available resources. Our population, which either by birth or adoption considers itself "fronteriza," must, in spite of prejudice from the interior, demand opportunities rather than request privileges.

The social sector of the border is dynamic and creative. It can be trained to complement its fund of experience with the necessary theoretical knowledge to run its own companies. This is especially true because the female worker with seven to ten years' experience in the export maquila has production experience which can be transferred to national priorities.

It is important that campaign promises be kept and that border companies formed by displaced women workers of the export maquila receive treatment equal to or better than that accorded the export maquila. Prompt authorization should be given to the existence of companies able to take advantage of the existing situation, not only to supply the border area but also to export their production freely or to enter the national market. It has been our experience that, given the conditions that exist between the different agencies responsible for the development of national companies and in particular of companies controlled by labor, it takes cooperatives anywhere from eight months to three years to acquire their registration permit. Further, the Secretaría de Comercio y Fomento Industrial should exercise the same flexibility and expediency in the issuance of permits for import, export and entry into the markets of the interior for national companies as are given to transnational companies.

In like manner, and once and for all, the border should become integrated into the national economy. This cannot happen through a strategy that has not worked—making national companies enter the border market—nor through allowing export maquilas to sell their finished product in Mexico. Rather it must happen through allowing truly national companies—national capital or in the hands of labor—to participate in the market of the interior.

A priority is to break the tax barriers. Borders and free zones of the country are at inconceivable cross purposes; indeed, borders and free zones live between *two* borders: one with the neighboring country, the other a tax border created through decree. We can no longer speak of integrating the border and the free zones through population. We are and will continue to be overpopulated, a problem that cannot be solved at the border for the central areas and the interior of Mexico. Neither can we become integrated by believing that by defending the language and the culture we will make the Mexican more Mexican. The Mexican "fronterizo," and even the Mexican who lives temporarily in the United States, feels himself to be, and is, profoundly Mexican. To integrate the border—and specifically to integrate Ciudad Juárez—into the economy and the country in general, it is necessary to cause the disappearance of Kilometer 28 or 20 where the tax barrier is located.

If the border is not economically integrated into the rest of the country and does not see its future as working to improve the situation of all Mexicans, it will have no alternative but to turn north, with all the risks this implies.

The social sector and the female workers of Ciudad Juárez are aware of the problems of the Sierra of the State of Mexico, of the Sierra of the State of Puebla and of the Sierra of the State of Guerrero.

Rather than competing within a marginal situation, the female workers in Ciudad Juárez, displaced from the export maquila, can increase production and improve quality. Their ability, production experience, and awareness of quality form a potentially dynamic combination with artisan, small manufacturing and other types of operation which are in the hands of workers or nationally capitalized.

A project has begun in Mexico through the INEA that raises hopes for creating jobs, for training workers, and for mobilizing existing resources of skill. To succeed, this project or any other must be fully supported. The secretariats must give it treatment equal to that offered the export maquilas. And that which was created by decree must be taken away by decree: the tax border. Determination and political will must integrate the border areas into the national economy.

The federal government and especially the Secretaría de Hacienda y Credito Público should give incentives to those nationally-capitalized or worker-controlled companies who are willing to use the experience of female workers displaced from the maquila. The training of female workers can and should be used not only for their own benefit, not exclusively for the benefit of border areas, but rather with broader vision as a mechanism to creatively integrate the production of artisans of the isolated areas of our country. In Chiapas, Michoacán, Nayarit, Guerrero, Puebla and the State of Mexico, artisan quality and ability can be combined with export-quality raw materials in new products for both export and import.

The Need for Marketing Skills: Two Examples

The request of the INEA also opens the possibility of training "fronterizos" as well as other groups in administration and marketing. We cannot continue trying to market in the manner we have done, especially if national industries are going to try to enter the export market.

In recent research done in Michoacán, artisans in workshops, as well as a FONART representative, were asked how many baskets of a certain type (the largest one displayed was chosen) could be delivered per month. The answer in every case was that all orders would be supplied; all the representatives said they would have no problem in providing this monthly amount. The concrete request was for 8,000 baskets a month. However, it was later confirmed through studying the previous year's production that the yearly production of baskets of every size by each of these artisans did not exceed 7,000.

Another example was the attempt to produce "standard sizes" in dresses and a shirt. (A very low quality fabric was combined with an embroidered appliqué of the highest quality.) To develop this project, a seamstress with no previous training was hired to create a pattern; and an unknown number of these dresses and shirts were made. Upon delivery of the order, a size 36 was tested which turned out not to be a size 36; the same happened with the rest of the sizes. So as not to discourage the workshop, the seamstress was asked to correct the sizes though it was recognized that the garments would never find a market at the higher price caused by this cost increase.

This same project could have been carried out by using a different procedure and truly integrating the country in production. With materials of export quality, the female workers on the border could effectively make the number of items required in all sizes and add a creative design in embroidery of the highest quality such as is already being produced. It is possible for the border area to become a national resource not only in labor but in business and marketing knowledge, especially "export expertise."

Conclusion

The national crisis, the new strategies and policies of export maquila companies, and the great differentials and enormous net profits made by these companies since February 1982 lead us to offer the options described above. Work is required, but work has been required of the Mexican for a long time. The will to work is already present; the information and expertise that are also needed can easily be provided. The political will, reflected in a dynamic and creative regulatory atmosphere, remains to be supplied. Through these we can take advantage of the only, perhaps last, possibility for Mexico's overcoming its crisis of justice and social peace. It is also the possiblity of solving in depth the problem of unemployment and marginality—through fully using the material and human resources available, and through uniting the efforts of the whole country, not excluding its border.

Part 2

Institutional Structures, Flows, and the National Economies

11
The Vicissitudes of the Mexican Economy and Their Impact on Mexican-American Political Relations

Olga Pellicer

I. THE OIL-BONANZA PERIOD AND PROPOSALS FOR A SPECIAL RELATIONSHIP

From 1977 to 1980, the image of Mexico in the United States is associated with interest in the oil deposits, with refined products and how to use them to satisfy American energy requirements, and with reflections on the desirability of seeking a "special relationship" between the two countries.

As is known, the oil program begun under the government of López Portillo permitted Mexican oil exploration works to be accelerated. This, added to highly novel techniques in the calculation of proven reserves, yielded spectacular results. Proven reserves—which had been on the order of six billion barrels in 1976—jumped to 16 million barrels by the end of the following year and by September 1978 had reached 20 billion.

The American media viewed with rising enthusiasm the increase in these figures. Beginning around the middle of 1977 they reported that, given the new petroleum wealth, private international banking interests had fully recovered their confidence in Mexico and were hastening to continue offering her credit. They also reported interest on the part of large oil companies in offering the equipment and technology required for rapid expansion of PEMEX. It is true that they also expressed certain misgivings; some, for example, expressed doubt as to the possibility of achieving significant gains in petroleum production given the distrust engendered by "PEMEX's known mismanagement."[1] However, as 1978 progressed and PEMEX's production program became known, the goals were announced to have been reached two years ahead of schedule, the doubts vanished and Mexican oil captured completely the imagination of the majority of commen-

177

tators on the energy problem in the American press. Headline stories on the subject appeared in the most influential newspapers and magazines in the business world.

Initial speculations on the Mexican-American energy relationship tended to overestimate, or oversimplify, the speed with which Mexican crude exports could be increased, and the possibility of their being channeled, fundamentally, to the United States. Awed at the vastness of the deposits discovered and the enthusiasm with which López Portillo's administration had embarked down the oil road, they came to the conclusion that the United States would find in Mexico a splendid alternative to oil imports from the Middle East and their attendant difficulties. In the first book to appear on the subject of the new Mexican oil bonanza published in the United States, *Mexican Oil and Natural Gas: Political, Strategic and Economic Implications*,[2] the author, in addition to maintaining the advantages to Mexico of achieving production levels on the order of 13.5 million barrels daily, entered on a long discourse concerning the benefits which would accrue to the United States by establishing a solid relationship in energy matters with its neighbor to the south.

In the American Congress, the first manifestations of enthusiasm for Mexican oil took place in the bosom of the Energy Subcommittee of the Joint Economic Affairs Committee. In hearings held in March 1978, several participants emphasized the critical importance of the Mexican discoveries, considered by some to be another Saudi Arabia.[3] Beginning at that time the subcommittee chairman, Edward Kennedy, became one of the main promoters of mobilization in favor of measures to foster the elevation of Mexican crude oil production. This was explicit in the letter sent to the Congressional Information Service requesting the formulation of a study, which appeared shortly thereafter, titled *Mexico's Oil and Gas Policy: An Analysis*.[4]

This publication was only an example of the numerous studies and press commentaries whose objective was to draw attention to Mexican oil potential for the United States and to pressure the Carter administration into formulating a "creative diplomacy"[5] capable of smoothing out the rough spots in Mexican-American relations which might obstruct a desirable *entente* in the matter of oil. "An effort is being made to ensure that our relations with Mexico are good," was the generalized opinion in those years.

Now then, at the beginning of the Carter administration there were notable differences of opinion between American sectors which, attracted by the oil discoveries south of the border, came out in favor of a careful and extra-special relationship with Mexico, and the executive agencies who handled, negligently or with outright clumsiness, central topics in Mexican-American relations. Examples are the scant attention paid to Mexico in the preparation and presentation of the Carter Plan to Stop Illegal Immigration into the United States; the alarm with which the nation's leaders in Washington reacted to measures taken in Mexico to increase exports in the automobile industry and, above all, the arrogance with which the Energy Department refused, in 1977, to approve prices for sale of Mexican natural gas which had been set by PEMEX with certain American companies. The result of all this was that, despite the goodwill manifested by Carter and López Portillo during their first meeting in February 1977, political relations between the two governments entered a period of strain, termed by some observers "an unhappy era" in the history of relations between Mexico and the United States.

Nonetheless, the effort by the news media and by members of Congress to draw attention to the oil riches south of the border, as well as the deterioration of the energy situation following the overthrow of the Shah of Iran in 1978, militated in favor of a change in policy by the American Chief Executive toward Mexico. In August 1978, abandonment of what a number of observers had termed "the disconcerting coolness toward Mexican oil" began. The first sign of this was a communiqué sent by the National Security council to a number of agencies in the executive branch, calling for a study to review the overall relationship with Mexico and propose new lines of action in the areas of trade, energy and migrant workers.[6] The topics which, according to this communiqué, were to be taken into consideration in order to evaluate and decide the relationship in the matter of energy, included highly significant directives suggesting the transcendency to be given to this relationship. There was, for example, discussion of "stimuli" which the United States might possibly use to induce PEMEX to expand its production . . . preferential access of Mexican oil into the American market, possibly at previously pacted prices . . . trade agreements, the exchange of American capital and agricultural goods in exchange for the flow of Mexican oil." This study, concluded in December 1978, was known as Presidential Review Memorandum No. 41 (PRM 41).

This document has been considered a turning point in the relations of the American Executive toward Mexico. The truth is that it was. During its gestation period, the majority of Latin American specialists focused their attention on Mexico; in addition, the document came under the personal attention of the President. This, in the view of American political scientists, is an indication of the high plane which Mexico occupied on the list of American foreign policy priorities.

Anyone expecting immediately a more effective and better-articulated policy toward Mexico would have been disappointed by the results. President Carter's visit to Mexico—in February 1979—was seen as one of the great failures in American diplomacy; it did little to advance the creation of a climate of friendship and understanding between the two countries and, save for the agreement to reopen negotiations on the sale of natural gas, produced no concrete results.

It is not, however, at presidential summitry, but at the general organization of bureaucratic groups charged with policy toward Mexico, and at the formulation of a new rhetoric concerning the desirability of "special" Mexican-American "agreements," that one must look to find the effects of the study which, for so many hours, dominated the attention of foreign policy experts in the United States government.

With regard to the first point above, it should be remembered that as a result of PRM 41 it was decided to create a special office for Mexican affairs, located in the State Department and headed by an "ambassador-at-large" with direct access to the President. Regarding the second point, it is not insignificant that the officer charged with heading up the study was Luigi Einaudi, Latin American advisor in the State Department and one of the true believers in the "common destiny of Mexico and the United States," which destiny was deemed not only "highly desirable" but "inevitable." Beginning with an appreciation of the depth and heterogeneous nature of the ties between the two nations (a fact undeniably true), Einaudi concluded by calling for a policy toward Mexico which did not parallel that formulated for other Third World countries. This idea of a "special policy," presented as one of the most attractive options in PRM 41, not only captured the imagination of the executive branch of the American government but, as we have pointed out since 1978, had been an idea that permeated the thinking of members of Congress and the business sector. The latter, for different reasons and purposes, began to think that the "unique" nature of the relationship between Mexico and the United States also demanded the formation and handling of "special agreements."

This preoccupation with a special relationship coincided with a period of accelerated growth in the Mexican economy, from which American interests benefited enormously. In fact, between 1978 and 1981, trade between the countries grew at an annual rate of more than 40 percent, turning Mexico into the third most important client of the United States. True, Mexican exports, and specifically her oil exports, increased significantly. But since imports of all manner of goods of United States origin grew even more, the result was a balance-of-payments surplus in favor of the latter, which by 1981 reached $5.8 billion.[7]

If Mexico was a fertile field for American exports, it was no less so for the expansion of direct investment. Beginning in 1977, these investments underwent one of the most significant increases in the recent history of the United States; new investment by that country grew from $321 million in 1976 to $1,622.6 million ($1.6226 billion) in 1980. Most of these new investments came from automobile manufacturers interested in shifting to Mexico certain phases of their production, especially the manufacture of motors and parts destined for export.[8]

Finally, the financial groups, who had evinced a certain wariness due to the state of the Mexican economy in 1976, quickly regained their optimism and hastened to grant credit to Mexico. *Fortune* magazine, an accurate barometer of the state of mind in the international banking industry, fully reflected its enthusiasm for the oil bonanza in a lengthy article published in 1978 under the title "Why Bankers Love Mexico."[9]

Beginning with the second half of 1981, new winds began to blow. Divers factors, both internal and external, led to a sudden aggravation of Mexico's economic and financial problems, creating in international financial circles a climate of considerable restlessness and uncertainty which cast doubt on this love for Mexico. In place of love came an alarmist image of the country emphasizing for one thing, the severity of the country's economic problems and, for another, the fragile nature of Mexico's political stability. In this context, reflections on the "special relationship" were relegated to a secondary plane of importance or disappeared altogether; and the Mexico which is presently discussed in the United States is that which could "cause problems" for American society.

II. THE ECONOMIC CRISIS AND THE NEW IMAGE OF MEXICO IN THE UNITED STATES

The reduction in demand and consequently in the price of oil that began in 1981 was sufficient reason for Mexico to lose her attractiveness to American society. There were, however, additional reasons not only for the loss of that attraction but for its being supplanted with outright disenchantment and concern over Mexican affairs. In fact, the dip in oil prices and the sharp increase in interest rates on the world market (which from 1978 to 1981 went from 6 percent to 20 percent), provoked a significant reduction in Mexico's capacity to meet either her increasing financial obligations outside the country or the high cost of imports. In the short term—given the confidence of international banks in the country's oil potential—easy access to sources of international financing was envisaged as a partial solution both to the problem of the slow decline in foreign revenues from exports (it is estimated that, in 1981, Mexico experienced a nearly $6 billion decline in oil sales outside her borders), and to the aggravation of the imbalance in the balance-of-payments account. At medium term, however, this situation caused not only the irrepressible growth of the foreign debt of Mexico, both public and private, but also a deterioration in the structuring of the foreign debt to the extent that the conditions for credit became more rigid. Thus, the burden represented by servicing the debt became greater and greater, given the increase in the short-term value of the debt and the accumulation of payments due for 1982. In January of that year, the Bank of Mexico estimated that the expenditure of foreign currency for interest payments during 1982 would be $10 billion, which led a number of international financial circles to estimate that Mexico would have to contract a net financing volume of $25 billion[10] in order to keep pace with the growth and avoid the necessity of renegotiating part of her debt.

In February 1982, the American press took it for granted that in Mexico the conditions which short months before had aroused the love of the bankers and the widespread enthusiasm of American investors had disappeared. The *New York Times* summed up the new situation at the beginning of a long article: "The four-year fiesta characterized by public expenditures, imports and foreign loans following confirmation of the oil discoveries has led to an excruciating hang-over and remorse over the excesses in debauchery . . . in a matter of months, the mood of economists and bankers has swung from optimism to a notable pessimism."[11]

The question which remained open was when and how there would occur what appeared an inevitable devaluation of the peso. Based on interviews with groups of businessmen, bankers and politicans, the *Wall Street Journal* stated that, taking into account the political cost of a devaluation and its impact on the inflationary process, it was unlikely that the government would go the devaluation route before the July presidential elections. The most desirable course of action was to accelerate the slide of the peso in such a way that, by the end of the year, it would have lost 30 percent of its value.[12] The flight of capital from Mexico, however, accelerated by warnings and observations in the American press, made this alternative impossible. A first devaluation of the peso occurred on February 18 in which the peso lost 45 percent of its value vis-à-vis the dollar.

While the extent of the February devaluation was more far-reaching than had been foreseen, it did not cause great criticism in the United States; it was an expected measure and, for many, a well-considered way of leaving to "market supply-and-demand forces" the determination of the rate of exchange. What was worthy of extensive commentary was Mexico's financial situation. A large number of articles pointed out that the Mexican Government urgently required international credit calculated at $28 billion for 1982. Now then, it was evident that the mood had changed in the financial markets. The majority of the bankers had lost their confidence in the Mexican economy, and while this did not permit consideration of a cutoff of credit to Mexico (the interest rates at stake there were too high to permit that), what was most probable was that new loans would be at shorter-term and higher interest.[13] Apropos of this latter point, a representative of the international banking circles stated that it was unthinkable to grant credits whose interest rates were not at least 1.5 percent above the London Interbank, or LIBOR, rate. In a word, then, the conclusion of a number of bankers interviewed by the American press was that it would be practically impossible for Mexico to obtain all the credit she required.

The skepticism reported above seemed to be exaggerated when, in July 1982, Mexico obtained a syndicated loan for $2.5 billion under terms less severe than had been predicted. This show of confidence did not, however, alter the frankly alarmist atmosphere within which the American press began to report; now the press addressed not only Mexico's financial questions, but also the inflationary spiral running loose in the country, the difficulties in the economic adjustment plan and, in summary, the outright chaos prevailing in the Mexican economy.

Two countries came to the minds of the observers in referring to Mexico's economic problems: Poland and Iran. Thus it was that in an article entitled "On the Brink of Disaster," *Newsweek* magazine stated:

America has a potential Poland on her borders; her name is Mexico.
... As is the case with Poland, the Mexican economy is in grave difficulty. It has been incapable of holding up the aspirations of the Mexican people and coping with the growing population. The Mexican economy now contemplates the collapse of one of its largest first. . . . Standards of living which are already low are now even lower.[14]

In turn, the problems of Iran were evoked in order to prove similitudes with the situation in Mexico.

The parallels and similitudes between Mexico today and Iran under the Shah are surprising. The distortions in Persian society caused by the Shah's "white revolution" were the same which have resulted from the industrialization of Mexico: incomplete and inefficient agrarian reform, heavy migration to the cities, exasperating problems of overcrowding and lack of housing, intolerable levels of inflation . . . nothing observed in Mexico is reassuring with regard to the fragility and the explosive nature of the forces existing there.[15]

Concern and distrust over the economic situation in Mexico was aggravated when a new devaluation occurred at the beginning of August; dollar accounts in Mexican banks were frozen and a dual rate of exchange implanted, this last being a policy which until then the Mexican government had considered taboo. At the same time, talks were begun with representatives of the international banking sector in order to renegotiate the Mexican public debt, calculated at that time at $80 billion; negotiations on an agreement with the IMF were begun; and help was sought from the Federal Reserve Bank of the United States. According to news reports, over the next twelve months short-term credits granted to Mexico for a total of $15 billion would fall due. If these were not renegotiated in order to extend their term, suspension of payments appeared possible.[16] Mexico's problems then went beyond considerations of her internal situation to give rise to genuine panic over repercussions in the international finance system. By the end of August 1982, the situation in the Mexican economy was seen by many to be the weakest link in a chain whose breaking could set off a crisis of major proportions in the capitalist system.

In these conditions, the decrees nationalizing the private banking industry and bringing monetary exchange under complete control, announced by President López Portillo in his last State of the Union Message in September, accentuated the disagreement over the situation in Mexico and hastened appeals in favor of a "responsible" policy capable of guaranteeing Mexico's compliance with her international financial obligations.

The usefulness of the measures adopted on September 1 in order to put an end to financial speculation which had broken loose in the country, to exercise greater control and permit the establishment of priorities in the use of foreign currencies, were unworthy of notice in the American press. The principal concerns expressed therein were the negative effect of the new policies on the negotiations already underway between the Government of Mexico and the IMF,[17] the distrust which had become widespread among foreign investors,[18] and the tensions these measures had created among the Mexican political elite and between government and business.[19] As far as American public opinion was concerned, the nationalization of the banks and the exchange controls, far from providing instruments to cope with the crisis, were a destablizing element making even more remote and complex the recovery process of the Mexican economy. The sensationalist news coverage of the Mexican economic disaster did not subside until the beginning of November when a Letter of Intent was signed with the IMF. Beginning then, all expectations turned to the political changing of the guard in Mexico, which would signal the beginning of a new era in the nation's economic policy.

As was to be expected, concern over economic questions conditioned the image of political events of 1982. Coverage of the election campaign in Mexico, which culminated on July 4 with the election of a new president for the 1982–1988 term, provided no place for meaningful reflections on the nature of the Mexican political system; nor did it note that the election, taking place within the framework of the new political reform of 1977, presented novel aspects which allowed certain conclusions to be reached concerning the possibilities for opening up a political regime which had been described as authoritarian.[20] What is true is that the campaign was one more pretext for the United States to emphasize the social problems in Mexico, point out the lack of credibility in the Mexican government, and decry the corruption running rampant in the country.[21]

Among the problems most frequently cited is the frustration of the people. They had set their hopes on oil and then, before "they have had the opportunity to enjoy the fruits of the oil riches, the Government says the good times are over."[22]

The consequent disenchantment has, according to the United States press, contributed to the second most serious problem in Mexican policy at the present: the loss of credibility of the government. "The difference between words and actions, between the ideology of a revolution and the deeds of the Government, grows daily. Mexicans are used to the Government saying one thing and doing another. This had led to misunderstandings, cynicism, frustration, and nihilism."[23]

These attitudes appeared to be soundly rooted in the Mexican middle class, an impression confirmed by the results of the July 4 elections in which an opposition party, the National Action Party (PAN), obtained a significant percentage of the vote among the well-to-do in the large urban cities. This stood out in the headline in the *New York Times* story reporting on the elections, entitled "The Middle Classes Vote Their Discontent."[24]

Another dominant theme in reports on Mexican political life has been that of corruption, a phenomenon which not only discredits those in power but brings into question some of the achievements attained with the oil bonanza.

All of these reports flow to the sea in the form of that concern which is presently widespread in the United States: the future stability of Mexico. The idea has been implanted in American groups interested in relationships with Mexico that the Mexican political system is incapable of coping with its social and political problems, aggravated by the thorny economic situation. A number of voices have expressed skepticism about a Mexican leadership whose incompetence they blame for the disorder into which the Mexican economy has fallen. This coincides with unrest about security problems which, according to the version of the Reagan Administration, is threatened by subversive activities originating in Central America. In a nutshell—for the media, and in certain State Department circles, as well as in the White House—the Mexico of 1983 is a country plagued with problems which could fall into the orbit of Central American destabilization.

Fear of a political crisis, however, does not lead to greater emphasis on special policies to ensure a harmonious relationship between the two countries; rather, these policies have lapsed. This does not mean that the "special" way in which the Mexican problems could affect the United States has been lost from sight. There is full awareness of the impact that these problems could have on border situations, on migratory movements, on the decrease in American exports and on the general stability of the financial system. There are, however, no indications that because of this situation there are plans to give Mexico a different or preferential treatment with regard to that given other countries. Now silent are the voices which in 1977 and 1979 asked that policy be planned on the basis of consideration of the special ties between Mexico and the United States, and taking into account that Mexico's problems are reflected in the United States more than those of any other country.

III

Having reached this point we can afford to vouchsafe certain reflections. The first is related to the nature, so volatile, of the forces within the United States militating in favor of a "special relationship" toward Mexico, "special" understood in the sense of a differential and more favorable policy. The voices advocating this policy emerged when the worldwide energy situation and the promise of Mexican oil provided arguments for greater attention to good relations between Mexico and the United States. However, with the exception of measures of an administrative nature, these voices did not influence the policies of the United States toward the central problems between the two countries, such as trade questions or immigration. In fact, trends have been imposed against so-called "unfair business practices" by Mexico and in favor of the application to our country of compensatory taxes and "graduation" and "reciprocity" criteria. Restrictionist forces, in fact, have been accentuated as in the Simpson-Mazzoli Act. With the reversal of an oil price evolution favorable to the United States, and with the outbreak of an economic crisis of major proportions inside Mexico, American concern for a "special relationship" tends to vanish, and in its place come alarmist visions of Mexico's future.

Our second reflection has to do with the way the Mexican system of politics is interpreted in the United States, despite that country's nearness and its interest in Mexico. Carried along, perhaps, by the alarm growing out of the situation in Central America, American observers fasten their attentions on the possibilities of social conflict and political destabilization (which no doubt exist). These observers set aside central elements of Mexican political life, such as the strength of the institutions of the masses, the executive branch's freedom of action—present, for example, in the days following the bank nationalization—and the launching of a political reform which offers possibilities of rechanneling discontent.

The difficulties or the impossibility of putting into practice a "special relationship" between Mexico and the United States, the lack of long-range projects to harmonize relationships between the two countries, and the once-over-lightly manner in which some American observers dismiss the Mexican political structure contribute to the difficulty of Mexican-American political relations in times both good and bad.

SUMMARY

During the period from 1976 to 1982, two great moments occurred in the economy of Mexico. The first of these was associated with the discovery of enormous oil deposits and the decision to turn the oil industry into the central axis around which a period of accelerated economic growth was to revolve; the second was related to the drop in the price of oil, the aggravation of financial problems and the unleashing of a severe economic crisis. Both of these moments have given rise to new and sharper perceptions of Mexico in the United States and caused certain subjects rather than others to occupy priority places on the agenda of bilateral problems between the two countries. The purpose of this treatise is to recapitulate these priority perceptions and subjects and, based on that recapitulation, form some general reflections concerning the nature of relations between Mexico and the United States.

Notes

1. See Olga Pellicer, "The Policy of the American Executive Branch Toward Mexican Oil, 1976–1982," in *Mexican Energy, Past and Present*, Miguel Wionczek, editor. Mexico, El Colegio de Mexico, 1982.

2. By Richard B. Manke, Praeger Publishers, New York, 1979.

3. The hearings ended on March 21, 1978. Beginning then, Subcommittee Chairman Edward Kennedy established as a priority objective attracting public opinion to the importance of Mexican oil. His interest in this matter is explained by his refusal to accept the thesis of then-Energy Secretary Schlesinger regarding the exhaustion of world oil reserves. In an article published in the *Washington Post*, entitled "Let a Hundred Oil Fields Boom" (November 20, 1978), Kennedy maintained that the error rested in not having sufficiently fostered oil exploration activities throughout the world. The Mexican oil discoveries supported his reasoning.

4. Prepared for the Senate Foreign Relations Committee and the Joint Committee for Economic Affairs by the Research Office of the United States Library of Congress. U.S. Government Printing Office, Washington, D.C., December 1978.

5. See Olga Pellicer, "The Rhetoric of Friendship in a Context of Contradictions," thesis presented to the International Relations Commission of the CLACSO, Puerto Rico, 1981 (mimeographed copy).

6. The text of the memorandum sent by Brzezinski to the branches of the executive, as part of formulating the document, was reproduced in *Inside D.O.E.: An Exclusive Weekly Report on the Department of Energy*, September 18, 1978. The Mexican-American directives were also to be included. As may be appreciated from the paragraph reproduced, the expectations, such as "preferential access to the American market by Mexican oil, possibly at previously pacted [sic] prices," were very high.

7. See Celia Toro, "Mexican-American Trade: the Unequal Reality and the Limitations on American Collaboration" in Olga Pellicer, editor, *Mexico's Foreign Policy: Challenges for the Eighties*, CIDE Collection of Essays on Political Studies, March 1983.

8. Data from the Foreign Investment Commission, Industrial Development and National Heritage Secretariat.

9. July 16, 1978.

10. Summary of the problems of 1982 and its reactions in the United States in *Declaration of Mexican Foreign Policy*, CIDE, October-November 1982; Department on International Policy; and Olga Pellicer, "The Good-Neighbor Relationship in Hard Times," in *Mexico's Foreign Policy: Challenges for the Eighties.*

11. "Mexico After the Fiesta," *New York Times*, February 14, 1982.

12. "Mexico Ponders the Peso Problem," *Wall Street Journal*, January 20, 1982.

13. *Wall Street Journal*, "Mexico's Debt Load Troubles Banks," April 21, 1982; "Mexico Unveils Plan to Narrow Budget Deficit," April 22, 1982; "Mexico is Weathering the Float of the Peso, but Problems Persist," February 1982; "Amid Mexico's Doomsayers, A Banker Bucks Trend with His Hopeful Outlook," April 23, 1982; "Alfa of Mexico Stops Paying Debt," April 28, 1982; *Business Latin America*, "Mexico's Maxidevaluation Corrects Some Problems but Raises New Dangers," February 24, 1982.

14. June 14, 1982.

15. "Mexico, A Nation Under Strain," *Los Angeles Times*, June 22, 1982.

16. "Mexico Seeks to Stop Paying Debt Principal"; "Treasury Bill Prices Soar After Rumors About Banks, Peso," *Wall Street Journal*, August 20, 1982.

17. "Widening Differences Between the IMF and Mexico Cloud Financial Rescue Plan," *Wall Street Journal*, September 8, 1982; "IMF Deal Stirs Protest," *Journal of Commerce*, September 13, 1982; "Mexico Said to Resist Curbs," *The New York Times*, September 9, 1982.

18. The observations carrying the most weight regarding the relations with American investors, as well as relations with the American Embassy in Mexico, were those that appeared as follows: "U.S. Could Draw Fire for Failing to Aid American Investors with Deposits," *Wall Street Journal*, September 9, 1982. This article reported parts of the text of the telegram sent by American Ambassador to Mexico John Gavin, discussing the measures taken on September first. Among other things, Gavin remarked that the measures announced "spell a decreased availability of foreign currency for imports and make more likely a moratorium on the payment of interests on the Mexican debt . . . in a word, the new change control will mean disaster."

19. "Mexican Businessmen Shaken by Crisis Measures," *Washington Post*, September 12, 1982; "Political Tensions Aroused in Mexico," *The New York Times*, September 12, 1982.

20. Very little has been written in the United States concerning the political reform in Mexico and its importance for channeling social discontent through opposition parties. An exception to this is the work by Kevin Middlebrook, "Political Change in Mexico" in Susan Kaufman, Editor, *Mexico-United States Relations, Proceedings of the Academy of Political Science*, Volume 34, Number 1, New York, 1981.

21. Three long articles appearing in American weeklies illustrate well this orientation: "Will the New Broom Sweep Clean?" in *Time*, July 12, 1982; "Mexico's Fading Promise" in *Newsweek*, July 5, 1982, and "Getting Mexico Moving Again" in the *New York Times Magazine*, July 4, 1982.

22. *Wall Street Journal*, June 8, 1982.

23. "Mexico's Disorder Is the Gap Between Dogma and Deeds," *Los Angeles Times*, July 4, 1982.

24. July 11, 1982.

12
The Welfare Economics of Labor Migration from Mexico to the United States

John M. McDowell

Introduction

The United States and Mexico comprise a region within which a laborer can, either legally or illegally, migrate from one country to the other. Normally, labor migrants, like manufacturing plants, may be expected to move to where their productivity is high and away from where their productivity is low. As a result, such migration is expected to raise total regional output, and therefore be economically beneficial to the two countries as a whole. However, this increase in welfare only occurs in the technical sense that the gainers from the migration process, generally assumed to be the migrants themselves and the indigenous population of the country of immigration, could compensate the losers, normally assumed to be the country of emigration, and still have something left over. Since institutional arrangements do not exist whereby such compensation can be made, and since most analysts propose a goal of national over regional objectives (though these objectives need not be inconsistent), most analyses of the welfare implications of international migration have either focused on migration's impact on the migrant's country of origin or on that of his country of destination.

This paper also examines the impact of emigration as a separate matter from that of the impact of immigration. This is partly done for clarity of exposition. In addition, often the issues of concern differ depending upon whose perspective is being considered. For instance, whereas aggregate per capita income levels and/or the country's overall rate of development are issues of primary concern in the "brain drain" discussions of migration's impact on the country of emigration, distributional impacts appear to dominate discussions of migration's impact on the country of immigration. Moreover, when migrants are characterized as skilled laborers, the focus of interest is generally on how this migration impacts on the country of emigration. On the other hand, with the migration of unskilled workers, impacts of primary concern generally occur in the country of immigration.

Labor Migration from Mexico to the United States

For purposes of exposition, a model is first developed to present a simple treatment of international migration. Laborers are viewed as attempting to maximize their incomes so that whenever there exists a wage differential between the United States and Mexico, workers respond by migrating from the country of low wage to the country of high wage.

Mexico, assumed to be the low-wage country and therefore the migrant's country of origin, is illustrated in Figure 1(a) and the United States in Figure 1(b). Each country is endowed with a fixed amount of labor and physical capital. The respective wage rates are determined by the intersection of the country's labor supply curve and the curve for the marginal product of labor. In the absence of international migration, Mexico's supply of labor is $S_{O,E}$ and in the United States the supply is $S_{O,I}$. Given the marginal product curves, the wage rates are $W_{O,E}$ and $W_{O,I}$, respectively. Mexico's aggregate income is represented by the area $O_E DBL_{O,E}$, of which labor receives the area $O_E W_{O,E} BL_{O,E,}$ and the return to owners of the capital stock is the area $W_{O,E} BD$. In the United States, total income is equal to the area $O_I L_{O,I} TU$, which is divided into labor's share, area $O_I L_{O,I} TW_{O,I}$, and capital owners' share, area $W_{O,I} TU$.

If transportation costs were negligible, and if other impediments to the free flow of international migration were nonexistent, then laborers would move from where their wage is relatively low ($W_{O,E}$) to where the wage is relatively high ($W_{O,I}$), continuing to do so until the wage differential is eliminated ($W_{I,E} = W_{I,I}$). As shown in Figure 1, $L_{I,E} L_{O,E} = L_{O,I} L_{I,I}$ individuals migrate with the new labor supply curves being $S_{I,E}$ and $S_{I,I}$, respectively. Although the existence of costs of migration and the presence of legal barriers to migration will result in a persisting wage differential between the countries, the general implications of the analysis that follows will not be altered.

The actual number of Mexican laborers who legally entered the United States from 1966 through 1978 is shown in Table 1. In general, the annual number of these workers increased through the mid-1970s and thereafter declined (with the exception of 1978). Illegal aliens constitute another important source of migrants to the U.S. The only available indicator of the trend in the flow of these migrants (i.e., apprehensions of deportable Mexican aliens) suggests a sharp rise since the 1960s in the number of illegal aliens residing in the

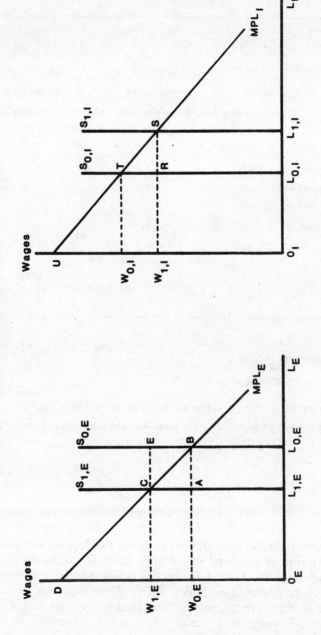

FIGURE 1   The Welfare Implications of International Migration

(a) Country of Emigration

(b) Country of Immigration

TABLE 1

Major Origin States for Undocumented Migrants to South Texas, 1976 - 1981[a]

State	(1) Number of Undocumenteds	(2) Percentage of Total Undocumenteds	(3) # of sample undocumenteds per 100,000 resident population, 1970[c]
Guanajuato (GTO)	210	21.0	9.25
Coahuila (COA)	167	16.7	14.98
San Luis Potosi (SLP)	126	12.6	9.83
Nuevo Leon (NL)	102	10.2	6.02
Zacatecas (ZAC)	92	9.2	9.67
Tamaulipas (TAM)	72	7.2	4.94
Others	231	23.1	0.59
Total	1000	100.0	2.07

[a] April of each year

[b] Total N = 1000 (see first column)

[c] Sample number in column 1 divided by state population in 1970, x 100,000.

Sources: Undocumented data: INS - 213 forms on apprehended aliens from INS District Office, San Antonio; Population data: 1970 Mexican Census.

U.S. However, precise estimates of the size of this flow are not available. Most estimates of the total illegal alien stock fall within a range of 3–12 million in the United States at any one time (see Interagency Task Force on Immigration Policy, 1979). These estimates seem quite high and have been the subject of considerable criticism. Díez-Canedo (1981, p. 30) suggests a "more likely figure is around 815,000" Mexican aliens in the United States.

The Impact of Emigration: The Case of Mexico

Static Analysis Without Distortions

As a result of the migration, earnings of each migrant increase from a wage of $W_{O,E}$ to $W_{O,I}$. One can therefore presume that, since the migration was voluntary, the welfare of each migrant has been improved. Considering now the nonmigrant population remaining in Mexico, Grubel and Scott argue that, for infinitesimal migration, the emigrant will neither harm nor help the nonemigrant population. This is because "the emigrant removes both his contribution to national output and the income that gives him claim to this share, so that other incomes remain unchanged" (1966, p. 270). However, this conclusion rests upon the assertion that persons are paid their marginal product. In general, this is not true because it is only the marginal worker who receives the full value of his marginal product, with all workers being paid only what the marginal worker is worth. As a consequence, as noted first by Aitken (1968), and Berry and Soligo (1969), for non-marginal or finite migration flows there is a "surplus" which is lost by the nonmigrants who remain in Mexico.

The foregoing argument is illustrated in Figure 1(a). The emigration of $L_{I,E}L_{O,E}$ individuals will raise the wages of nonemigrant laborers from $W_{O,E}$ to $W_{I,E}$. The total income of nonemigrant labor becomes $O_EW_{I,E}CL_{I,E}$, of which $W_{O,E}ACW_{I,E}$ is redistributed from owners of capital who have their income reduced by $W_{O,E}BCW_{I,E}$ as a result of the migration. Since $W_{O,E}ACW_{I,E}$ is smaller than $W_{O,E}BCW_{I,E}$, there is a loss of total income represented by the area ABC. Thus, as a result of the migration, the total income available to those who remain in Mexico is reduced from $O_EL_{O,E}BD$ to $O_EL_{I,E}CD$ and owners of factors of production made relatively more abundant by emigration (i.e., capital) find the relative factor prices turned against them.

The fact that the migration results in a reduction in the total as well as overall average income of the nonemigrant population is generally accepted as evidence that the welfare of those left behind is adversely affected by international migration. However, the redistribution of income within Mexico illustrates a basic difficulty involved in ascertaining that a burden or a benefit is created by the migration—some individuals benefit and some lose. Therefore, in spite of the illustrated total income losses, it is theoretically possible that Mexico's aggregate welfare could rise. Such an event would occur when $L_{I,E}L_{O,E}$ laborers emigrate and the increased welfare of the remaining laborers brought about by the addition to their income of $W_{O,E}ACW_{I,E}$ exceed the loss of welfare of capital owners whose income is reduced by $W_{O,E}BCW_{I,E}$.

In addition, even though it is possible that a net burden is imposed on those remaining at home, an economic loss cannot accrue to

Mexico if the welfare of the migrants is credited to their country of origin. In terms of Figure 1(a), the total income of migrants increases by ABEC, which is more than the loss of capital income at home (=ABC). Therefore, the total income of Mexicans (including that of migrants) is increased by area CEB. This point is of particular relevance in differentiating between the impacts of permanent vs. temporary migration flows. With temporary migration, it would seem appropriate to include the welfare of migrants in that of the native population remaining at home. As a consequence, the migration process itself is more likely to be judged beneficial from the viewpoint of Mexico.

The above implications concerning migration's impact on those individuals who remain in Mexico can be altered if the migrants are assumed to own some portion of Mexico's capital stock. A general approach to such a two-factor emigration analysis allows for the emigrants and nonemigrants to have capital-to-labor endowments which differ from one another—one group being capital rich and the other capital poor. Johnson illustrates that if either the capital-rich or the capital-poor group migrates and takes its endowment of capital with it, "the other group is made worse off than before, except in the trivial case where both groups are initially endowed with the same capital-to-labor ratio" (1967, p. 400).[1] The extent of damage done to those remaining (i.e., a reduction in total as well as average income) will depend on returns to scale, elasticity of substitution between factors of production, and the extent to which emigration alters the overall capital-to-labor ratio. If Mexico's aggregate production function is subject to increasing (decreasing) returns to scale, those remaining behind would suffer additional (smaller) losses from the reduction of scale resulting from emigration. In addition, income losses are an increasing function of the absolute difference between the ratios of capital-to-labor taken along by the emigrants and that existing in the economy. Finally, the losses are a decreasing function of the elasticity of substitution of factors of production.

The necessity of some loss to the nonmigrant group rests on the assumption that the emigrants take all their capital with them. While the human capital invested in skilled people necessarily migrates with them, physical capital need not. Berry and Soligo (1969) illustrate that, if the emigrants are owners of capital which they left invested in their country of origin, drawing the income on it in their new country of residence, the remaining population can actually benefit from the migration.[2] Furthermore, if the migration ultimately results in increased capital investments by migrants (perhaps upon their return) in Mexico, the nonmigrant population will benefit.

Analysis with Market Distortions and/or Externalities

The presence of market distortions and/or externalities can result in a misallocation of resources within and among countries and thereby affect the welfare of nonmigrant populations. The existence of externalities refers to the effects a person's activities have on the well being of others and for which he is neither compensated (if the impact is positive) nor charged (if the impact is negative). It is often argued that highly skilled individuals produce positive externalities for society so that their emigration tends to produce large uncompensated losses.

Although there is general acceptance of the belief that international migration may entail a loss in a situation where positive externalities exist, there is considerable controversy as to what constitutes a "genuine" externality as well as the precise quantitative nature of such effects. Grubel and Scott (1966) and Johnson (1967) stress that the externality of concern is something which is peculiar to the emigrant personally and not in his professional capacity. This is because, if the externality attaches to the profession rather than the individual, the emigration of the individual will deprive the country of the externality only until he is replaced by another member of the profession. On the other hand, when the externality is attached to the individual (e.g., extraordinary qualities of leadership, originality of thought, inventive ability, etc.), not only short-run but permanent-irreplaceable losses are incurred by the society through the individual's departure. However, many authors have objected to this argument regarding "genuine externalities." For instance, Thomas (1967), rather than dismissing the importance of the short-run adjustment costs, suggests that "the immediate adaptation of resources to the removal of highly skilled emigrants (retraining, for example) may entail considerable frictional losses . . . which . . . may be far from negligible" (pp. 490–91). Therefore, the loss imposed on Mexico due to the existence of externalities attached to the emigrants' profession depend on the extent to which the emigrants can be substituted for by other members of the society. If emigrants are not easily replaced, and they do not return to Mexico, the losses could be high.

Another possibility of international migration entailing a loss is provided by the technological externalities specifically associated with education. That is, the burden from a "brain drain" argument is construed to rest on the assertion that there are spillover benefits from investments in education which are lost to a region if later emigration occurs. The residents of Mexico obviously lose from emigration to the extent that the emigration of educated people deprives them of tax revenue in excess of the governmental services that would have had to be provided to the emigrants had they remained at home. For instance, if the currently working generation pays the cost of education of the young through its taxes, and in return expects to be compensated (or supported in its old age) by taxes on the incomes of the young after they have graduated, the emigration of the young after completion of education deprives the elders of their expected returns and thus constitutes a loss.

In addition, if the Mexican government attempts to redistribute income via a progressive tax and a regressive spending structure, then the presence of the opportunity of emigration for the highly skilled reduces the ability of the government to pursue such a policy. Hamada (1975) illustrates this point in the context of the optimal income taxation. Note, however, the problem here (i.e., the per capita welfare in an open economy with opportunity for emigration is "strictly inferior" to the per capita welfare in the closed economy) stems from the distorting nature of the brain drain. Namely, not all the workers but only workers of the highly skilled category are allowed to move.

A final example of where the migration may impose a loss on Mexico concerns the possible existence of a less than perfect price system. The early theoretical analysis of the welfare effects of international migration was based on the neoclassical assumptions of full wage flexibility. Bhagwati and Hamada (1974) make a departure from this assumption by postulating that salary levels of educated labor are fixed "by international emulation and associated union-fixation or wage legislation" (p. 23) and thus allowing unemployment in the Harris-Todaro fashion. Within the context of this model, Bhagwati and Hamada illustrate that the emigration of educated labor can lead to unfavorable effects on national income, per capita income and unemployment (absolute and relative) of educated and uneducated labor. Of course, if the emigration does not produce the unemployment, but rather is partially a response to domestic unemployment, then migration from the pool of unemployed (or underemployed) Mexican workers will not result in substantial losses to Mexico.

The Impact of Immigration:
The Case of the United States

Impact on Present Incomes

Immigration's impact on the level of absolute and relative income in the United States is illustrated in Figure 1(b). The immigration of $L_{O,I}L_{I,I}$ individuals will raise the total income of the U.S. indigenous population from area $O_I L_{O,I} TU$ to $O_I L_{O,I} RSU$ (this latter area being the new aggregate income less the income received by immigrant workers).

There are also redistributional effects induced by immigration. While the total income to capital owners increases (from $W_{O,I} TU$ to $W_{I,I} SU$), the income of native laborers declines (from a wage of $W_{O,I}$ to $W_{I,I}$ and from a total income of $O_I L_{O,I}$ to $O_I L_{O,I} RW_{I,I}$). This redistribution of income occurs because of the substitutive and complementary effects produced by immigration into the country. In the case illustrated in Figure 1(b), all laborers are assumed to be homogeneous and migrants do not own physical capital (or if they do, they do not migrate with their physical capital). Therefore, since the migrants' labor is substitutable for native labor and capital is complementary with labor, the relative earnings of native owners of capital will rise, while native labor earnings fall.

The above redistribution argument is easily extended to analyze the differential impact of immigration on various groups in the domestic labor market. Consider, for instance, the case of three factors of production: capital, skilled labor, and unskilled labor. Within the context of such a model, Chiswick (1982) suggests that immigration of either type of labor will decrease the marginal product (and therefore wage) of the type of labor skill possessed by immigrants, and increase the marginal product of both capital and the other type of labor.[3] If immigrants are less skilled than the average U.S. worker, immigration will increase the aggregate earnings of the U.S. population as a whole. But, while the per capita income of skilled workers and capital rise, the average earnings of the low-skilled indigenous workers fall.

The empirical evidence on the impact of immigration on the earnings of native labor is not abundant and what is available provides a wide range of estimated effects. For example, Wise (1974) found that termination of the *bracero* program raised wages by between 12 percent and 67 percent, relative to the levels that would have otherwise prevailed. On the other hand, Barton Smith and Robert Newman (1977) found immigrants to have only a relatively small impact on domestic wages. In 1970, there was an 8 percent difference between the earnings of Mexican-Americans who resided in Houston, where presumably few immigrants were present, and earnings of Mexican-Americans who resided close to the Texas-Mexico border in areas of substantial concentration of immigrants. Their evidence also tends to verify the hypothesis that low-skilled domestic workers are significantly more impacted than high-skilled domestic labor by the presence of low-skill immigrant labor, though again, the suggested impacts appear to be less severe than commonly believed. Grossman (1982) also suggests that immigration has a relatively modest impact on the total earnings of native workers. Assuming that the characteristics of immigrants are similar to those of U.S. legal immigrants employed in 1969, Grossman finds that the effect (with fully flexible wages) of a 10 percent increase in the flow of immigrants to the U.S. is to reduce native wages by roughly 1 percent.

The longer-term consequences of immigration must also take into account the effects arising from the general increase in the amount of labor relative to capital in the economy as well as any change which may occur in the overall composition or mix of labor skills. If immigrants bring less capital with them than is owned by the average member of the indigenous population, the aggregate capital-to-labor ratio will fall and wages decline relative to the rental rate of capital. The rise in the rate of return to capital provides incentives for more domestic investment. The greater the increase in capital stock, the smaller will be the ultimate decline in the wage received by native workers relative to the return on capital.[4] In addition, the increase in the wage differential between low- and high-skilled workers, which results from the inflow of low-skilled migrants, will set in motion another set of adjustments. Members of the indigenous population who are on the margin between choosing to invest in the human capital necessary to become highly skilled workers, and not to engage in such training and thus remain low-skilled workers, are now more likely to become high-skilled workers. Over time, immigrants will also adjust the level of their skills.[5] As natives and immigrants adjust, and their proportions become increasingly more skilled, the wage differential between low- and high-skilled workers will narrow. The more rapid this adjustment process, the more cushioned the impact of immigration on the relative earnings of domestic workers.

In addition to impacting on wages, immigrants may affect domestic employment and labor force participation rates. Widespread disagreement exists concerning these impacts of immigrants on domestic workers. It is likely that immigration's short-run impact on domestic employment will differ from its long-run impact. In many U.S. industries, domestic wages may be inflexible downward in the short run. Consequently, if immigration leads to a situation of excess supply for certain types of labor, those immigrants who do find jobs will do so at the expense of domestic workers. George E. Johnson (1980), around a range of parameters he believes to be most plausible, suggests "a labor market displacement effect that is only around 10%" (p. 335).[6] However, Grossman (1982, p. 601) suggests that this "rigidity of domestic workers' wages is likely to occur only in the immediate short-run" and, in the longer term, all wages are flexible to adjust.[7] Thus, whereas in the short run the adjustment to immigration may be primarily through natives' employment changes, the long-run adjustment is totally through relative price changes.

Market Distortions

Among the many effects allegedly induced when migration occurs in the presence of market distortions, perhaps the most controversial, and currently most debated, are those which concern migration's impact in the presence of an income transfer system. Governments may attempt to redistribute income via a progressive tax and regressive spending structure. Such government taxing and spending policies can create a difference between an individual's net real wage (i.e., actual wage minus any tax payments plus any benefits received that are financed through the general tax system) and his marginal contribution to national product. With a truly effective progressive tax system, the net wage may be expected to exceed the marginal product of labor for the poor and to be less than the marginal product of labor for the rich. Therefore, if immigrants are relatively poor, a progressive tax system tends to induce an adverse impact on the welfare of the original residents.

Although transfer payments are often suggested as a negative offset to any positive effects of immigration, it is not universally accepted that migrants constitute a net burden on the public transfer system. Julian L. Simon (1982) suggests that the difference between other welfare payments to immigrants and to natives is small compared to the difference in Social Security payments and, since the distribution of immigrants when they arrive has more workers and fewer dependents than the distribution of native population, immigrants, on net balance, contribute to natives through the Social Security and support-of-education transfer payments.[8] Simon goes on to argue that migrants contribute to the cost of national defense, reducing the cost to each original resident without reducing the amount of defense provided. Simon concludes that "immigrants have an overall positive effect through these other transfers" (p. 336).

Even if immigrants do have an overall positive effect through the various public transfer systems, this does not necessarily mean that all areas or groups in the United States are positively affected. Immigrants tend to concentrate in specific geographical areas. Large concentrations of immigrants in particular locations could have negative impacts on these locales through various local transfer systems. Of course, if immigrants have an overall positive effect (including Social Security and federal tax payments), the gainers could compensate the losers. However, there is the question as to whether such a compensation actually occurs.

SUMMARY

The welfare implications of international migration have been shown to depend on several factors. Generally, one can assume that the migrants themselves gain by migrating. However, the impacts on the natives in the receiving and sending countries are less clear. The assessment of these impacts will depend on whether one considers the welfare of the respective native population as a whole or particular groups within the population; on the specific characteristics of the migrants (temporary versus permanent and skilled versus unskilled); and on one's judgment of how important is the presence of market distortions and exernalities.

If a substantial number of skilled laborers permanently migrate from Mexico to the United States, this would tend to have a negative impact on those remaining in Mexico. Several reasons are provided above for drawing this conclusion. However, the available evidence does not point to this being the proper characterization of the labor migrating to the U.S. Recent flows of legal migrants have been proportionately less skilled. If we further assume that the average illegal migrant is less skilled than the average legal migrant, and that the number of illegal aliens has increased since the mid-1960s, there would seem to have been a substantial decline in the overall skill level of migrants who entered the U.S. from Mexico. The migration of a less skilled worker results in a smaller reduction to Mexico's domestic output, entails smaller losses due to externalities associated with either the migrant personally, his occupation, or his education, and presents a less serious problem to government efforts to redistribute income. Furthermore, if, as is generally presumed, illegal migration is more temporary in length, the welfare of the migrants should be included in that of the native population remaining in Mexico. This would add to the impression that the welfare of Mexico has been positively affected by the recent migration flows of labor to the U.S.

The immigration of labor into the United States will tend to increase the total income of U.S. residents. However, immigration may also have important redistributional impacts on domestic laborers. The available evidence does not suggest that these impacts are substantial. But one cannot conclude that the impacts are insignificant. Since the migration's overall impact on the U.S. appears to be positive, appropriate compensation measures could be made to maintain the level of welfare of those natives who are adversely affected by the migration. If such compensation is not possible one could conclude that the relative gains of the migration process to the U.S. have declined somewhat in recent years. This is especially true if one puts a particularly large weight on the importance of the redistributional impacts of migration.

Notes

1. If migrants and nonmigrants are endowed with the same capital-to-labor ratio, then, while Mexico's total income is reduced, the average income of the remaining residents is not altered by the migration.

2. The nonmigrant population will become better off if the wage-rental ratio rises (falls) and the emigrants who leave their capital behind have a greater (lower) ratio of capital owned per person than nonemigrants. For instance, when emigrants are capital rich and take their financial claim to their capital with them but leave a sufficient amount of their capital behind to raise the overall capital-labor ratio, the nonmigrant group will become better off (i.e., higher average income) with emigration.

3. The increase in the marginal product of the other type of labor assumes that low- and high-skilled labor are complements in the production process. Evidence on the issue of complementarity vs. substitutability of various types of labor is not abundant; therefore making judgments based on such evidence is somewhat hazardous (see Killingsworth, 1983).

4. Johnson (1980, p. 340) considered the case of large scale immigration of low-skilled workers and concluded that, if capital adjustments are sufficiently large to keep the marginal product of capital constant, the "big gainers,

compared to the no capital adjustment case, are high-skilled workers" whose wages increase 43 percent due to the capital adjustment.

5. The immigrants' adjustment may also involve a transition from the status of temporary to permanent settlement, which in turn may pose some additional difficulties in the United States (see, for example, Piore, 1979).

6. Johnson's evidence also suggests that one has to make very extreme assumptions about demand and supply elasticities (i.e., that the former is very small and the latter very large) in order to obtain a displacement as large as 50 percent.

7. In the short run, when native wages are assumed to be inflexible, Grossman estimates that a "10 percent inflow of immigrants induces only an 8/10 of a percent fall in native employment" (1982, p. 601).

8. Concerning illegal immigrants, North and Houstoun found that 73 percent of illegal aliens had federal income tax withheld and 77 percent paid (but did not collect on) Social Security tax. Moreover, the proportion who use welfare is small. (See North and Houstoun, 1976.)

References

Aitken, Norman D., "The International Flow of Human Capital: Comment," *American Economic Review,* June 1968, 58 (3, Pt. 1). Pp. 539–545.

Berry, R. Albert, and Ronald Soligo, "Some Welfare Aspects of International Migration," *Journal of Political Economy,* September/October 1969, 77 (5). Pp. 778–794.

Bhagwati, Jadish, and Koichi Hamada, "The Brain Drain, International Integration of Markets for Professionals and Unemployment: A Theoretical Analysis," *Journal of Development Economics,* June 1974, 1 (a). Pp. 19–42.

Chiswick, Barry R., "The Impact of Immigration on the Level and Distribution of Economic Well-Being," in *The Gateway: U.S. Immigration Issues and Policies.* Edited by Barry R. Chiswick. Washington, D.C.: American Enterprise Institute, 1982. Pp. 298–313.

Díez-Canedo, Juan, "A Different Perspective on the Mexican Migration to the U.S.," unpublished manuscript, February 1981.

Grossman, Jean Baldwin, "The Substitutability of Natives and Immigrants in Production," *Review of Economics and Statistics,* November 1982, 64, (4). Pp. 596–603.

Grubel, Herbert G., and A. D. Scott, "The International Flow of Human Capital," *American Economic Review,* May 1966, 56 (2). Pp. 268–274.

Hamada, Koichi, "Efficiency, Equality, Income Taxation and the Brain Drain," *Journal of Development Economics,* September 1975, 2 (3). Pp. 281–287.

Interagency Task Force on Immigration Policy, *Staff Report,* Washington, D.C.: U.S. Government Printing Office. 1979.

Johnson, George E., "The Labor Market Effects on Immigration," *Industrial and Labor Relations Review,* April 1980, 33 (3). Pp. 331–341.

Johnson, Harry G., "Some Economic Aspects of Brain Drain," *Pakistan Development Review,* Autumn 1967, 379–409.

Killingsworth, Mark R., "Effects of Immigration into the United States on the U.S. Labor Market: Analytical and Policy Issues," in *U.S. Immigration and Refugee Policy.* Edited by Mary M. Kritz. Lexington: Lexington Books, 1983. Pp. 249–268.

North, David S., and Marion F. Houstoun, *The Characteristics and Role of Illegal Aliens in the U.S. Labor Market: An Exploratory Study.* Washington, D.C.: Linton and Company, 1976.

Piore, Michael J., *Birds of Passage: Migrant Labor and Industrial Societies.* Cambridge: Cambridge University Press, 1979.

Simon, Julian L., "The Overall Effect of Immigrants on Natives' Incomes," in *The Gateway: U.S. Immigration Issues and Policies.* Edited by Barry R. Chiswick. Washington, D.C.: American Enterprise Institute, 1982. Pp. 314–348.

Smith, Barton, and Robert Newman, "Depressed Wages Along the U.S.-Mexico Border: An Empirical Analysis," *Economic Inquiry,* January 1977, 15(1). Pp. 51–66.

Thomas, Brinley, "The International Circulation of Human Capital," *Minerva,* Summer 1965, 5 (4). Pp. 479–506.

Wise, Donald E., "The Effect of the Bracero on Agricultural Production in California," *Economic Inquiry,* 12. Pp. 547–558.

13
Explaining Origin Patterns of Undocumented Migration to South Texas in Recent Years

Richard C. Jones

Introduction

A persistent puzzle runs through a great deal of the literature on Mexican undocumented migration—why do some areas of the country send large numbers of migrants to the U.S., while adjacent areas send relatively few? The question has been raised several times (Cornelius, 1978, p. 21; Roberts, 1980, p. 6), but never answered satisfactorily. Frequently, origin patterns are treated as interesting curiosities with little bearing on impact issues, but in fact migrants from different Mexican states and localities differ significantly in their socioeconomic and demographic status, and thus in their impacts on U.S. destinations as well as on Mexican origins (Jones, 1982, 1983). Furthermore, it is obviously valuable for policy-makers at all levels in the U.S. to know how proposals to curtail this immigration would affect particular sectors and regions of Mexico—that is, if we care at all about future social and economic stability in that country.

A simplistic answer to the puzzle is that undocumented migrants come from the poorer economic strata in relatively backward regions; they have been the population hardest hit by recent economic crises in Mexico. This answer appears on the surface to have some support. During the 1970s and early 1980s, a series of events in Mexico have accelerated the "push" forces at rural origins: leveling off of "Green Revolution" productivity increases (Cross and Sandos, 1981, pp. 62–63); government emphasis on large-scale commercial grain and fiber operations versus small-farm agriculture (Cross and Sandos, pp. 63–73); industrial location policy which has strengthened the position of Mexico City and its satellites vis-à-vis regional cities (Scott, 1982, pp. 107–110); the focus on petroleum exploitation at the (frequent) expense of peasant agriculture; and four devaluations of the peso between 1976 and 1982. Studies by Frisbee (1975) and Jenkins (1977),

203

furthermore, suggest that these "push" factors, measured in terms of agricultural wages and productivity in Mexico, clearly outweighed "pull" factors in the U.S. as determinants of Mexican undocumented flows to this country in the early 1970s. Finally, recent studies suggest—in line with theoretical expectations (Lee, 1966)—that in response to such "push" forces, migrants have indeed been negatively selected at the origin. Both Cornelius (1978, p. 20) and Roberts (1980, p. 6) note that migrants tend to come from the lower half of the income distribution in their communities, though they are not at the bottom. Various village studies, by their very selection of sites (Las Animas, Zacatecas: Mines and de Janvry, 1982; Acuitzio del Canje, Michoacan: Wiest, 1979; Villa Guerrero, Jalisco: Shadow, 1979; and Los Altos, Jalisco: Cornelius, 1976), focus on more isolated, backward areas of the country and of their respective states; thus, one is left with the strong inference that it is the *less-developed* parts of a state that send migrants to the U.S.

In this study, it will be shown that the aforementioned negative-selectivity argument does not hold: i.e., the *municipios* which sent undocumented migrants to South Texas in the late 1970s tended to be of above average socioeconomic status in their respective states and overall. Nevertheless, a two-step selectivity process is evident: (1) Historic economic forces have promoted undocumented migration to South Texas from traditional primary production subregions of north-eastern Mexico; these subregions have higher-than-average income and urbanization levels owing to their former importance, but have declined in recent decades. (2) Among the *municipios* in these subregions, propensity to migrate to the U.S. is indeed related to lower income and lower urbanization levels. This second step implies that the factors which compel emigration from certain Mexican subregions and not others are different from the factors which determine the magnitude of migration from those subregions. These findings are explained in detail below, and implications for U.S. policy are drawn.

Relative Characteristics of Sending Municipios

Based on the relevant literature, we would expect Mexican undocumenteds to originate in relatively poorer, less-dynamic areas of their respective states. Regarding the South Texas undocumented migration stream, these would be the less-progressive areas of such states as Guanajuato, Coahuila, San Luis Potosi, Nuevo Leon, Zacatecas, and Tamaulipas, which together account for 76.9 percent of the total undocumenteds to South Texas according to INS records of deportable aliens between 1976 and 1981 (Table 1).

INS data (I-213 forms) indicate that only 37 *origin municipios* (most recent residence in Mexico) in the above states accounted for 50.8 percent of the total apprehensions of Mexicans in the San Antonio

TABLE 1

Labor Migrants from Mexico to the United States

Year	Immigrants With Occupation		Temporary Workers Admitted		Total Workers		
	Total	Skilled	Total[1]	Skilled[2]	Total	Skilled	Percent Skilled
1978	38,491	2,244	2,164	975	40,655	3,219	7.9
1977	18,137	1,193	1,881	904	20,018	2,097	10.5
1976	21,624	1,087	1,632	871	23,256	1,958	8.4
1975	21,338	1,141	2,216	882	23,554	2,023	8.6
1974	23,222	818	2,666	1,297	25,888	2,115	8.2
1973	22,564	1,060	2,230	1,037	24,794	2,097	8.5
1972	20,682	1,048	2,248	1,386	22,930	2,434	10.6
1971	15,288	858	1,546	1,253	16,834	2,111	12.5
1970	12,238	679	1,433	1,167	13,671	1,846	13.5
1969	12,893	711	1,309	1,080	14,202	1,791	12.6
1968	13,844	957	1,474	1,298	15,318	2,255	14.7
1967	12,334	1,043	1,250[3]	1,071	13,584	2,114	15.6
1966	9,707	855	955[3]	835	10,662	1,690	15.9

Source: Immigration and Naturalization Service, Annual Report, various years.

Notes: [1]Temporary workers admitted under section 101(a)(15)(H), Immigration and Nationality Act, in class H(i) and H(ii).

[2]Class H(i), which is workers of distinguished merit and ability.

[3]Excludes Mexican farm laborers admitted under class H(ii).

District over the period 1976–1981. Over half of these (19) were in Coahuila and Guanajuato (Table 2). The "flow densities" are highly variable among these *municipios.* High flow densities are associated with both border and interior *municipios,* and every state exhibits at least one *municipio* in the highest category. High densities are associated both with urban and with rural *municipios.* In summary, no clear differentiation by state, urbanization level, or part of Mexico appears in Table 2.

Having identified these 37 *municipios* (identified hereafter as "sending *municipios*"), the question is this: how do they differ in socioeconomic status from the averages for their respective states? Utilizing available

TABLE 2

Principal Municipios of Origin ("Sending Municipios") of Undocumented
Migrants to South Texas, 1976–1981[a]

Municipio and State		Number of Undocumenteds	Flow Density: # of Sample undocumenteds per 100,000 population, 1970[b]	
Acuña	COA	22	67.69	
San Juan de Sabinas	COA	25	66.01	
Rio Grande	ZAC	22	62.15	
Piedras Negras	COA	29	62.10	
Apaseo el Grande	GTO	12	56.35	
Mier y Noriega	NL	3	40.83	HIGH
Allende	GTO	25	38.58	FLOW
Monteczuma	SLP	5	34.13	DENSITY
Dolores Hidalgo	GTO	9	32.70	(>20)
Matehuala	SLP	14	28.43	
Nuevo Laredo	TAM	42	27.78	
Moroleon	GTO	9	26.60	
San Felipe	GTO	15	26.22	
Juventino Rosas	GTO	8	25.18	
Apaseo el Alto	GTO	13	21.35	
Sabinas	COA	5	17.13	

(continued)

TABLE 2   (continued)

Municipio and State		Number of Undocumenteds	Flow Density: # of Sample undocumenteds per 100,000 population, 1970[b]	
Rio Verde	ZAC	9	15.76	
Guanajuato	GTO	10	15.31	MEDIUM
Cerritos	SLP	3	15.10	FLOW
Ojo Caliente	ZAC	3	14.71	DENSITY
San Pedro	COA	9	12.36	(10-20)
Jalpa	ZAC	3	12.18	
Dr. Arroyo	NL	5	11.66	
Valparaiso	ZAC	5	11.37	
San Luis Potosi	SLP	27	10.08	
Torreon	COA	19	7.58	
Zacatecas	CAZ	4	6.86	
Monterrey (5 mcpos.)	NL	83	6.84	
Musquiz	COA	3	6.54	
Celaya	GTO	9	6.11	LOW FLOW
Monclova	COA	5	6.11	DENSITY
Valle de Santiago	GTO	4	5.73	(<10)
Rio Bravo	TAM	4	5.60	
Matamoros	TAM	9	4.83	
Reynosa	TAM	7	4.64	

(continued)

TABLE 2   (continued)

Municipio and State		Number of Undocumenteds	Flow Density: # of Sample undocumenteds per 100,000 population, 1970[b]
Fresnillo	ZAC	4	3.86
Leon	GTO	10	2.78
TOTALS		508	–

[a]April of each year. Only those 37 municipios with ≥3 undocumenteds in sample are included in the table.

[b]Total N=1000.

Source: I-213 forms from INS District Office, San Antonio.

indices from the 1970 Mexican Census, we can outline certain theoretical expectations as follows:

1. The sending *municipios* will be below average in median income and in farm income.
2. The sending *municipios* will have an above average percentage of their population living in urban areas.
3. The sending *municipios* will exhibit above average personal income inequality.
4. The sending *municipios* will exhibit lower rates of lifetime immigration, i.e., a smaller proportion of their populations born out-of-state.

Thus, the comparisons are between the (1970) average characteristics of a state's sending *municipios* and the (1970) average characteristics for the state overall. So that particular *municipios* are not over- or under-represented in the sending *municipio* averages, characteristics of each *municipio* are weighted by that *municipio's* proportion of undocumented migrants to South Texas. This ensures, for example, that a very populous *municipio* such as Leon, Guanajuato, which had a very few undocumented migrants in proportion to its size, is not over-represented when the averages are calculated.

The results of this exercise are surprising (Tables 3 and 4). In general, the sending *municipios* exhibit higher incomes, more urbanized populations, less income inequality, and greater in-migration rates—just the reverse of expectations. Only in Guanajuato are the sending *municipios* consistently of lower status; and in Zacatecas, the income and agricultural variables (but not urbanization) are approximately equal between sending *municipios* and the state as a whole. The ratios between the sending *municipios* and the state are particularly high for San Luis Potosi and Tamaulipas (Table 4), due to the fact that undocumenteds from these states come disproportionately from the cities of San Luis Potosi, Matamoros, Reynosa, and Nuevo Laredo. On the other hand, in Guanajuato relatively few migrants come from cities such as Leon, Celaya, or Irapuato; thus, the ratios are low. In summary, undocumented migrants appear to be positively selected at the origin, not negatively selected.

This conclusion is based on at least three assumptions. First, we assume the sending *municipios* are indeed the true ones, instead of simply nearby urban *municipios* cited by the undocumenteds (to INS officials) because they would be more familiar or higher-status. There is little indication of any systematic bias in this regard, with the exception of (probably) slightly inflated figures for border cities in Tamaulipas and Coahuila (see below). Second, we assume that the averages we have been comparing really do reflect differences between undocumented migrant populations and overall populations in a state. Is it possible, for example, that the higher-status *municipios* also have the most income inequality such that the poorest populations are at a greater disadvantage vis-à-vis the wealthiest, thus stimulating their migration? If so, migrant characteristics would not be reflected by *municipio* averages. This scenario has little support either, because in our *municipio* data, income inequality is poorly (and negatively) related to median income ($r_s = 0.328$). There is no reason to expect that averages by type of *municipio* are not proportional to average differences between undocumented and total populations of the respective states. Third, we assume that the migration process is selecting from among migrants with different characteristics, rather than the migration process determining those characteristics; i.e., is it possible that U.S. migration improves economic status? There is some support for this argument in that better-off *municipios* are that way partly because of prior migration to the U.S. This begs the question, however, because our data reflect migration decisions made in 1976–1981 versus socio-economic characteristics in 1970; the latter decisions could not impact the *municipios* in 1970, even though the argument might be valid for 1980 *municipio* characteristics (not yet available from the Mexican Census).

TABLE 3

A Comparison of Socioeconomic Characteristics Between Sending Municipios and

Overall, by State (1970 Mexican Census Data)

State	(1) Median Income, in Pesos/Month		(2) % of Agric. Labor Force Earning < 200 pesos/mo.		(3) % of Labor Force in Agriculture[a]		(4) % of Population Living in Places of ≥10,000[b]		(5) Income Inequality = $(Q_3-Q_1)/Q_2$[b]		(6) % of Population Born Out-of-State	
	Sending Muni-cipios	State as a Whole	Sending Muni-cipios	State as a Whole	Sending Muni-cipios	State as a Whole	Sending Muni-cipios	State as a Whole	Sending Muni-cipios	State as a Whole	Sending Muni-cipios	State as a Whole
Guanajuato	361	418	42.1	35.6	53.5	45.0	35.0	42.5	1.216	1.440	3.59	5.57
Coahuila	801	682	11.5	15.0	18.4	28.6	85.0	65.3	1.084	1.160	12.72	12.33
San Luis Potosi	510	353	36.8	46.9	30.4	51.0	61.4	30.1	1.269	1.601	7.94	6.52
Nuevo Leon	916	871	12.1	24.5	9.8	15.6	74.2	62.6	0.943	1.042	28.84	23.60
Zacatecas	336	329	46.8	43.8	59.4	61.3	30.3	15.9	1.500	1.386	3.75	4.59
Tamaulipas	871	495	9.7	21.0	15.6	31.3	91.2	62.4	1.196	1.022	30.56	21.87
All 6 states	639	560	28.4	33.6	23.1	35.9	63.0	43.5	1.163	1.368	14.01	12.65

(continued)

TABLE 3   (continued)

[a]Percentage of labor force reporting income which was engaged in agriculture.

[b]The quartile deviation of income divided by the median income (in pesos per month). Calculated from tabular data in Mexican Census.

Source: Mexican Census, 1970.

TABLE 4

Ratio Between Socioeconomic Status of Sending <u>Municipios</u> vs. State as a Whole

		Characteristic[a]				
	(1)	(2)	(3)	(4)	(5)	(6)
State	Median Income	% of Agric. Labor Force Earning $\geq$ 200 pesos/month	% of Labor Force in Non-Agricultural Activities	Urban-ization	Income Equality	% Born Out-of-State
Guanajuato	0.86	0.90	0.85	0.82	1.19	0.64
Coahuila	1.17	1.04	1.14	1.30	1.08	1.03
San Luis Potosi	1.44	1.19	1.42	2.04	1.27	1.22
Nuevo Leon	1.05	1.16	1.07	1.19	1.11	1.22
Zacatecas	1.02	0.95	1.05	1.91	0.93	0.82
Tamaulipas	1.76	1.14	1.23	1.46	0.85	1.40
All 6 states	1.14	1.08	1.20	1.45	1.18	1.11

[a]Ratios of > 1.0 indicate that sending <u>municipios</u> are of higher status on the characteristic than the state as a whole; of < 1.0, that sending <u>municipios</u> are of lower status. Variables 2, 3, and 5 are redefined so that they reflect status directly instead of inversely, as in Table 2.

<u>Source</u>: Calculations by author from Table 3.

Historical Regional Forces and Undocumented Migration

How can this positive selectivity at the *municipio* level be explained? One basic characteristic of most of these *municipios*, which stands out when they are mapped (Figure 1), is that they are in zones of traditional primary production. The zones were once prosperous, even leading the nation in the production of particular raw materials, but in recent decades they have declined. Today, they are above-average economically owing to their past prominence, yet they suffer from unemployment and wage depression owing to recent setbacks, compelling emigration to the U.S. These zones are discussed in turn, and shown on Figure 2. The discussion draws heavily from West and Augelli (1976, Chapter 11).

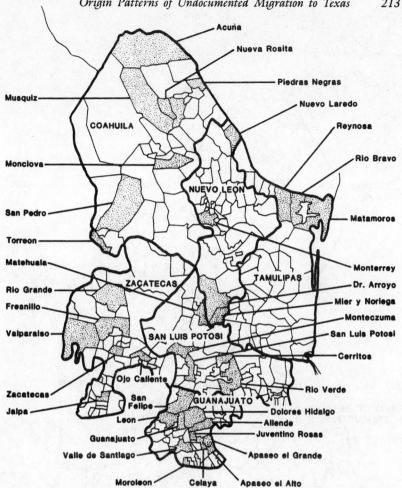

FIGURE 1.   <u>Municipios</u> with ≥3 Undocumented Migrants to South Texas, 1976 – 81
(INS files)

Municipios con ≥3 Emigrantes Indocumentados al Sur de Texas, 1976 – 81
(archivos de INS)

1. The Zone of Metals Production includes parts of the states of Zacatecas, San Luis Potosi, and Guanajuato. In the 1880s, this zone produced 90 percent of Mexico's mineral exports in the form of silver and gold; and after 1900, lead and zinc were mined intensively, peaking around 1940. Since World War II, foreign competition, lowered prices, and depleted mines have brought a continuous decline.

214

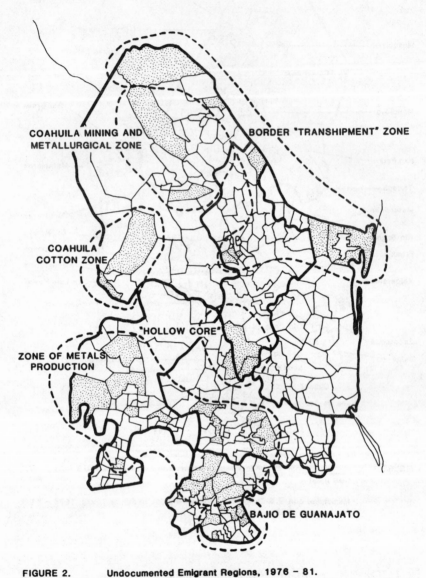

FIGURE 2.   Undocumented Emigrant Regions, 1976 – 81.

               Regiones de Origen, Emigracion Indocumentada, 1976 – 81.

2. *The Bajio de Guanajuato,* once the breadbasket of Mexico, has in recent years been faced with competition from wheat produced on huge plots in the northern oases and beset with rural population pressure. In addition, mechanization and land consolidation have put many small farmers off their land. The Bajio illustrates positive selectivity even though the major zone of emigration in Guanajuato, the north, does not.

3. *The Coahuila Cotton Zone,* the first irrigated cotton project of its size in Mexico, and one of the first collective *ejidos,* initiated this important domestic and export crop in Mexico in the 1930s. Cities such as Torreon and Gomez Palacio trace their growth to this period. In recent decades, excessive pumping of irrigation water, competition from irrigated projects elsewhere, and worldwide depression of cotton prices have led to a decline of production and employment in the region.

4. *The Coahuila Mining and Metallurgical Zone* owes its existence to two factors: local deposits of metallurgical coal, and proximity to the major steel centers of the north—especially Monclova, a planned iron and steel plant built in 1944, which is Mexico's largest. This zone has continued to grow, but with the Las Truchas plant (begun in 1971 in coastal Michoacan and utilizing local iron ore and coal from Colombia), competition has been stiffer. Furthermore, the urban centers grew faster than the steel/coal industries could absorb the new labor force. As a result, unemployment and emigration have occurred.

5. *The "Hollow Core"* is an exception to the previous four zones, in that it was not a traditionally dynamic area. Instead, emigration from here reflects extreme poverty, proximity to the U.S., and a tradition of migration to Monterrey as well as to the U.S.

6. *The Border "Transshipment" Zone* is also an exception, even though its easternmost end (Matamoros-Reynosa) is an important cotton zone that has stagnated. Emigration from this zone principally reflects the inability of border cities to absorb the migrants who have come there in anticipation of jobs in industry, trade, and transportation; as well as kinship networks between border Mexico and South Texas which have strengthened since the Revolution.

These observations remain impressionistic, but they illustrate how the forces influencing migration selectivity do not operate instantaneously, but over years and decades. The map also shows broad areas where emigration to the U.S. is minimal. Some of these areas—for example, southern Coahuila, northern Nuevo Leon, northeastern Zacatecas, central-western San Luis Potosi—are sparsely settled and too poor to send many migrants; others (e.g., southern Tamaulipas) have more dynamic commercial economies, with adequate jobs for their populaces.

Migrant Flow Densities and Their Determinants

A question unanswered in the preceding analysis is as follows: among the *municipios* sending undocumenteds to South Texas in the late 1970s, what factors operated to determine the magnitude of flows? Does the flow density vary according to the economic characteristics discussed earlier and, if so, how does it vary? This test makes use of the six characteristics discussed in Tables 3 and 4, measured for each of the sending *municipios*, plus distance, defined as mileage from the center of the *municipio* to the nearest point on the Texas border. The number of cases in this test is 32 instead of 37; five *municipios* with unusually large flow densities (the first five in Table 2) are eliminated from the analysis. The reason for this is that their magnitudes are large enough to suggest bias in the data—i.e, inflated values for the three Coahuila border *municipios* due to their misspecification as origins by some migrants; and the probability that Apaseo el Grande (GTO) and Rio Grande (ZAC) are high owing to INS raids on particular sites which captured members of the same family and village. Simple and multiple linear correlation is performed for the seven independent variables versus the dependent variable (flow density) for the 32 *municipios*.

The results are again surprising (Table 5), in that the lower status *municipios* among the 32 send migrants at a higher rate. Income (two measures) is the strongest selective force in both the simple and multiple correlation results. Thus, negative selectivity does appear when we focus only upon these relatively high-status sending *municipios*. A final figure (Figure 3) shows that the highest flow densities are associated with interior states and *municipios*, which have lower socioeconomic status; while the lowest figures are associated with border and border-state *municipios*, which are much better off.

Conclusions and Implications

As stated in the introduction, these results suggest a two-step selectivity process. The first step is positive, in that *municipios* with a history of dynamism but recent stagnation send undocumented migrants to the U.S. These *municipios* are relatively developed but stagnant. The second step in the selectivity process is negative; i.e., among the positively selected sending *municipios*, the emigration rate (flow density) to the U.S. is an inverse function of socioeconomic status. Thus, there is initially a threshold for migration, for which selection is positive; but once the decision to migrate is made, the selection process favors the less well-off subareas among these.

Thus, the factors which compel undocumented migration to the U.S. from Mexico—historical forces which affect relatively well-off zones—may differ from those which determine the relative magnitudes of migration among *municipios* of the sending zones.

TABLE 5

Correlation Analysis: Undocumented Flow Density

vs. Seven Characteristics for 32 Mexican <u>Municipios</u>, 1970s [a]

Characteristic (1970)	Simple r$_p$ with Flow Density	Beta Coefficient in Multiple Regression
Median income	−0.511	−0.713
% of agricultural labor force earning <200 pesos/mo.	0.560	0.569
% of labor force in agriculture	0.431	−0.286
% of population living in places of ≥10,000	−0.389	0.238
Income inequality	0.248	−0.072
% of population born out-of-state	−0.345	−0.073
Distance to U.S. border	0.214	−0.419

[a]Multiple R of flow density <u>vs.</u> all six independent variables = 0.621 (R^2 = 0.386)

Source: Calculations of author.

There are several implications to be drawn from these results. This paper offers additional proof for the argument that the benefits from undocumented migration do not reach the poorest regions and sub-populations in Mexico. Like many government programs, these benefits do not reach the lowest-status persons in the society. In addition, programs to induce economic development in the poorest parts of Mexico may actually accelerate undocumented migration, in that these programs will give potential migrants the desire and the means to travel to the U.S. Finally, the positively selected nature of undocumented migrants suggests that the streams may be more discretionary than previously thought. That is, migrants are chiefly moving to opportunities in the U.S. rather than away from problems in Mexico. All in all, the undocumented population of the future should be relatively high-status, ambitious, and careful about job pathways. The

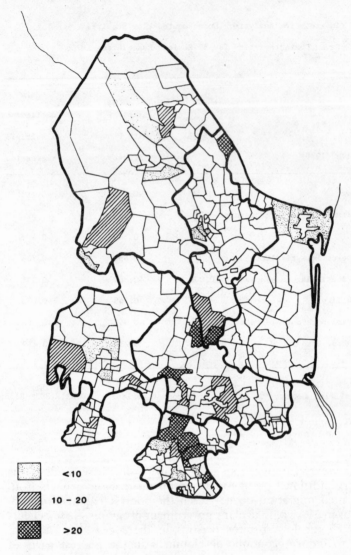

	< 10
	10 – 20
	> 20

FIGURE 3.   Flow Density of Undocumented Migration to South Texas, 1976 – 81, in Sample Respondents per 100,000 population of <u>municipio</u> (only <u>municipios</u> with ≥3 migrants in INS Sample)

Flujos de Emigracion Indocumentada al Sur de Texas, 1976 – 81: Numero de Respondentes por 100,000 de la poblacion del municipio (considera solamente los municipios con ≥3 emigrantes en la muestra INS)

impacts of such migrants will doubtless be greater than those of the traditional rural migrant of the past.

References

Cornelius, Wayne A. *Mexican Migration to the United States: The View from Rural Sending Communities* (Cambridge, Mass.: Center for International Studies). 1976.

Cornelius, Wayne A. *Mexican Migration to the United States: Causes, Consequences, and U.S. Responses* (Cambridge, Mass.: Center for International Studies). 1978.

Cross, Harry E., and James A. Sandos. *Across the Border: Rural Development in Mexico and Recent Migration to the United States* (Berkeley: Institute of Governmental Studies, University of California, Berkeley). 1981.

Frisbee, Parker. "Illegal Migration from Mexico to the United States: A Longitudinal Analysis," *International Migration Review*, Vol. 9, pp. 3–13. 1975.

Jenkins, J. Craig. "Push/Pull in Recent Mexican Migration to the U.S.," *International Migration Review*, Vol. 11, pp. 178–189. 1977.

Jones, Richard C. "Undocumented Migration from Mexico: Some Geographical Questions," *Annals, Association of American Geographers*, Vol. 72, pp. 77–87. 1982.

Jones, Richard C. "Changing Patterns of Undocumented Mexican Migration to South Texas," submitted to *Social Science Quarterly*. 1983.

Lee, Everett S. "A Theory of Migration," *Demography*, Vol. 3, pp. 47–57. 1966.

Mines, Richard, and Alain de Janvry. "Migration to the United States and Mexican Rural Development: A Case Study," *American Journal of Agricultural Economics*, Vol. 64, pp. 444–454. 1982.

Roberts, Kenneth D. *Agrarian Structure and Labor Migration in Rural Mexico: The Case of Circular Migration of Undocumented Workers to the U.S.* (Austin: The Institute of Latin American Studies, The University of Texas at Austin). 1980.

Scott, Ian. *Urban and Spatial Development in Mexico* (Baltimore: Johns Hopkins University Press, for the World Bank). 1982.

Shadow, Robert D. "Differential Out-Migration: A Comparison of Internal and International Migration from Villa Guerrero, Jalisco (Mexico)," in Fernando Camara and Robert V. Kemper, eds., *Migration Across Frontiers: Mexico and the United States* (Albany: State University of New York at Albany, Institute for Mexoamerican Studies), pp. 67–83. 1979.

West, Robert C., and John P. Augelli. *Middle America: Its Lands and Peoples* (Englewood Cliffs, N.J.: Prentice-Hall). 1976.

Wiest, Raymond E. "Implications of International Labor Migration for Mexican Rural Development," in Camara and Kemper, eds., op. cit., pp. 85–97. 1979.

14
Industrialization, the Flow of Technology, and Economic Solvency and Independence

Mariano Bauer

Introduction

On the basis of the concept of the added value that processing confers to raw materials, one of the policies accepted as leading to prosperity and economic solvency for a country is that of industrialization.

The value-added road leads—in principle—to the substitution of imports and eventually to the competitive export of manufactured products. However, expectations of prosperity and economic solvency offered by the value-added road fail if it is necessary to import technology at every stage of production, as is the case in most of the developing countries. In the historical context of the industrial development of these countries, it is clear that the lack of an appropriate scientific and technological infrastructure has systematically deepened economic dependency and subordination, preventing the attainment of a reasonable interdependency with the developed countries.

In effect, the increasingly evident failure of economic expectations is due in great measure to not having considered, along with the industrialization process, a development of the nation's scientific and technological capabilities that permits innovations in the technologies acquired as well as participation in the development of new finished products and future technologies. To continue down this road leads to a mirage of modernization, since the entire process implies a deficit which requires the subsidizing of cheap labor and, ergo, low standards of living for most of the population.

For this reason the developing country must cease considering basic and applied research and technological development as luxuries, and recognize them instead as essential and basic parts of the development project.

We present below some data on the industrial development of Mexico and its scientific and technological infrastructure. The information does not purport to be exhaustive, but simply indicative of the problems which the country faces. Finally, we suggest some proposals which could help developing countries avoid—or, rather, escape from—what we have termed the pitfall of the value-added road.

A Bird's Eye View

The development of Mexico between 1975 and 1981 was remarkable, reaching one of the highest growth rates in the world—between 7 percent and 9 percent annually. The oil boom, however, gave rise to an unbalanced growth, distorting the industrial structure and the balance of payments. The country's debt grew without limitation as we counted on the price of petroleum to continue increasing. The importation of nondurable and capital goods was diversified, and the contracting of services abroad increased unnecessarily.

The drop in oil prices, and in the prices of other products exported by Mexico due to the worldwide economic recession, brought about a radical change in the country's situation, leaving it in the critical state in which it now finds itself. The growth rate for 1982 was −1.1 percent, and for 1983 it will surely be negative again.

With regard to the transfer of technology, we note the following data.[1] In 1979, there were 8,257 transfer contracts registered, of which 23 percent were between Mexican companies, although this does not imply that this technology was developed locally. Fifty-two percent of these contracts were with the United States, while the remaining 25 percent were with other countries. Of the 4,305 technology transfer contracts with the United States, 52 percent were in alleged priority areas for the nation. From this same source, we have the following: 6,293 companies in Mexico acquired diverse technologies in 1981. Among these companies—of which 53.2 percent are in high priority areas—73.5 percent do not carry out technological developments.

As another indicator of Mexico's high degree of technological dependency we have the fact that her ratio of adaptation-and-development expenditures to purchase-of-technology expenditures is 0.2, whereas in advanced countries this ratio exceeds multiples of 10. Twelve thousand technology transfer agreements were registered in 1982, but only 3,000 national patents were issued.

The lack of a scientific and technological infrastructure in Mexican industry is evident when one analyzes the two indicators that determine the state of research and development in a country: human and financial resources.

In Mexico there are 59 organizations that carry out research and development, but only half of these have any direct bearing on industry. Eighty percent of the resources earmarked for science and technology may be found in the Mexico City metropolitan area, and 44 percent of the total investment is concentrated in four places (IMP, INEN, PEMEX and UNAM). As far as human resources are concerned, this represents only 2.4 persons per 10,000 involved in research as assistants, students, or researchers. In Argentina this figure is 5.6; in the United States, 26.0, and in the Soviet Union, 53.0.

With respect to financial resources, at present only 0.5 percent of the GNP goes to research and development. In highly developed industrial countries, this value is between 1.8 and 2 percent.

Moreover, the administration of these resources in Mexico in 1976 assigned 67.4 percent of their total expenditures to salaries, 13.5 percent to scientific equipment and operating materials and 19 percent to the lease of space and the purchase of buildings and land.[2] In any case, the current devaluation will serve to accentuate the disparity between what goes to salaries and what is allocated for operating materials and equipment, thus slowing many research projects.

The best example of the problematical situation exposed here may be the petrochemical industry. Certainly, hydrocarbons constitute one of the main resources and wealth of the nation. The use of a part of these resources (9 percent of the total extracted in 1982) as a source of feedstock for the chemical industry produces the highest dividends, thanks to value added, and thus has been intensified in the last few years. Between 1977 and 1981, refining capacity was increased by 57 percent and basic petrochemical production by 132 percent. There are 84 basic petrochemical plants in operation, producing 41 different products. In 1982, 400 plants produced 600 products and employed 90,000 workers.[3]

Eighty-five percent of the domestic demands are satisfied, but the remaining 15 percent represents a deficiency not only quantitative but also qualitative (some products are not produced), creating bottlenecks at different stages. In addition, most of the 41 basic petrochemical products available, for the most part, pose serious marketing problems, since the industrial system is not prepared to continue the chain of chemical processing required to reach the final consumption stage. Whenever the final stage is achieved, it is based on imported processes, technology and capital goods.

It would be interesting to evaluate the expenditure along these lines imposed by the necessity of using products at the initial stage of the value-added route.

In the hydrocarbon area, the bulk of research and development is represented by the Instituto Mexicano del Petroleo, where industrial processes now in use and under license in foreign nations, have, in fact, been developed. The IMP's present budget, however, reaches only six billion, five hundred and thirty million pesos (US$43.5 million), of which only about 3.5 percent, or US$1.5 million, is allocated for basic process research. This can be compared to the estimated $14 billion income from oil sales and the relative amounts invested in research and development in the United States, as follows: 0.4 percent of gross sales, or 6.6 percent of gross income in the oil industry, and 2.4 percent of gross sales, or 44.6 percent of gross income in the chemical (excluding pharmaceutical) industry.[4]

The road looks desolate as regards getting out of the trap in which we are stuck as a consequence of a development pattern in which our industrial capacity increased 15 percent annually, but expenditures for the acquisition of technology were three times as great.

How to Get Out of the Trap

The fundamental requirement for not getting any further into the trap, and for eventually getting out of it, is not more outside aid, but a change in internal economic policy, although more outside aid could be very helpful. Essentially, the country must decide to support, firmly and continuously, both basic and technological research directed toward participation in the discovery and development of future technologies. It must encourage the creation of an innovative capacity for the use of present technology and the design of new finished products.

This surely requires greater resources than have been invested up to now. It should be mentioned that, because of a shortage of highly qualified personnel, the investments could not be large enough to seriously threaten the budgets assigned to the country's short-range problems. But to reduce such budgets, as is presently being done under the pretext of responding to economic crisis, would be penny-wise and pound-foolish. Scientific and technical progress is slow, and requires continuity, without which knowledge rapidly dissolves, and restoration is much more expensive than the original saving.

Let us point out that the large investment made in the education of a scientist or a highly qualified technician is lost if he or she, discouraged, decides to leave the country or to go into a different field.

Since we have abundant quantities of hydrocarbons, we suggest that an example of new policy might be the establishment of a petrochemical development plan, providing the mechanisms required to crystallize an intensive, continuous, coordinated and supervised effort based on a systematic investment commensurate with the available oil resources in this country. Such an integrated plan must take into consideration industry-oriented research and development, basic scientific research, and the education of personnel.

Some of the advantages of an integrated plan operating together with a preestablished, permanent, and aggregate allocation of resources are the following:

• The continuity of projects is guaranteed.

- Pressure to manage annual budgets, regardless of circumstances, is eliminated. This is a situation which leads to distortion and to unnecessary expenditures.
- The economic capacity to fund costly stages of development is created (for example, prototypes and pilot plants).
- Human resources would be directed toward technical and scientific areas which have recently been weakened.

We therefore propose that the country set aside a certain fixed percentage of its foreign (oil) income to create a Permanent Petrochemical Development Fund.

It is clear that this concept of an integrated plan is applicable to other areas and should be implemented as soon as possible.

Finally, we turn to the activities which a country such as the United States could undertake in order to support the real modernization of a country on the road to industrialization. We find ample and interesting suggestions in a study prepared by the National Research Council at the request of the State Department and entitled, "U.S. Science and Technology for Development: A Contribution to the 1979 U.N. Conference." Since this document deals with a number of countries in different stages of development, some of its proposals do not apply to Mexico and others would not be acceptable. In general, while its orientation is adequate, its proposals lack the desired scope and depth, however.

Limiting ourselves to the problem of industrialization in a country such as Mexico, the specialists underscore two principal points for U.S. initiatives:

1. encouraging the development of a creative capacity and the use of technology by the PVD (*país en vías de desarrollo,* or developing country)
2. easing access to the technology of industrialized countries.

Much American technology requires no right-to-use payment, while a great part of technology developed with governmental assistance is normally in the public domain. Accordingly, it is suggested that an effort be made to disseminate this information and to seek help from universities, from government and private laboratories, and from industry, in the adaptation and transfer of specific technologies. The specialists further propose actions to increase the capacity of the PVD to choose a suitable technology and even, in some cases, to negotiate contracts where payments are, in fact, required. At no time, the authors state, does the document go as far as the overall negotiations proposed by the group of 77.

The first point, which seems to lead in the most interesting direction for us, deals, however, with the concept of "appropriate technology" for a PVD. This implies that Border Technologies are not considered. It is further alleged that, considering that almost all innovations are generated in developed countries, these developments may not be technologically or economically adequate for a developing country.

To accept our present situation as irremediable would be equivalent to resignation to backwardness, with evident industrial and economic disadvantages.

The National Research Council document surely is a source of ideas and projects which, with adequate modifications, could prove of great help to a developing country in reaching its legitimate goals.

SUMMARY

The industrialization of an underdeveloped country as a means to prosperity and economic independence is based on the concept that processing adds value to raw materials. The value-added road leads— in principle—to the substitution of imports and, eventually, to the competitive exportation of finished products. It is only then that the industrialization process will lead to a reasonable economic interdependency with the developed countries. Otherwise, it serves only to accentuate existing dependency and subordination. In order to avoid such a pitfall, the developing country must urgently plan for investment in its scientific and technological infrastructure in accordance with the magnitude of the industrial investments already made. For this purpose it must also seek the support of the developed countries, including the United States. In this paper we present several alternative mechanisms and possibilities for cooperation.

Notes

1. "Annuario Estadístico: Inversiones Extranjeras y Transferencia de Tecnología." SEPAFIN 1981. ("Statistical Yearbook: Foreign Investment and Technology Transfer.")

2. "Política Nacional de Ciencia y Tecnología," 1976. ("National Science and Technology Policy.")

3. "ENERGETICOS," August 1982.

4. International Business Week, July 1982.

15
Hazardous and Toxic Substances as a Part Of United States–Mexico Relations

Howard G. Applegate
C. Richard Bath

Introduction

Environmental issues have often played significant roles in United States–Mexico relations. Perhaps the most celebrated case is the salinity of the Colorado River, but there are a host of other issues involving environmental questions that have plagued relations between the two countries over the years.[1] An environmental issue of more recent origin is the question of hazardous and toxic substances in relations between Mexico and the United States. There can be little question that these substances will have a decided impact on economic relations between the two countries. The incredible growth of the chemical industry in the last 50 years has generated acute anxiety throughout the world about the consequences of the use of hazardous and toxic substances.[2] There is a genuine problem at the outset and that is the definition of a hazardous and toxic substance. Such a definition is not easy to determine. It would appear that those who are concerned with these substances in international relations base their definition on whether such a substance has been declared by a government agency to be, indeed, hazardous. For example, Francine Schulberg defines a hazardous product "as a product that is prohibited for sale in the United States or whose sale is highly restricted, as with prescription drugs or restricted-use pesticides. The prohibition or restriction could result because the product has not met some statutory requirement or because of an affirmative finding by a regulatory agency that the product poses dangers to health, safety, or the environment."[3] Specifically excluded are narcotics, radiological or biological products, firearms, or tobacco. Such a definition relates primarily to export policy for the United States and may be unduly restrictive for the purposes of this paper. An additional problem, as will be seen shortly,

226

is that using a governmental agency classification under the current regulatory climate may disguise truly harmful products. The Reagan administration does not appear to be in any haste to classify or test the potential hazards of such materials.[4] First, a look at the United States regulatory framework with some discussion of the international policy implications will be presented. Then a shorter review of Mexico's regulatory framework will be followed by a discussion of some of the critical issues involving hazardous and toxic substances in U.S.-Mexico relations.

Regulation of Hazardous and Toxic Substances in the United States

The primary focus of this review of United States regulatory efforts for hazardous and toxic substances will be on export policy; that is, on regulatory efforts to control the export of these materials to other nations. However, domestic policy cannot be ignored, mainly because of the United States–Mexico border. The border brings into play domestic policy, as in state regulatory efforts by Texas, Arizona, New Mexico, and California, and these have a decided impact on United States–Mexico relations.

There are seven major laws which affect export of hazardous materials.[5] Perhaps most important for U.S.-Mexico relations is the Federal Insecticide, Fungicide, and Rodenticide Act (FIFRA). FIFRA requires the Environmental Protection Agency (EPA) to oversee a registration system for domestically produced pesticides. Under 1978 amendments to FIFRA, the EPA is required to notify a country of the export of pesticides not registered for use in the United States. The Toxic Substances Control Act (TSCA) charges the EPA with regulation of materials that pose a threat to health or the environment. However, TSCA does not apply to exported substances unless they pose a threat to the United States through reimportation. The Food, Drug, and Cosmetic Act authorizes the Food and Drug Administration (FDA) to protect U.S. public health by regulating misbranded or adulterated drugs, medical devices, food, food coloring, and cosmetics. Most of the power to regulate covers domestic use, and when these products are exported they are simply required to be labeled for export and not to violate the laws of the recipient country. The FDA also is required to inspect food and drugs coming into the United States to protect public health. Three other laws are the responsibility of the Consumer Products Safety Commission: the Federal Hazardous Substances Act, the Flammable Fabrics Act, and the Consumer Products Safety Act. The first covers the domestic production and sale of substances that are toxic, corrosive, irritants, strong sensitizers, flammable, combustible, or packaged under pressure. Also included are hazardous toys. The Fabrics Act is self-explanatory. The CPSC covers products that pose some personal danger to the user. It should be noted that the export provisions of all three of these acts are extremely weak and call for little more than notification to the recipient country that the product could be dangerous. Finally, and most recently, the Export Administration Act of 1979 gives the President a variety of controls over exports.[6] The EPA did not give specific powers to the President to regulate the export of hazardous substances but President Jimmy Carter used the broad grant of power to issue an Executive Order in January, 1981, to include hazardous substances. Shortly after assuming office, President Reagan rescinded the order, so it is a bit unclear presently whether EPA could be used by the President to control the export of such substances.

The regulatory framework is made a bit more complex because in addition to the EPA, FDA, and CPSC, several other agencies play a role in export policy. The Commerce Department oversees foreign trade and is always interested in any restrictions that might be placed on U.S. exports. The State Department is concerned with the implications for foreign policy and is specifically charged under FIFRA and TSCA with notification to foreign governments of the export of materials covered by these acts. An agency that has a direct interest in imports and exports with Mexico is the Department of Agriculture, which is not often mentioned by those analyzing export policy but certainly is important in relations with Mexico. Upon occasion other governmental agencies may become interested, i.e., the Office of Special Trade Representative. Finally, the states are specifically charged with domestic regulation of FIFRA and TSCA.

The regulatory problems facing the EPA in enforcing FIFRA and TSCA are enormous. FIFRA was initially placed under the USDA, but as amended in 1972 the EPA was given jurisdiction. Both the 1972 and 1978 amendments ostensibly strengthened the hand of the EPA in regulation, but the agency has had great difficulty in effectively regulating chemical use. Not the least of its problems is the enormous, unparalleled increase in the sheer number of chemicals created in the last 30 years. It is estimated that well over 40,000 pesticides have fallen under the jurisdiction of the EPA and the vast majority of them have been the result of scientific developments in the last two decades. The EPA simply has been inundated with an incredible workload in its efforts to regulate pesticides effectively. Under the Reagan administration an effort has been made to streamline the process of registering pesticides but there is genuine concern that a less thorough scientific investigation, caused primarily by a dramatic reduction in the number of personnel in the EPA, may have put some potentially harmful products into use.[7] Another problem with FIFRA (as well as other legislation relating to the environment) is that its renewal is currently stuck in Congress. Major interest groups are involved, including the chemical industry and the AFL-CIO. A House of Representatives bill would have permitted individuals injured by violations of pesticide use to sue in the courts and was greatly favored by the AFL-CIO and farm migrant workers. The American Farm Bureau Federation and various chemical industry groups opposed that provision and it was dropped from the Senate version. The Senate looked more favorably on industry's position requiring stringent deadlines for registration of pesticides with state agencies, whereas the states thought this would interfere with their need to protect public health and safety.[8] Given the current stalemate between the Republican-dominated Senate and the Democratic-controlled House, it is difficult at this juncture to determine what will be the outcome for FIFRA.

An additional problem is pointed out in a General Accounting Office report on the need for stronger enforcement to prevent the misuse of pesticides.[9] The 1978 amendments to FIFRA gave the states primary responsibility for enforcing FIFRA, and the GAO report concludes that the states are not doing a very good job of enforcement. The GAO found that questionable enforcement actions had been taken by the states, that there was insufficient and inadequate investigation and monitoring of pesticide use, that FIFRA's registration process was being circumvented through special local needs provisions, that enforcement actions were inconsistent, and that the states generally did not share EPA's enforcement philosophy.[10] The latter was due to the placement of regulation in the state departments of agriculture where a clear conflict of interest emerged. For example, pesticide regulation in the border states of Texas, Arizona, and California is essentially within the states' department of agriculture. In addition there is a tremendous diversity in commitment to enforcing FIFRA. California, for instance, in 1980 had about 250 people in its regulatory effort with a budget of $2.3 million.[11] Texas had an estimated full-time staff of 38 with a budget of approximately $1.5 million.[12] At the other end of the scale, Arizona employed two inspectors and a clerk with a total 1980 budget of $45,000 for its enforcement program.[13] The conclusion reached by the GAO is that in the state enforcement of FIFRA the public's health simply was not being protected.

Concern for the export of hazardous materials arose in 1977 as a result of the disclosure that children's clothes treated with TRIS, a carcinogen, while banned in the United States, were being exported and there was no authority to prevent such exports. As a result, hearings were held in the Congress and major efforts were made to change federal policy to include some provisions for regulation of exports.[14] Subsequently, President Carter formed the Interagency Working Group on a Hazardous Substances Export Policy chaired by Esther Peterson, Special Assistant to the President for Consumer Affairs.[15] In her testimony before the Congress, Chairperson Peterson identified six major areas of concern:

1. The United States' moral responsibility to regulate hazardous exports must be balanced against other nations' rights and willingness to protect their own citizens.
2. The United States must protect the health and safety of its citizens from the possibility of reimportation of banned products.
3. United States policy must reflect the fact that the use of the domestically banned product might be justified in other countries in view of their economic, social, and cultural conditions.
4. An export policy must take into account the domestic economic burdens regulations may impose.
5. There is a need to coordinate with international organizations and foreign governments in information sharing and the development of an international export policy.
6. Policy formulation must take into account the practicality of enforcing policy.[16]

In spite of the Presidential commitment to develop an export policy, the working group could not develop a formulated policy, mainly because of a hopeless division brought on by opposition from the Departments of Commerce and Agriculture.[17] It should be noted that throughout the various hearings over export policy, the major concern was over the moral role of the United States in selling products to other countries which were regarded as harmful to its own citizens. The Reagan administration has made absolutely no attempt to implement such a policy.

One regulatory problem that demands further investigation is the process by which the EPA notifies the State Department of the export of hazardous and toxic substances and the State Department then, in turn, notifies the appropriate foreign ministry of the recipient country that the product is being exported. Little is currently known of how effective this process actually is, but there are indications that it may not work very well. For example, in a recent (February, 1983) response to a student question at a conference at Texas A&M University, Ambassador to Argentina Harry Schlaudeman indicated that there were technical problems in transmitting the EPA reports. The student had been concerned about the moral responsibility of the United States in exporting such material and Ambassador Schlaudeman, ignoring the moral question involved, stated that his embassy simply did not have the technical capacity to translate the EPA reports into Spanish for the Argentine government. A House Committee concluded in 1978 that the State Department "has failed to coordinate an effective notification program."[18] Quoting a GAO report, the Committee concluded that in regard to notification of the export of pesticides, the recipient country was not supplied sufficient information in a manner which could lead to effective oversight of the pesticides. Another incident, familiar to this writer, points out another problem.

The El Paso Independent School District removed asbestos from pipes in its schools, given the health threat posed to students. The asbestos ended up in a dumpsite in Ciudad Juarez across the border. There is some concern that the Mexican official who received notification of the toxic material was the very one who ended up disposing of it! Whether the notification process was followed is unknown; certainly far more research is necessary in order to clarify the notification process.

A final comment is in order with respect to participation in the international regulatory efforts for hazardous substances by the government of the United States. There are four major organizations attempting to develop international policy.[19] The International Agency for Research on Cancer (IARC) is assembling worldwide data on environmental causes of cancer. The United Nations Environmental Program supervises the International Register of Potentially Toxic Chemicals (IRPTC) to develop data on potentially toxic chemicals. Two European organizations, the Organization for Economic Cooperation and Development (OECD) and the European Economic Community (EEC) are both actively involved in developing standards for registering hazardous materials and notifying European countries of their export and use.

Initially the United States was supportive of these international efforts; however, recent actions of the Reagan administration, in keeping with a general withdrawal from international organizations, bring into question the international commitments of the United States to regulate hazardous and toxic substances. For example, the OECD had developed a system known as Minimum Premarketing Data (MPD) as a uniform system for testing potentially toxic chemicals. Ten European countries accepted MPD, but in November, 1982, Anne Gorsuch, administrator of the EPA, told the OECD members that the United States would not subscribe to MPD and would stick with the far less stringent provisions under TSCA for U.S. chemical manufacturers.[20] In May, 1981, the United States was the only country in the World Health Organization to vote against an international code of standards for the marketing of baby food. And most recently, the United States cast the lone dissenting vote (the vote was 146–1) against a resolution in the UN General Assembly for protection against harmful products.[21] A review of the FIFRA import and export provisions says:

> The section on imports and exports is noteworthy in that it gives minimal export safeguards to foreign countries receiving pesticides from American producers and seems explicitly to embrace a *caveat emptor* philosophy, whereas it gives this country, and its pesticide industry, maximum protection from imports of pesticides not in compliance with U.S. pesticide laws. . . . In short, the United States continues to dump abroad pesticides whose use would not be permitted domestically, and

records of the subject are most difficult to obtain even for EPA, much less the public at large.[22]

It is readily evident that the marketing of U.S. goods has taken precedence in the Reagan administration over any moral concern with the export of hazardous and toxic substances. Indeed, one finds very little evidence that the United States is currently at all concerned with problems posed by hazardous and toxic substances in international relations. For that matter, other producers in the developed world, especially Great Britain and Switzerland, do not appear willing to restrict exports either.[23]

The Regulatory Framework in Mexico

Mexican governmental concern for environmental issues emerged in the early 1970s, primarily as a result of concern for air and water pollution. In 1971 the Congress passed the Federal Law for the Prevention and Control of Environmental Contamination as the legal basis for environmental protection. In this law, Chapter 4 dealt with soil pollution and included Article 24 which stated, "the Federal Executive shall limit, regulate, and when necessary, prohibit the use of all substances such as insecticides, herbicides, fertilizers, defoliants, radioactive materials, etc., when its improper use may cause contamination."[24] The following year the *Subsecretaria de Majoramiento del Ambiente* (SMA) was created within the Ministry of Health and Welfare to enforce the federal law. (Incidentally, in the Mexican system, no role is assigned to state and municipal agencies for environmental regulation although, at least theoretically, all such agencies are to file the equivalent of an environmental impact statement.) Within the SMA, subagencies were established to deal with air and water pollution as well as the general consequences for environmental health but, so far as can be determined, no subagency was established to handle hazardous substances. In fact, regulation under Art. 24 appears to have been left in the Ministry of Animal Husbandry.[25] In December, 1981, a new Federal Law for Protection of the Environment was passed. The section covering hazardous substances was expanded and criminal sanctions were included for violations. The administration of President Miguel de la Madrid has created a new *Secretario de Desarrollo Urbano y Ecologia* with the SMA subsumed under it. Since Mexico has tended to link environmental problems with urban development, it would seem that problems relating to hazardous and toxic substances, unless specifically related to water pollution, are handled by agencies concerned with agricultural development such as the Ministry of Agriculture and Irrigation (SARH).

At this juncture it is almost impossible to assess the performance of the Mexican government in regulating the use of hazardous and toxic substances. Regulation of air pollution has been found to be ineffective.[26] A recent series of articles in *Excelsior* dealing with environmental problems in Mexico City, while not specifically referring to hazardous substances, also condemned government regulatory efforts.[27] Further, the leader of a group of environmental engineers in Mexico severely castigated the government for its inability to control pollution and blamed the inability on politics.[28] Several incidents point out what is probably a very low level of both regulatory effort and concern for the impact of hazardous and toxic substances on the environment or on public health. For example, it is well known that the development of the petroleum industry in the South is having a horrendous impact on the rivers and on the fishing industry in the state of Tabasco. Eventually such pollution could pose a threat to the shrimp industry in the Gulf of Mexico; and it should be quickly pointed out that much of that shrimp is exported to the United States. One of the more interesting pieces of research encountered for this paper is by two Mexican scientists who tested for levels of organochlorines in bays located off the coast of Sinaloa.[29] They found extremely high concentrations of DDT, DDE, and DDD in oysters, shrimp, and lobsters in these bays and estuaries. It is ironic because the pesticides are largely used to protect winter vegetables subsequently marketed in the United States. There is genuine concern that the Gulf of California is becoming highly polluted from these pesticides and, indeed, it has already encountered the deadly phenomenon of red tides.

The head of the SMA in 1982, Manuel López Portillo (cousin to then President José López Portillo) acknowledged that there was widespread use of pesticides and herbicides that were prohibited in the United States.[30] He pointed out that their use was especially heavy in the North where products were grown to be exported to the United States. His major concern was that high levels of residues would prevent the export of such products to the United States. He added that the SMA and SARH were working on a new law which would regulate the use of pesticides and herbicides. Another interesting case involves the use of Galecrom, a pesticide developed by the Swiss firm, Ciba-Geigy, to use in the cotton industry.[31] The Berne Commission stated that the pesticide should not be used without gloves, masks, and protective clothing, but it is acknowledged that Mexican workers are using none of them because of the cost involved. As a result, Mexican workers were found with residues 60 times higher than permitted by Ciba-Geigy and 3,000 times greater than permitted by the World Health Organization. However, from a regulatory point of view the article stated that the *campesinos* refused to complain of any sickness for fear of losing their jobs. All of these incidents, as well as others mentioned, suggest that there is very little effective control over the use of hazardous and toxic substances in Mexico, especially in agriculture.

Hazardous Substances in United States–Mexico Relations

No attempt will be made to treat exhaustively the subject of hazardous substances in U.S.-Mexico relations; rather a few well-known, and some not so well-known, incidents will be discussed to see if a pattern emerges of their overall impact on relations between the two countries. Perhaps the most notorious case involved the use of herbicides to spray marijuana and opium fields in Mexico during the 1970s. The United States, in an attempt to stem the tide of drugs coming from Mexico, provided the Mexican government with equipment and material, including the herbicides 2,4,5-T, 2,4-D, and paraquat.[32] Drug Enforcement Administration agents accompanied Mexican pilots using helicopters provided by the United States and employing the latest infrared aerial photography developed in Vietnam to detect and spray fields throughout Mexico. The program was a decided success but attracted attention because some of the marijuana sprayed with paraquat could have arrived in the United States and threatened the health of U.S. smokers. (It should be mentioned that the long-range consequences of the use of 2,4,5-T, as in Vietnam, are just beginning to be understood and they could pose severe threats to human health in the areas sprayed in Mexico.) The office of Senator Charles Percy, as well as the National Organization for the Reform of Marijuana Laws (NORML), began making inquiries into the use of paraquat in Mexico in 1977 and encountered stiff opposition from the State Department. In fact, the State Department initially denied any U.S. involvement whatsoever in the Mexican eradication program, but subsequent legal maneuvers eventually resulted in the need to file an Environmental Impact Statement for aid of that nature. One of the more interesting aspects of this case was the stonewalling by the State Department over the role of the United States in the program. One can only speculate that it was over concern for the sensibilities of Mexicans regarding U.S. governmental activities within their country, as well as recognition that such a program, if well-known, could be attacked as an infringement on sovereignty.

A far more complex issue is the use in Mexico of pesticides banned in the United States for use in production of vegetables and fruits. In 1978 the Subcommittee on Foreign Agricultural Policy of the Senate Committee on Agriculture, Nutrition, and Forestry held hearings on inspection standards of vegetables imported into the United States.[33] The reasons for the hearings may have been disguised, since the Subcommittee Chairman, Richard Stone, a known supporter of the Florida tomato growers, was probably more interested in protecting the interests of Florida growers than in any disclosures regarding either use of pesticides in Mexico or inspection standards of U.S. government agencies. The Florida tomato industry has carried out a long campaign against Mexican growers and has left no stone unturned in efforts to handicap the import of Mexican tomatoes. Nevertheless, the hearings are important in terms of delineating the roles of various actors involved, including governmental agencies and interest groups, in an incredibly complex situation. Governmental agencies included the Departments of Agriculture; State; Health, Education, and Welfare; Commerce; Treasury; and Labor, as well as representatives of the EPA, the FDA, and the Office of Special Trade Representative.

It becomes glaringly evident that Mexico is using pesticides banned for use in the United States on products that are imported into the United States. It is also painfully evident that U.S. inspection of these imported goods is none too rigorous. As a result, potential threats to U.S. public health are high. A wide range of pesticides, including Monitor, parathion, and diazinon, are used in the production of winter vegetables and fruits in Mexico.[34] As a result, at various times during 1977–1978, shipments of peppers, tomatoes, strawberries, squash, and other produce were stopped by either the FDA or state authorities. Several points should be made about the inspection process itself. First, the samples actually tested of the incoming products are very small. For instance, for 1977 the FDA inspected one sample for over nine million pounds of asparagus coming into the United States, 122 samples for 108 million pounds of strawberries, and 160 samples for 810 million pounds of tomatoes.[35] Second, it is doubtful that the analytical process itself is very good for detection of certain chemicals. The *Los Angeles Times* reported that out of 279 pesticides registered for use in the United States, only 80 can be detected by routine analysis.[36] Furthermore, out of 71 pesticides used in the Culiacan area, the center of winter vegetable production in Mexico, 16 cannot be detected using current analytical methods.[37] Finally, there is some concern that Mexican growers are aware of the tests used by U.S. inspectors and change the use of their pesticides to escape detection.

A General Accounting Office report attacked the FDA inspection process in 1979.[38] The audit showed that the FDA detected 90 violative shipments of produce in 1977 but released 50 of them for public consumption before tests were complete. In one case, a shipment of dried eggs was released although subsequent analysis detected traces of PCB, a highly toxic substance.[39] The GAO report concluded:

1. Half of the imported produce found to contain pesticides was marketed without penalty and consumed by the public.
2. FDA tests for pesticides are incomplete and can detect only about one-third of the pesticides in use.
3. Many pesticides used in foreign countries are not registered for food use in the United States, and the hazards the pesticides pose to consumers have not been evaluated fully by the FDA.
4. Because of an incomplete testing program, the FDA cannot assure that imported food is not in excess of established tolerance.

5. The sampling program is inconsistent and spotty.
6. Importers who violate standards by marketing pesticide-adulterated foods face no penalties.

Clearly, the public health of the United States is not being protected, and blame can be shared by Mexican producers, U.S. importers, and governmental agencies.

One of the more interesting developments in pesticide use is the close cooperation that has developed between governmental agencies and interest groups on both sides of the border. In response to a question from Senator Stone directed towards the FDA concerning its knowledge of the use of pesticides in Mexico, the FDA noted that to improve communication with Mexico, a Mexican Liaison Officer had been established in the Dallas office.[40] This office maintains close contact with the Director General for Vegetable Sanitation and the Mexican Pesticide Laboratory in Mexico City. FDA discourages the use of certain pesticides, provides information about tolerance levels, and also engages in some technical training of laboratory technicians. The FDA pointed out, however, that it had no knowledge of the types of pesticides actually exported from the United States to Mexico.

It also became evident that the Mexican government does not directly control the producers. It is the producers themselves that establish and certify exports.[41] At the national level the *Union Nacional de Productores Hortalizas* (UNPH) is the governing body. In Sinaloa the *Confederacion de Asociaciones Agricolas del Estado de Sinaloa* is the principal agency.[42] The president of the UNPH, J. Cuahuatemoc Bernal, stated that his organization policed itself and had stopped certain farmers from exporting products violating residue standards.[43] He added that the UNPH tries to educate its members in U.S. regulations concerning pesticide use and itself inspects shipments leaving Mexico. What this would appear to indicate is that within Mexico the producers are self-regulating, and one suspects that there is little governmental interference or regulation of pesticide use. Perhaps one of the reasons it is difficult to determine the process of governmental regulation of hazardous and toxic substances is because it is non-existent.

Two additional problems should be mentioned regarding pesticide use. First, there are some genuine threats to the health of farm workers in both countries.[44] Although there is little direct evidence of misuse in Mexico, stories are often told of pesticides being improperly stored or labeled, and of workers not having adequate protective devices and clothing. In Culiacan, boys as young as 13, wearing only shorts, routinely hand spray pesticides on produce destined for the United States. Mexican law prohibits anyone under 16 from doing this work. The boys are from families called *canaleros*—canal people. They live along the canals used for irrigation. After a day's work, the spray tanks are rinsed in the canals, people wash in the canals, and canal water is used in cooking. The official Mexican attitude is summed up by one official: "When technicians of the law go on saying we need to fine violators, or to close down their operations, we are seen as interfering with national progress."[45] In Ciudad Juarez very high levels of DDT were found in blood specimens of residents in the central city and the investigators were hard-pressed to explain them since they were not close to agricultural fields. It was discovered that one of the local *curanderos,* or folk medicine practitioners, was selling amulets to ward off evil spirits by hanging them around the neck. They contained a powder which was found to be DDT. There is also genuine concern for Mexican fieldworkers, both legal and illegal, who may encounter pesticide poisoning in the United States.[46] At this juncture the extent of possible pesticide poisoning among field workers is simply not known.

Another interesting development is the possibility that pesticides banned for use in the United States are being illegally imported back into the United States. Recent studies have indicated "hot spots" in Arizona, New Mexico, and Texas of high levels of DDT and its residues, and the speculation is that some farmers have obtained DDT illegally from Mexico.[47] Mexico has continued to produce DDT. Certainly the border is permeable enough and if farmers wanted to use banned products they would encounter little difficulty.

Yet another issue involving hazardous and toxic substances is the relocation of U.S. plants in Mexico because of potential health threats posed to workers. At the outset it should be understood that Mexico, because of its unemployment problem, invites such industry, but there should be some concern in the United States that what is being exported is dangerous to health. The full extent to which U.S. firms are relocating in Mexico because of safety regulations posed by the United States is not fully known; nonetheless, it has occurred. One example is asbestos plants. With the knowledge that asbestos was a cancer threat to workers, several U.S. producers relocated in Mexico. One was AMATEX, the American Asbestos Textile Corporation which relocated in Ciudad Juarez.[48] When a newspaper reporter made known to health officials that workers in the plant had none of the protective clothing required for asbestos production, they rushed to the plant but apparently had little impact. One of the more interesting problems is that the SMA officials who were required to measure the level of asbestos in the air simply did not have the necessary equipment to do so. Similarly, the plant of a U.S. firm making fluoride gas also emits gases which have killed vegetation around the plant but there is no way for the SMA to measure and test the emissions. One suspects that other U.S. firms are located in Mexico and may be producing substances which are hazardous to both workers and the public, but far more research is needed in this area before even tentative conclusions could be reached.

The question of what is considered hazardous is most complex. The lead study done in El Paso–Ciudad Juarez found children with elevated blood lead levels showing subtle neuropsychological difficulties but no overt symptoms of lead poisoning.[49] As a result of these findings, several European nations lowered acceptable blood lead levels in children. The United States still is debating the matter. Studies with pesticides have also shown physiological and neuropsychological changes in persons chronically exposed to high levels of pesticides.[50]

One of the objectives of the U.S.-Mexico Border Health Initiative is to alert clinics and doctors to the overt symptoms of pesticide poisoning. It may be, however, that sub-clinical symptoms pose greater threats, not only to workers handling pesticides but also to the public consuming foods contaminated with the chemicals. As yet, neither country has shown any sign of dealing with this problem.

A tragic problem is that both organochlorine and organophosphate pesticides are lipid soluble. Since both mother's milk and animal milk are high in lipids, these compounds can be passed on to children even when the mothers are no longer exposed to the compounds.[51]

A possible threat to the environment is illegal dumping of toxic substances in Mexico. Presently there is little evidence that such dumping is occurring, but one should not be surprised if it does happen. Indeed, there is one recorded case of illegal dumping in the interior of Mexico.[52] In March, 1981, a 75-year-old American, Clarence Nugent, was arrested by Mexican officials and charged with illegally dumping some 260 drums of toxic chemicals, including 42 drums of PCBs, in the state of Zacatecas. The chemicals were sent to Houston to be conveyed to Mexico and arrived in Zacatecas by railroad. An EPA official stated that loopholes in the law permitted such dumping, but an unnamed source said the primary reason for the arrest of Nugent was that he had failed to pay the necessary bribes to the appropriate officials. In any case, Mexico asked the United States to assume the responsibility for cleaning up the mess. The disposition of the case is unknown. Given the current status of U.S. policy towards the dumping of toxic wastes and the illegal dumping of such materials within the United States itself, it would come as no surprise to anyone to discover that toxic substances from the U.S. were being dumped in Mexico.

Finally, mention should be made of the availability of substances banned in the United States to its own citizens across the border. In some cases these substances are accepted in Mexico and may be purchased by anyone. An interesting example is the contraceptive Depo-Provera which is prohibited in the United States, but readily available in Mexico and apparently consumed by U.S. citizens living along the border.[53] Given the incredible population expansion in Mexico, it could be argued that any contraceptive should be welcomed since the social consequences of an unbridled birth rate may be greater than the threat posed over the long run to users. On the other hand, it should be pointed out that U.S. agencies specifically charged with protecting the health of its public cannot do so in a border setting. Another interesting example, while not directly involving a hazardous substance, is the alleged cancer cure, laetrile, which was the subject of much publicity in the United States. Incidents involving the alleged miracle cure once again point out the regulatory problem for U.S. agencies along the border, and one suspects many other examples could be found.

SUMMARY

This brief review of hazardous and toxic substances in United States–Mexico relations points out several factors. Perhaps most notable is that these substances are relatively new as issues in international relations and there is, as yet, no satisfactory mechanism for handling them either in the global arena or in terms of bilateral relations. What needs to be stressed is that many of these substances pose long-range threats to human health and the environment and there should be genuine concern today to prevent these future threats. The policy framework in the United States is characterized by a proliferation of both laws and agencies involved in the regulation of toxic and hazardous substances, especially as they relate to U.S.-Mexico relations. The laws governing the export of materials are weak and do not severely sanction those who might export dangerous materials.The international position of the Reagan administration is not supportive at all of any international regulation of these substances and, inceed, it does not appear willing to stop the export of such materials. A major problem, as in the case of other environmental issues in U.S.-Mexico relations, is the federal system which leaves much enforcement to the states. For various reasons, including lack of personnel and an unfavorable regulatory climate, the states have not been very effective in controlling dangerous substances.

If anything, the regulatory framework in Mexico is worse. In spite of formal laws relating to the environment, there is very little effective enforcement, especially in regard to hazardous and toxic substances. At least in the case of agricultural products destined for exports, producers appear to be self-regulating. One result is that there are probably many, many cases of health threats posed to agricultural workers that are not known or catalogued. Given the level of economic development, Mexican authorities may feel they do not have, or cannot obtain, the necessary resources to control hazardous and toxic substances effectively. Such a shortsighted policy may, in the long run, provide for disastrous consequences.

Thus far several issues have arisen in bilateral relations between the two countries. Neither country has a strong moral position and both can be faulted for not taking into consideration effects on the public health of activities in the other. Certainly the United States should make every effort to control effectively the export of hazardous and toxic substances, and Mexico should make every effort to prevent the use of such materials when they pose a threat to human health. Neither country appears ready to take strong stands for environmental public health. In the long run this means that future conflict involving hazardous and toxic substances is highly likely.

Notes

1. See, for example, three editions of the *Natural Resources Journal* entirely devoted to environmental issues along the United States–Mexico border: Vol. 17, No. 4 (October, 1977); Vol. 18, No. 1 (January, 1978); and Vol. 22, No. 4 (October, 1982).

2. The best review of the fantastic growth in the problem of hazardous and toxic substances is the Annual Report of the Council on Environmental Quality, e.g., Council on Environmental Quality, *Ninth Annual Report* (Washington: GPO, 1978).

3. Francine Schulberg, "Comment: United States Export of Products Banned for Domestic Use," *Harvard International Law Journal*, Vol. 20, No. 2 (Spring, 1979), p. 332.

4. *Christian Science Monitor*, December 29, 1982.

5. This section relies heavily upon Schulberg and Mary Patricia Azevedo, "Trade in Hazardous Substances: An Examination of U.S. Regulation," in Seymour J. Rubin and Thomas R. Graham (eds.), *Environment and Trade: The Relation of International Trade and Environmental Policy* (New Jersey: The American Society of International Law, 1982), pp. 135–153. It should be pointed out that the Resource Conservation and Recovery Act (RCRA) is not covered in this review. However, RCRA could eventually play a role in regulating the dumping of toxic wastes outside the country.

6. Azevedo, pp. 140–141.

7. *Christian Science Monitor*, December 29, 1982.

8. *El Paso Times*, January 2, 1983; also, House of Representatives, Subcommittee on Department Operations, Research and Foreign Agriculture of the Committee on Agriculture, *Hearings on the Federal Insecticide, Fungicide and Rodenticide Act*, 97th Congress, 1st Session, 3 Vols., June 16, 1981, June 18, 1981, February 4, 1982.

9. General Accounting Office, "Stronger Enforcement Needed Against Misuse of Pesticides," Report to the Congress, CED-82-5, October 15, 1981.

10. Ibid., pp. i–ii.

11. Ibid., p. 46.

12. Ibid., p. 72.

13. Ibid., p. 39.

14. United States House of Representatives, Committee on Government Operations, *Report on Export of Products Banned by U.S. Regulatory Agencies*, 95th Congress, 2nd Session, October 4, 1978.

15. *Business America*, June 30, 1980, pp. 14–16.

16. Cited in Schulberg, p. 336.

17. David Weir and Mark Schapiro, *Circle of Poison* (San Francisco: Institute for Food and Development Policy, 1981), p. 63.

18. House, *Report on Export of Products*, pp. 20–21.

19. See Philip Alston, "International Regulation of Toxic Chemicals," *Ecology Law Quarterly*, Vol. 7, No. 2 (1978), pp. 397–456; also Sam Gusman, et al., *Public Policy for Chemicals: National and International Issues* (Washington: The Conservation Foundation, 1980).

20. *Science*, December 3, 1982, p. 982.

21. Ward Morehouse, "Out of Step at the U.N.," *Christian Science Monitor*, January 5, 1983.

22. William A. Butler, "Federal Pesticide Law," in Erica L. Dolgin and Thomas G. P. Guilbert (eds.), *Federal Environmental Law* (St. Paul: West Publishing Co., 1974), p. 1271.

23. *Christian Science Monitor*, May 10, 1983.

24. For a discussion of the Mexican legal position, see Julian Juergensmeyer and Earle Blizzard, "Legal Aspects of Environmental Control in Mexico: An Analysis of Mexico's New Environmental Law," *Natural Resources Journal*, Vol. 12, No. 4 (October, 1972), pp. 380–412; Lucio Cabrera Acevedo, "Legal Protection of the Environment in Mexico," *California Western International Law Journal*, Vol. 8, No. 1 (Winter, 1978), pp. 22–42; and Americo J. Flores Nava, *Breves Consideraciones sobre Derecho Ambiental* (Mexico, D. F.: Ed. Tlacatecutli, 1981).

25. Juergensmeyer and Blizzard, pp. 590–591.

26. C. Richard Bath, "U.S.-Mexico Experience in Managing Transboundary Air Resources: Problems, Prospects, and Recommendations for the Future," *Natural Resources Journal*, Vol. 22, No. 4 (October, 1982), pp. 1147–1168.

27. *Excelsior*, Series on urban problems, January 17, 18, 20, 22, 1983.

28. *Excelsior*, January 24, 1983.

29. Lilia Albert and Victor Manuel Armiente, "Contaminacion por plaguicidas organoclorados en un sistema de drenaje agricola del estado de Sinaloa" (n.p.: n.d., mimeographed).

30. *Excelsior*, February 3, 1982.

31. *Excelsior*, February 28, 1983.

32. *Science*, February 24, 1978, pp. 861–864; also Richard B. Craig, "La Campana Permanente: Mexico's Antidrug Campaign," *Journal of Interamerican Studies and World Affairs*, Vol. 20, No. 2 (May, 1978), pp. 107–131.

33. United States Senate, Subcommittee on Foreign Agricultural Policy of the Committee on Agriculture, Nutrition, and Forestry, *Inspection Standards of Vegetable Imports*, 9th Congress, 2nd session, May 25, 1978.

34. Ibid., pp. 69, 79–82.

35. Ibid., p. 84.

36. *Los Angeles Times*, September 1, 1980.

37. Ibid., September 3, 1980.

38. General Accounting Office, "Better Regulation of Pesticide Exports and Pesticide Residues in Imported Food is Essential," CED-79-43, June 22, 1979; also *Dallas Morning News*, February 15, 1981.

39. *Dallas Morning News*, February 15, 1981, p. 18.

40. U.S. Senate, *Inspection Standards of Vegetable Imports*, pp. 86–87.

41. Ibid., p. 67.

42. For the activities of UNPH and CAADES, see David R. Mares, "Agricultural Trade: Domestic Interests and Transnational Relations," in Jorge

I. Dominguez (ed.), *Mexico's Political Economy* (Beverly Hills: Sage, 1982), pp. 79–132.

43. *Dallas Morning News*, February 15, 1981, p. 18.

44. See, U.S. Department of Health, Education, and Welfare, "Pesticide Residue Hazards to Farm Workers," HEW Report II 76-191. The proposed United States–Mexico Border Health Institute specifically addresses the problem of treating migrant farm workers for pesticide poisoning within the United States.

45. *Los Angeles Times*, April 27, 1980.

46. See, for example, *Los Angeles Times*, November 21, 1980.

47. Donald R. Clark, Jr., "DDT Hot Spots in New Mexico and Arizona," Unpublished manuscript, Patuxent Wildlife Research Center, 1982.

48. *El Paso Times*, April 3, 1978, and April 4, 1978.

49. P. J. Landrigan, R. W. Whitworth, R. W. Baloh, N. W. Staehling, W. F. Barthel, and B. F. Rosenblum, "Neuropsychological Dysfunction in Children with Chronic Low-Level Lead Absorption," *Lancet*, I, No. 7909 (1975), pp. 208–212.

50. P. M. Tocci, J. B. Mann, J. E. Davies, and W. F. Ed Mundson, "Biochemical Differences Found in Persons Chronically Exposed to High Levels of Pesticides," *Industrial Medicine*, Vol. 38, No. 6 (1969), pp. 188–195; E. P. Savage, J. A. Lewis, and L. H. Parks, "Chronic Neurological Sequelae of Acute Organophosphate Pesticide Poisoning: A Case-Control Study," EPA 540/9-80-003, GPO; E. W. Owens, Health Effects of Organophosphate Pesticides in Man: A Case-Study Approach, Mimeographed, 27 pp.

51. J. V. Bell, G. R. Van Petten, P. J. Taylor, and M. J. Aiken, "The Inhibition and Reactivation of Human Maternal and Fetal Plasma, Choline Esterase EC-3.1.1.8 Following the Organophosphate Dichloroase," *Life Science*, Vol. 24, No. 3, pp. 247–254; M. K. J. Siddiqui, M. C. Saxena, A. K. Bhargava, T. D. Seth, C. R. Marti, and D. Kutty, "Agrochemicals in the Maternal Blood, Milk, and Cord Blood: a Source of Toxicants for Pre-nates and Neonates," *Environmental Research*, Vol. 24, No. 1 (1981), pp. 24–32.

52. *New York Times*, March 20, 1981.

53. *El Paso Times*, January 16, 1983.

16
Bilateral Admiralty Relations Between Mexico and the United States

Genaro Carnero Roque
Adolfo Aguilar Zinser

Since time immemorial, the sea has played a strategic role in the development of nations. The major powers—Portugal, England, and Spain—gained much of their power from mastery of the sea. It was the seagoing fleets of these powers that gave them force and power in the time of their greatest dominance.

Today, legislation applied in the divers nations and admiralty regulations is considered one of the major macroeconomic factors. Bilateral relations often come up as priority, and often conflictive, topics. The explanation for this lies in the fact that the dynamic forces in contemporary international society assign primary importance to the overwhelming problem of establishing new laws and a new international code governing the use and exploitation of marine resources. Laws heretofore permitting almost unlimited freedom of use of both renewable and non-renewable resources have been discarded and all but invalidated. The situation tends to be exacerbated when problems arise between countries with differing degrees of economic development.

With the culmination of the Third United Nations Conference on Sea Rights in December 1982, establishment of a legal code was achieved, applicable to all uses of the sea and dealing equitably with the aspirations and needs of the Third World. The code establishes guidelines and mechanisms for the peaceful solution of controversies. Notwithstanding, the problems which have arisen within the framework of bilateral relations between Mexico and the United States remain unresolved because of differences in the enforcement criteria adopted by each of these nations.

Put another way, while Mexico's admiralty philosophy has always been in harmony with the precepts established by International Law, the United States—in the majority of cases—has tended to favor the interests of international pressure groups. In this sense, far from adhering to the progressive principles emanating from the New Sea Law, the United States has attempted to coerce other nations in search of international profits.

Unfortunately, this policy—with its variants—of our neighboring country has been tolerated by Mexico for many years of her history and the results have not been favorable to the Mexican people. It is sufficient to remember the most extreme case, that of the Guadalupe Hidalgo and La Mesilla treaties imposed on Mexico, which deprived her not only of an enormous part of her territory but also a vast littoral extension.

Beginning in the 1970s, the Mexican government has striven to consolidate the nation's marine boundaries, and to protect the utilization and conservation of her natural resources. However, all of her efforts in search of equitable solutions to various admiralty problems have been blocked by the posture of vested economic interests, reflecting the policy of the United States government.

Viewed from this perspective, the most controversial themes in the admiralty relations of these nations embrace, on the one hand, the problem of fishing for highly migratory species (yellow-fin tuna) in the Pacific Ocean and, on the other hand, the Territorial Limits Treaty of 1978, especially as it concerns the Gulf of Mexico.

With regard to the problem of highly migratory species, conflict arises from the inequitable fishing-quotas system prevailing in the Interamerican Tropical Tuna Commission. This body was established in 1949 between Costa Rica and the United States, with Mexico joining it in 1964. Among the functions of the ITTC is that of regulating the exploitation of that species so as to maintain the populations of fish schools at sufficiently abundant levels to permit them to be exploited to the maximum extent. To this end, a quota system has been established, based on the concept that each member nation's volume of catch is determined by the strength of its fleet and the indices of its fish hauls. Without a doubt, under such a criterion the nation benefiting the most is the United States, in view of the differing degrees of economic development of the member nations and to the fact that the United States has more advanced technology as well as the world's largest tuna-fishing fleet. Thus, "in the period from 1975 to 1978, this nation was assigned more than 50% of the total quota." The upshot of this was that in 1978, of the 198,391 tons comprising the quota worldwide, the United States used 104,495 tons.

On numerous occasions the government of Mexico requested that ITTC modify these criteria by using formulae increasing the shares of other signatories' respective tuna-fishing fleets, since the largest concentration of tuna schools are located in the ocean waters along the coasts of Mexico and Costa Rica. At the ITTC meeting held in

San José, Costa Rica, in 1977, Mexico proposed the establishment of quotas based on the following: (1) the length of the coastline of each country with regard to the entire area covered by the treaty (we refer here to the area under the control of the Yellow-Fin Tuna Commission); (2) the nearness of this species to the coasts of the country in question, in determining which consideration should be given to the geographical center of the area involved; (3) the relative consumption of this species in each country; and (4) the volume of the catch obtained by the nation's fleet during the year prior to the establishment of quotas. These criteria seemed to be most proper, but Mexico's motion was never accepted, in spite of the fact that its third and fourth points tended to favor the interests of the United States.

The legal differences between our two nations were aggravated beginning with three episodes: (a) the establishment, in 1976, of the Exclusive Mexican Economic Zone; (b) Mexico's withdrawal, in 1977, from the Interamerican Tropical Tuna Commission; and (c) adoption by the United States in March, 1977, of a fishing conservation and administration zone.

In fact, with Mexico's withdrawal from the ITTC, free access was denied to foreign tuna-fishing vessels within the 200-sea-mile space off Mexican coasts since, as of 1976, Mexico has exercised sovereignty over all of her resources within that area. Accordingly, the highly migratory species did not escape from Mexico's jurisdiction. Beginning in 1980, regulations were formulated covering the charges for license-fees required for fishing expeditions and the exploitation of the above-mentioned species. These quotas reached $1,250 pesos per vessel for trips of up to 60 days, and $1,380 pesos for each net ton of catch taken by the vessel.

This situation was not viewed favorably by the American fishermen who, far from asking that their government negotiate with the government of their neighboring country, began carrying out illegal fishing raids in Mexican waters. This in turn led to vessels being impounded and fines being paid to the Mexican government.

Given this situation, the reaction of the Carter Administration was to decree an economic embargo on all U.S. tuna imports from Mexico. President Carter's action went as far as the remission by the United States government of the fines assessed to vessels fishing in Mexican waters in violation of the regulations. This was an unmistakable sign of the *carte blanche* which American fishermen received from the Carter Administration and was, in fact, a stimulus to continued illegal fishing raids in Mexican waters.

Four points seem clearly to prove that the facts are on Mexico's side and that her position in this problem is right.

First, Paragraph Four of Article V of the Statutes of the Interamerican Tropical Tuna Commission reads, verbatim, as follows: "At any time following the expiration of a ten-year period beginning the date that this article takes effect, any of the parties hereto may give notification of its intention to repudiate it." Mexico exercised her rights and withdrew from that body in 1977.

Second, Mexico's Exclusive Economic Zone, or shelf, of 200 miles has been constituted since 1976, and the minutes of the Third Sea Conference show that no exception is made for highly migratory species within that zone. Mexico therefore is within her rights in permitting or refusing to permit the fishing of said species. That is, the Exclusive Economic Zone does not include freedom of fishing for other nations, and this right is regulated by the policies of, and negotiations with, the seacoast nation itself.

Third, Mexico, in accordance with Article 64 of the Third Sea Conference, has from the beginning insisted on the modification of regulations regarding the fishing quotas established by the only regional body existing in this matter.

Finally, Mexico has never denied foreign vessels the right to fish in her territorial waters, in accordance with the international principle of "permissible capture," and has established fees for such fishing.

In spite of the foregoing, the controversy between Mexico and the United States regarding this matter has remained practically stalemated. From the legal point of view, the solution is surely within reach of the parties to the dispute. In accordance with the provisions approved by the Third United Nations Sea Rights Conference, under which the highly migratory species are not excluded from the Exclusive Economic Zone, the seacoast country in question is within her rights in pemitting, or in refusing to permit, tuna-fishing in said area. To this end, that conference itself recommended, in its Article 64, that the orderly exploitation of these resources be achieved by the signing of regional and mutually beneficial treaties.

Despite her decision to withdraw from the Interamerican Tropical Tuna Commission, Mexico in no way opposes the signing of such agreements. She feels, however, that any international treaty should be clearly equitable with regard to the economic requirements and rational exploitation of a signing nation's resources. The signing of a bilateral agreement actually would place these problems in clearer perspective. As things stand, the United States claims preferential treatment for her fishermen, who obviously have greater technical and financial resources for capturing large quantities of tuna. Under such conditions, the problem goes beyond the legal limitations and rests in the general sphere of political and economic relations with the United States.

At present, the price of tuna in the United States has risen considerably, and the solution to the problem would involve an increase of the supply of tuna in that market. Ending the embargo on exports from Mexico is thus inimical to the interests of the American tuna industry. Mexican tuna would be cheaper for the American consumer, thus affecting the profit margins of the American industry.

Mexico's insistence on protecting the resources in her Exclusive Economic Zone, on the other hand, leads to the capture of American tuna-fishing vessels in Mexican waters and constitutes a latent political problem which could have an impact on the general climate of relations between the two countries, and unleash political confrontations of greater scope.

Another as yet unresolved issue involves the sea borders between Mexico and the United States. While both countries have indicated that they claim jurisdiction to a distance of 200 miles off their respective coasts, in actual fact the Bilateral Limits Treaty has not taken effect. That is, the sea borders exist *de facto*, but not *de jure*.

On May 4, 1978, Mexico and the United States entered into a Sea Limit Treaty, signed by then-Mexican Foreign Secretary Santiago Roel and his American counterpart, Cyrus Vance, Secretary of State. This treaty constituted the ratification of the exchange of communications from November 1976, in which both countries accepted, temporarily, sea limits between 12 and 200 nautical miles into the Gulf of Mexico and the Pacific Ocean, and accepted the "practical and equitable" nature of contiguous international boundaries. This treaty was held to be of the utmost importance, since it regulated equally both the Continental Shelf boundaries and those of the ocean floor.

In December 1978, the Mexican Senate, acting in accordance with the Mexican Constitution, ratified this treaty, which then lacked only ratification by the United States Senate to become binding. In fact, in 1979, this document was sent to the United States Senate by then-President Carter, for its "advice and consent." The Senate referred it to its Foreign Relations Committee for study, and that same year the committee approved, unanimously and without debate, a favorable resolution recommending that the treaty be ratified in plenary session.

At that time everything appeared to be going smoothly and completion of the steps required for the Sea Limit Treaty to take effect were considered a foregone conclusion. This, of course was not lost on the American oceanic companies, both oil and mining, doing business internationally. Professor Hollis D. Hedberg of Princeton University—in the hearing held by the Foreign Relations Committee of the United States Senate in June 1980—went to great pains to undermine ratification of the treaty, stating that the treaty "should be rejected, due to the fact that the limits proposed in principle were *inequitable and undesirable* as regards mining resources and to the fact that it would cause the United States to lose, without a *just or valid* reason, a deep-water area with probable sources of energy having enormous value in the future."

According to a study performed by the United States Geological Survey (USGS), geological conditions in the Gulf of Mexico favor the existence of crude oil and natural gas in an area covering a surface of approximately 152,660 square kilometers. Estimates of resources fluctuate between 2.24 and 21.99 billion barrels of crude and 5.18 and 44.40 trillion cubic feet of natural gas. It is worth mentioning that this study was carried out in six zones, among which is the bank of the Río Grande, including that part of the Continental Shelf off the coast of Tamaulipas, the Campeche slope, the Lost Belt, and the "Abisal" Basin of the Gulf of Mexico, with special emphasis on the border areas referred to in the treaty as the Sigsbee Pit. These resources therefore are in waters under Mexican jurisdiction; Dr. Hedberg's statements regarding the loss of said resources by the United States were out of order.

On the other hand, the Limitations Treaty of 1978, in its Article 1, establishes geodetic boundaries creating in the central part of the Gulf of Mexico a triangular area of approximately 40 square kilometers, hanging toward the Mexican Exclusive Economic Zone but belonging neither to Mexico nor to the United States. Put another way, this zone is considered as being on the high seas, with the characteristics corresponding to such an area; consequently, its non-renewable resources would be considered a "common inheritance of humanity." Had this area not been defined, the center of the Gulf of Mexico could be divided between the two countries in accordance with the documents of the Third Sea Conference in its section on Locked-in Seas.

In this matter, both nations agreed to await the results of that conference. Mark Feldman, legal counsel to the State Department during President Carter's administration, pointed out that "in the central part of the Gulf of Mexico there is a space . . . with no fishing limitations established between the two countries. In this area the coasts of the two opposite countries facing each other are separated by more than 400 miles. . . . For the present we have not drawn the limits of the area, since the continental shelf limitation is a question presently under active negotiation in the Third Sea Conference."

Accordingly, the posture assumed by the government of the United States—that of keeping the treaty bottled up for six years—is unjustified. This treaty has never represented an attack on the interests of the United States Government; on the contrary, all its terms are in accordance with International Admiralty Law, as confirmed by the resolution of approval of the Foreign Relations Committee of the United States Senate.

What is worth commenting upon, however, is the interest of international companies (among them, U.S. Steel and Lockheed Missiles) in appropriating for themselves the central zone of the Gulf of Mexico, the Sigsbee Pit. This area, as we have said, is rich in hydrocarbon deposits.

The posture assumed by the present administration—that of President Reagan—appears to be in line with that of international mining and ocean-going companies, who claim access to non-renewable resources in areas covered by the still unratified Ocean Limits and Waters Treaty in the Sigsbee Pit. By having refused to ratify the Third Sea Conference Accords regulating nonrenewable resources, especially those outside the jurisdiction of nations, the United States has prevented, or at least indefinitely postponed, the possibility of finding the most adequate and equitable channels of negotiation to resolve this controversy with Mexico.

In any event, President Reagan has not made the necessary effort to obtain Senate ratification of the Limitations Treaty of 1978. Had he done so, he would have taken the first step toward bilateral negotiation in the matter of the Sigsbee Pit resources.

It is evident that relations between Mexico and the United States involve a complex of highly different levels, spheres and matters of constant negotiation. The economic, commercial, financial, political and—of no mean importance—social questions derived from migratory waves, presuppose constant revision of agreements, permitting gradual adjustment to changing circumstances. It is impossible to prescribe general agreements of universal application. The changing and dynamic character of this asymmetrical and frequently conflicting relationship demands of both countries understanding and calm political behavior. Sterile confrontations and unnecessary showdowns must be avoided.

Within this framework, it should be supposed that the basic agreements between two neighboring states—that is, those involving precise and inalterable geographical definition of their respective national jurisdictions—could by now be fully settled. The expansionist nature of the American policies, most especially manifested during the 19th century as an impulse toward territorial expansion, unleashed the machines of war which—as has been pointed out—cost Mexico a substantial part of her territory. More than a century later, Mexico and the United States still have not agreed upon their territorial boundaries involving sea and ocean space and the exploitation of the resources therein.

Marine rights have taken on greater importance in recent years due, on one hand, to changes in international law which Third World countries have hailed as protecting their resources and, on the other hand, to new technological possibilities for exploiting resources which were inaccessible a few decades ago. The international community has had to broach—under these new circumstances—the difficult political, legal and economic problems of international oceanic order. Mexico and the United States cannot escape these facts, and the new principles and regulations which now are universally in legal effect must be incorporated into the definitive establishment of the sea boundaries between the two countries. However, the resistance of the United States government, and certain private sectors in that country, to recognizing the rights of Third World countries in this field has been singularly high-handed with regard to Mexico.

From the strictly political point of view, the achievement of equitable agreements between Mexico and the United States in admiralty questions should be a high-priority matter. This is clearly a fundamental subject in any relationship between neighboring countries. If not resolved, it clouds the general climate of negotiations between them. The present divergence in this field, then, could mean the presentation of conflicts that cannot be confined within the sphere where they arise, given the intensity and complexity of bilateral relations. The attitude assumed by the United States clearly demonstrates the existence of political and economic standards and principles growing out of the undeniable historical achievements of the Third World. If Mexico and the United States have so far failed to resolve questions in the matter of sea boundaries, it is clear in the final analysis that it is because of the configuration of economic interests. This configuration is similar to those in other spheres of the relationship, where reaching agreements also proves difficult and hazardous.

Mexico's posture has not been inflexible or unrealistic; on the contrary, she has constantly sought to meet with the United States at the negotiating table concerning sea rights. Willingness to negotiate does not, however, imply that Mexico will abandon her rights to those resources which are indisputably hers.

References

Carnero Checa, Genaro. *USA 1776-1976, Alborada y Crepúsculo (Dawn and Dusk)*. Ediciones Siglo XX; Lima, Peru, 1976.

Carnero, Roque G.; Alicia Kerber; Miguel Mendez; and Margarita Peña. *México y Estados Unidos ante la Tercera Confemar: Resultados e Implicaciones. Rev. Informe No. 3* ("Mexico, the United States, and the Third Sea Conference— Results and Implications." Revised Report No. 3"). CEESTEM, Mexico, 1982.

Graig, J. Calkimas; and P. Thomas *Distribución Geográfica de las Capturas de Atún Aleta Amarilla en el Océano Pacífico, La Flota y las Estadísticas Globales de Captura 1975-1978* ("Geographical Distribution of Yellow-Fin Tuna Catches in the Eastern Pacific Ocean, Fleets and Overall Catch Statistics 1975-1978"). CIAT, La Jolla, California, 1981.

Vargas, Jorge. *El Golfo de México y el Informe Continental del U.S. Geological Survey* ("The Gulf of Mexico and the Continental Report by the U.S. Geological Survey"). Page-one political supplement to *Uno Más Uno*, No. 27, February 28, 1982.

Vargas, Jorge. *Límites Marinos, Una Línea Extrañamente Discontinua*. ("Sea Limits: A Strangely Discontinuous Line"). Page-one political supplement to *Uno Más Uno*, No. 16, December 13, 1981.

Epilogue

Eliseo Mendoza Berrueto

It would be inappropriate simply to end this book with the final paper for in no sense has our long-term task been completed, even though the papers presented here mark a huge step toward mutual understanding. Instead of dwelling on where we have been, however, I should like to close this volume by pointing to where we wish to go. *The U.S. and Mexico: Borderland Development and the National Economies,* like its predecessor, *Regional Impacts of United States-Mexico Economic Relations,* comes from an on-going collaboration between scholars in the two countries. I emphasize the word on-going to reflect the fact that the business of exploring issues and topics of mutual concern is not something that can be outlined at one or two planning meetings, developed at a major conference, and then summarized in a single book—or even in two books. The task of building a dialogue between scholars with often markedly different perspectives is a long-term proposition. Any collaboration, and ours is no exception, starts slowly. There is an initial period where individuals simply get to know one another and where scholarly concerns are mapped out in general and often tentative terms. This initial stage is followed by a second one which demands clarification of terms, the opening of channels of communication, and the often uncomfortable task of coming to grips with questions of national pride, personal conviction and other matters of substantial delicacy.

These two stages would be difficult enough if the subject of the collaboration were static. But when the focus is on something as dynamic as U.S.–Mexico economic relations, the glue that holds the enterprise together must be strong indeed. In the case at hand, participants have managed to stay on course; our focus continues to be squarely on systematic approaches to questions of regional analysis, but the specific problems addressed and solutions offered have evolved to reflect changes in both Mexican and U.S. economies and redefinition of interregional concerns that are reflective of changing economic and political climates.

We are now in the process of growing into yet another phase in our development. Plans are being formulated for a second seminar

251

that will provide the opportunity to structure a third conference. Some things will stay the same: we will continue to encourage vigorous analytical approaches to regional perspectives on U.S.-Mexico economic relations, we will continue our insistence that discussions be frank and open, and we will maintain our practice of including established scholars from both countries. It would, however, be a mistake to assume that the future record will be little more than simply a slightly modified version of the established one. As we move ahead, our agenda will reflect changes in the socioeconomic and political environment, it will demand that we challenge the conventional wisdom lest we become complacent, it will emphasize the inclusion of new faces, especially those of junior scholars, and it will place a premium on joint research—research which emphasizes close and regular collaboration beween Mexican and U.S. scholars who share specific enthusiasms. In short, the publication of this book represents a major step in our efforts to promote appreciation of problems of mutual concern but it is an intermediate step in a much longer journey. We have not reached our final destination, which is the full understanding of U.S.-Mexico relations, but we have made substantial progress; and the prospects for even more progress in the future remain bright indeed.

Contributors

Adolfo Aguilar Zinser, Centro de Estudios Económicos y Sociales del Tercer Mundo

Howard G. Applegate, Department of Civil Engineering, University of Texas at El Paso

C. Richard Bath, Department of Political Science, University of Texas at El Paso

Mariano Bauer, University Energy Program, Universidad Nacional Autónoma de México

Jorge A. Bustamante, Centro de Estudios Fronterizeros del Norte de Mexico

Genaro Carnero Roque, Centro de Estudios Económicos y Sociales del Tercer Mundo

Alfonso Corona Rentería, Universidad Nacional Autónoma de México

Haynes C. Goddard, Universidad Autónoma de Nuevo Leon, Monterrey, Mexico, and Department of Economics, University of Cincinnati

Joseph Grunwald, Brookings Institution

Niles Hansen, Department of Economics, University of Texas at Austin

Richard C. Jones, University of Texas at San Antonio

Kevin F. McCarthy, Rand Corporation

John M. McDowell, Arizona State University

James T. Peach, Department of Economics, New Mexico State University at Las Cruces

Olga Pellicer, Centro de Investigación y Docencia Económicas

Luis Suarez-Villa, Program in Social Ecology, University of California at Irvine

Jesús Tamayo, Centro de Investigación y Dociencia Económicas

Guillermina Valdes-Villalva, Centro de Estudios Fronterizas del Norte de Mexico

Index

Tourism, 5–6, 85, 93(n7), 116, 152
Toxic substances. *See* Hazardous substances
Toxic Substances Control Act (TSCA) (U.S.), 227, 228
Trade, 27, 79, 81–82
    national debt and, 88–89
    peso devaluations and, 84–85
    regional, 94(n19)
    regulations, 26, 133, 138(n36)
    See also Imports; Oil
Transboundary cooperation in Europe, 12–13, 14, 15
Transnational companies. *See* Maquiladoras
Transportation, 20
TSCA. *See* Toxic Substances Control Act
Tucson, Ariz., 3, 4(table)
Twin plants. *See* Maquiladoras

Ugalde, Antonio, 11
Unemployment. *See* Employment
United States
    Department of Agriculture, 228, 230
    Department of Commerce, 228, 230
    Department of State, 228
    environmental regulations, 227–232, 239
    immigration impact in, 22–23, 24, 29, 196–199
    income distribution in, 61–79
    industry, 44, 45–49(table), 50–55
    labor, 25, 27, 28, 29

United States–Mexico Border Health Institute, 242(n44)
United Nations
    Conference on Sea Rights, 243, 246, 248, 249
    Environmental Program, 231
Union Nacional de Productores Hortalizas (UNPH), 236
Urbanization, 5, 203
Urquidi, Victor, 27
Uruapan, 32–39
"U.S. Science and Technology for Development," 224

Value added, 122, 130, 136(n15), 143(table), 159, 220
Values systems, 10, 22
Vance, Cyrus, 247
Van Wass, Miguel, 165, 170
Villarreal, A., 146, 149, 150
Villarreal, Sofia Mandez, 27

West, Robert C., 212
West Germany, 13, 112(table)
Williams, E. J., 40, 132
Wise, Donald E., 197
Women
    emigrants, 169–170
    in labor force, 28, 128–129, 132, 137(n21), 137(n22), 142, 161–163, 165, 167, 170–173
    older, 170
    organization of, 163
    as undocumented workers, 170
    unemployed, 161–162

Yellow-Fin Tuna Commission, 245
Youth. *See* "Cholo" movement

Zacatecas, 32–39